Lowrider Space

Aesthetics and Politics
of Mexican American Custom Cars

LOWRIDER SPACE

Ben Chappell

UNIVERSITY OF TEXAS PRESS AUSTIN

Unless otherwise noted, all photographs in this book were taken by the author.

Portions of this book appeared in earlier stages of development in the following books and journals: *Technicolor: Race, Technology, and Daily Life*, edited by Alondra Nelson and Thuy Linh N. Tu (New York: New York Univ. Press, 2000); *Mobile Crossings: Representations of Chicana/o Cultures*, edited by Anja Bandau and Marc Priewe (Trier, Germany: Wissenschaftlicher Verlag Trier, 2006); *Cultural Dynamics* 18, no. 3 (2006); and *City and Society* 22, no. 1 (2010).

The text of Latino Comedy Project's "Chuy in the Sky" sketch appears by permission of Teatro Humanidad Cansada. The text of the raulrsalinas poem "Via Crucis 150" appears by permission of Resistencia Bookstore and Red Salmon Arts.

Requests for permission to reproduce material from this work should be sent to:

Permissions

University of Texas Press

P.O. Box 7819

Austin, TX 78713-7819

www.utexas.edu/utpress/about/bpermission.html

The paper used in this book meets the minimum requirements of ANSI/NISO Z39.48-1992 (R1997) (Permanence of Paper).♾

Library of Congress Cataloging-in-Publication Data

Chappell, Ben, 1971–

Lowrider space : aesthetics and politics of Mexican American custom cars / Ben Chappell.

p. cm.

Includes bibliographical references and index.

ISBN 978-0-292-73786-0 (cloth : alk. paper)—ISBN 978-0-292-73787-7 (e-book)

1. Mexican Americans—Social life and customs. 2. Mexican Americans—Cultural assimilation. 3. Lowriders—Social aspects—United States. 4. Automobiles—Social aspects—United States. 5. Automobiles—Societies, etc.—Social aspects—United States. 6. Popular culture—United States. I. Title.

E184.M5C3837 2012

973'.046872—dc23   2012007465

To my family.

Contents

ACKNOWLEDGMENTS
IX

INTRODUCTION
1

I. CRUISING SPACES
31

II. INSIDE OUT
The Ambivalent Aesthetics
of Lowrider Interiors
64

III. AUTO BODIES
101

IV. WORK
The Producer as Author
136

V. NEITHER GANGSTERS
NOR *SANTITOS*
168

CONCLUSION
201

NOTES
207

REFERENCE LIST
217

INDEX
235

Acknowledgments

First and foremost, this book would not exist without the generosity of the low-riders of Austin, Texas. Names are concealed here to protect the innocent and the guilty alike, but if you are reading this and remember me hanging around the park, the car wash, and Riverside Drive, then I owe you my thanks for your hospitality and patience. I hope you feel that my efforts in the book are worthy and that we will have more chances to discuss it. In particular, among those who welcomed me to the scene very early on and made an effort to stay in touch over the years are Juan Gonzalez, Robert Guerrero, Alex and Mona Vargas, and Adrian Romero, whose photographs also enrich this book (see more at www.flacosfotos.com). Your friendship extended well beyond helping me with this project, and I will always be grateful.

I was extraordinarily fortunate to assemble a dissertation committee whose members modeled both intellect and kindness: Richard Flores (my adviser), Douglas Foley, Stephen Hoelscher, José E. Limón, Kathleen Stewart, and Pauline Turner Strong. Deborah Kapchan, Stuart Goosman, and David Montejano supported the project at key moments, whether or not they knew it. My fellow graduate students at the University of Texas formed a community that was a central event in my life and that I still miss. Before that, I had crucial proto-ethnographic experiences that set me on a path that I had no idea would be-

come a professional one, thanks especially to the family of Julio Chulín in Ix-
tacomitán, Tabasco; the Urban Life Center of Chicago; and my teachers Paul
and Mary McKay, Laurel and Paul Neufeld-Weaver, Virginia Boyle, and Scott
Cheesbro.

Fieldwork was financed at various times and to various degrees by the
Wenner-Gren Foundation (grant #6600), the University of Texas, the Rhonda
Andrews Memorial Fellowship, the Virginia Foundation for Independent Col-
leges Mednick Fellowship, Bridgewater College, and JAK Films. I am grateful for
it all. When I came back to the Eastside for research after having moved away,
dear friends opened their homes to me, including Jennie Burger and Bill Fagel-
son, Jim and Melissa Biggs Coupal, Heather Mathews and Andrew Otwell, Peter Haney and Laura Padilla, and Mieke Curtis and Kemal Namver. I made one
critical field trip in an aging but unstoppable Volvo station wagon belonging to
my father-in-law, John Janzen. In addition to the lowriders and neighbors who
are depicted in this text, I benefitted directly from the tutelage of Juan Valadez,
Miguel Guajardo, and Thomas Cruz, and their company over breakfast tacos at
Hernandez Café. I am grateful for all this support.

The long gestation of this book was helped along by many opportunities to
speak about it, including at Eastern Mennonite University, Bethel College, the
University of Illinois, the University of Kansas, the University of Central Arkan-
sas (virtually), and Haskell Indian Nations University. For these audiences and
deadlines, I am indebted to Moira Rogers, Mark Sawin, Christian Early, Betsy
Kuznesof, Adam Frank, Julia Good Fox, Dale Schrag, Marc Perry, Gilberto Ro-
sas, and Virginia Dominguez. My colleagues at the University of Kansas have offered limitless support and comradeship, especially my mentor, Sherrie Tucker,
and my chair, Cheryl Lester. The write-on-site events that Tonya Golash-Boza
instigated were vital to the last stage of this project. Others animated the writing process by commenting specifically on parts of the text, including Anthony
Corbeill, Jacob Dorman, Ruben Flores, Tanya Hart, Christina Lux, Yajaira Padilla, Ayu Saraswati, Akiko Takeyama, Dave Tell, and Jessica Vasquez. I am grateful to William Nericcio and an anonymous reviewer for the University of Texas
Press for their generous critique and encouragement, and to Allison Faust and
the team at the University of Texas Press for patience and diligence. Everyone
named here and many others contributed to this book, but it is no one's fault
but my own.

My parents, Terry and Bobbie Chappell, gave me life, breath, and freedom,
all of which were necessary for writing anything at all, and so much more. I

am grateful to my sisters and extended family on every side for all manner of support, including helping raise my children when they could. I am inspired by Calvin and Felix Janzen Chappell and grateful for their patience and confidence in me. Without the companionship, love, and intellectual teamwork I share with Marike Janzen, this book would have been one of the least important of many things that would not have turned out the same way.

Lowrider Space

Introduction

"Come on, Ben, you can ride with me." Taking Eddie up on the invitation, I followed him through the crowded, sprawling parking lot. It was around midnight on a summer weekend in Austin, Texas, and the lot we stood in, off East Riverside Drive, was packed with cars and people. The police were mysteriously absent from Riverside, emboldening the owners of custom cars to gather in the lot outside a closed bingo parlor to cruise around and show off their rides. A couple hundred people stood around watching gleaming vehicles creep between rows of parked cars and knots of conversation. Chrome and custom paint shone under streetlights while stereos throbbed with bass-heavy Texas hip-hop. Every now and then a thump and clank resounded as a car lifted by hydraulics bounced its front end in the air and fell to the pavement again. Across the parking lot, near a nightclub blaring electronic *cumbias* for a different crowd, an engine roar was followed by the squeal of tires as someone burned out. I glanced over to see a clean but apparently uncustomized truck lurching forward as smoke rose from its wheel. Standing beside me, Arturo shook his head disapprovingly. "See?" he said. "Once they hear that, then the cops come and we gotta go."

Though there was no sign of the cops so far, Eddie was heading out, having decided he fancied a cruise around downtown. I climbed into his car, a 1970s

Monte Carlo in which he had installed a powerful hydraulic system. Eddie had also cut the roof off with a torch. I climbed into the shortened, swivel-mounted seat on the passenger side and was surrounded with blue velvet upholstery on the dashboard and door. After starting the engine, Eddie touched a switch to lift the hydraulics a bit, then dropped the car, and the suspension springs bounced three or four times. I steadied myself with an arm on top of the open window.

As we drove west on Riverside toward downtown, we saw why the police were leaving the lowriders alone. A multiple-car accident on the interstate highway that divides Austin west from east had drawn a line of patrol cars on the side of the road near the wreck. Yet this was a temporary distraction: it would be only a matter of time before they headed back in the direction of the bingo parking lot. Leaving this scene behind, we cruised toward Congress Avenue. As we turned north to cross the bridge, the cityscape of downtown unfolded dramatically before us. The summer night sky was glorious overhead, and in the wide-open car, it felt as if you could take in the whole panorama at once. Moving into downtown, we were quickly surrounded by the full drama of "going out," as crowds flocked to the Sixth Street bar district. When we stopped at a light, it looked as though a couple of Anglo male college students who had apparently already enjoyed a fair amount of nightlife were swaying threateningly toward one another on the sidewalk while female companions made showy efforts to restrain them: "It's not worth it, Drew!" A friend of one of the impaired combatants looked at us as if making an aside from the stage, and said, "This isn't good." The light changed, and we left this entertainment behind, turning back toward the Eastside and enjoying appreciative looks from pedestrians as we took in the view of the city and weekend excitement from the chopped Monte Carlo.

《 》

A lowrider is an automobile customized in a popular aesthetic style (Kirschen-blatt-Gimblett 1995), which is practiced mostly but not exclusively by Mexican Americans in the U.S. Southwest.[1] A lowrider is also a person who participates in that style of customization by modifying his or her car with such adornments as custom wheels—wire spokes are usually considered "traditional" (see Figure 1.1)—an accessorized interior, a high-wattage stereo system, and elaborate and sometimes figurative paint jobs on the car body. Various kinds of mechanical customizations are another feature of lowrider aesthetics. The quintessential

Figure I.1. 1964 Chevrolet Impala lowrider on spokes.

mechanical modification is a hydraulic suspension, powered by a rack of batteries in the trunk and controlled from the driver's seat with switches, that allows the wheels to bounce or "hop" vertically off the ground. Beyond customizing cars, lowriding is a social practice: local scenes coalesce around the streets
and parks where lowriders gather to cruise, display their rides, and socialize.
Lowriders create aftermarket economies of barter, trade, and resale for cars,
parts, and labor. Lowriding also involves competitive car shows where rides are
judged for their aesthetics and hydraulic capabilities, earning their owners trophies, cash, notice in the pages of lowrider publications, and occasionally the
right to compete in the annual *Lowrider Magazine*–sponsored car show in Las
Vegas, which is the effective national championship of lowriding. Through all
of these manifestations, lowriding has remained a site of Mexican American
cultural authority for several generations of participants.[2]

The argument of this book is that everyday lowriding is best understood as
a material, space-making practice. To view lowriding as a production of space
illuminates both the politics of lowrider practice and the personal attachment
that lowriders feel for their idiom. Historically associated with urban barrio
communities, lowriding is entangled in the politics of place-identity and spatial constructs such as the public sphere. When lowriders put their distinctive
aesthetics on display in streets and parking lots, they affect their surroundings,

taking part in the ongoing production of social space and the inscription of particular sites as identified places. Further, lowrider cars acquire personal, social, and cultural meanings as well as political valence and emotional force—all of which I refer to as lowrider "significance"—in part from their location and proximity to other things.

One of my own earliest memories of lowrider style is of an encounter through the medium of text, a particular kind of text designed to serve a specific production of space: as an Anglo middle-class high school student in Ohio, I was reading the novelization of Dennis Hopper's 1988 gang-exploitation film *Colors* (Norst 1988). No literary scholar, I still noticed that whenever the narrative took its protagonist cops into the hoods of Los Angeles, the scene was painted by descriptions of traffic. When this landscape needed a "barrio" feel, the author mentioned lowriders. Like the glimpse of a passing snake in a suspenseful cinematic jungle scene, lowriders played the role in that story of an ominous mobile presence, integral to their setting and imbuing it with threat. I am not even sure I knew what kind of vehicle or person "lowrider" referred to. But it was abundantly clear that whatever or whoever these things were, they were being presented as part of the menacing environment of a particular place. In the elaborate logic of exoticization, this place was meant to entice and fascinate me, even as I was meant to fear it and thus to assent to an array of social measures organized to keep the barrio at a safe distance from my own home—measures including the work of LA cops, depicted with gritty, violent, and hypermasculine heroism in Hopper's film.[3]

Contrast this with the idyllic reminiscences that people shared with me much later in interviews, their own memories of lowrider cars as a familiar presence in childhood. For example, a lowrider I call "Roman" for the book said:

> We didn't have actually what you call a basketball court, it was just a pipe
> with a, a piece of backboard and a rim. So all the local neighborhood
> guys that were my age then, and younger, would hang out there and play,
> play basketball. So whatever they were driving and whatever their friends
> were driving, would show up and park outside [. . .] And as a kid, those—I
> was always fascinated by shiny wheels and uh . . . cause these guys had
> the things *I* liked. [. . .] I had an uncle that had a lot of friends that were
> into the lowrider scene. [. . .] My father always had those cars . . . always
> had a four-door Impala, a two-door, whether if it was a '63 year model,

'64. He always had those cars. [. . .] I would see my dad working on them and I got really familiar with them.[4]

Things have changed since I was in high school, curiously consuming urban popular culture at a distance. Kids of diverse backgrounds in the Midwest are now much more aware of lowriders, and not just as the threatening presence they were used to represent as part of the 1980s gang scares. If more people know what a lowrider is, though, that does not mean they have grasped the significance that Roman attributed to this particular automotive aesthetic as part of his remembered landscape of home. Nor have the ascriptions of gang culture and criminality to lowriders ceased or become more accurate. Perhaps most of all, as it has become widely recognizable, even marketable, the lowrider car style remains exotic to many observers, while its relation to the spatial politics of everyday life in a diverse and stratified U.S. society remains more or less taken for granted rather than thoughtfully critiqued.

By the time of my conversation with Roman in 2001, I had followed a circuitous route to the University of Texas and to a critical and reflexive version of anthropology that eventually made a certain corner of the academy feel like a home for me. Among other things, that meant I was trained to recognize the social relationships involved in research and to resist the titillation of exoticism that treated people's ordinary lives as spectacle. I understood my work to include accounting not only for differences in social position but also for the common material existence that I shared with people whom I would approach as a researcher, an arrangement that enmeshed us all in established political-economic relations and circuits of cultural production and exchange. Whether my fascination with popular aesthetics by this point had left exoticism behind is a question that still requires vigilance and perhaps always will, since the history of anthropology proves that professionalization is no inoculation against it. But at least I could claim increased awareness of the issues and the implications of my curiosity, and I was pursuing other motives than those prepared for me by Hopper's Hollywood. With that training, I went to meet some lowriders.

Going "to the field" is a spatial ritual at the core of modern anthropology. It presumes that research is a process of moving from one's "home" into a space of difference—"the field"—and returning to process the results of an encounter with Others (see Gupta and Ferguson 1997). This intellectual production of space and difference has been subjected to important and incisive critiques that undercut the assumption that the world is naturally divided into discrete areas of culture (Gupta and Ferguson 1992). These critiques not only shed light on how such boundaries have been historically constructed and enforced, but also challenge students of society to recognize the informal or de facto boundaries that mark out social divides within "a place." According to the maps of academic area studies, I conducted my ethnography in "the same place," that is, without leaving the town, let alone the country, where I had prepared as a student. Yet even critical scholars or those who have been strong advocates for the cultural validity of "marginal" places around the globe at times needed reminding that there is not one "Austin."[5] As I orchestrated opportunities to meet and spend time with lowriders, I shuttled between a privileged space of knowledge production, where I was working to establish a legitimate place for myself, and spaces where that budding credibility meant little. I came to understand how spatial arrangements of difference were not only the product of power and knowledge, but the medium through which those forces worked as well. Though the lines of "difference" that I crossed to practice research were determined by all the usual suspects—culture, political economy, race, and so forth—they were materialized as boundaries between sites of social space.

Lowriders are not responsible for this spatial arrangement, but they intervene in it. The space that lowriders make and the means by which they make it offer glimpses of a general process of cultural practice as spatial production. The immediate implication of this argument is that contrary to prevailing sociological definitions, culture is not only or even principally a set of meanings and values. Processual and poststructural moves in anthropology in the last decades of the twentieth century exposed some of the limitations of any static notion of culture as a system, a code, or a set of rules (Abu-Lughod 1991; Ortner 1984; Rosaldo 1993), yet even with the preferred adjectival form—speaking of "the cultural" rather than "a culture" (Appadurai 1996)—there is a persistent habit in scholarship and everyday discourse to imagine this dimension of human life in terms of ideas or propositions to be expressed. In other words, the notion that culture is something conveyed or transmitted by practices or texts enjoys the status of common sense, and cultural products such as customized cars are approached as expressions of something otherwise concealed behind or beneath them, like the script of a play or an army's marching orders.

Material practices such as lowriding challenge cultural theory to account for their significance in ways other than their representational or expressed content. The kind of significance that is a central concern of this book is the so-cial weight invested in practices that generate distinctive contexts by marking and arranging things and by affording particular embodied experiences. Thus, my aim is to explore lowriding as an event in the production of social space, the materialization of "social being" (Lefebvre 1991, 102). More broadly, the concern is with culture not so much as communication but as a process of producing "spatial fields" (Munn 1996).

This raises theoretical questions about the workings of identity and politics. When a lowrider builds a car and cruises it, or when lowrider car clubs take to the streets, they do so within history, which is to say that they act within economies of territory and social franchise that are framed by historical relations of inequality and the requirements of "government" in the broadest sense (Foucault 1991; see also Inda 2005). It may not be an expressly "political" identity that motivates each lowrider to build a car, but by merely existing, lowriders engage in larger struggles to create room for themselves in a diverse and stratified urban social landscape. By crafting "autotopographies" (González 1995), spatial versions of individual and group identity, they render space significant and produce spaces in which to perform acts of signification. Thus, cultural practice and spatial production are mutually constitutive.

In that light, beyond documenting everyday lowriders in a particular time and place, the book also enters into dialogue with other studies that have depicted expressive culture as intervening in contested spatial formations, not only in Mexican American Texas, but also within a broader range of minoritized people's cultural production, and particularly in cities creased by fault lines of race and class, among others.[6] Spatial theory provides some of these researchers with the language to understand what happens when audiences encounter identified cultural forms like hip-hop music and dance or graffiti writing in the public: among other effects, it forces them to confront the question of who has authority over urban space and hence over "the city" (Austin 2001). My work on lowriders began as another step in this collective project to document and theorize how people of color have developed cultural vernaculars that engage the politics of their social and spatial locations.

And yet even while referencing this spatial politics, scholarship of popular culture in general does not always respond to the challenge posed by Jody Berland two decades ago: to account for cultural practice as being not only potentially *about* space-and-place, but also a material process that occurs *in* specific spatial formations and, indeed, something that happens *to* social space. Critiquing what was at that time a scholarly silence on the spatiality of music, Berland argued for a materialist approach that takes performance to be integrally bound up in the production of space. After quoting a sound engineer talking about how a particular recording mix would sound on a car stereo system, Berland asks:

> Why is the literature on pop music, like that on other genres, other media, so often empty of cars, not to mention elevators, offices, shopping malls, hotels, sidewalks, airplanes, buses, urban landscapes, small towns, northern settlements, or satellite broadcasts? . . . Why is music so rarely conceived spatially . . . ? (1992, 39)

Appearing in the landmark volume *Cultural Studies*, Berland's piece was surrounded by other arguments that sought to draw out the significance of various forms of popular culture by examining the meanings they transmit, the consciousness that they signal, or the political economies in which they participate. Berland's polemic suggests, however, that analysts ask not what a popular practice represents so much as what it does. Following Berland, I propose that beyond serving as a mere vehicle for content, cultural forms such as music and the material aesthetics of car customization take part in the production of their contexts.

To pursue the implications of this proposition is a materialist project that prior generations of scholars have justified, even if they have not always followed up on it. What, for instance, would it mean to take Stuart Hall at his word that "popular culture is neither, in a 'pure' sense, the popular traditions of resistance to these processes [of social reproduction]; nor is it the forms which are superimposed on and over them," but is, instead, "the *ground* on which the transformations are worked" (1981, 228)? No less, what of Norma Alarcón's notion of consciousness not as abstract, but as a "*site* of multiple voicings" (1991, 38), or Carlos Vélez-Ibáñez's account of a "basic tenet of the [U.S.-Mexico borderlands] region" being "the struggle for survival and the search for *place and space*" (1996, 221)? How can scholars take such phrases not as metaphorical but as speaking to actual desires and efforts to gain "a piece of *ground* to stand on" (Anzaldúa 1987, 23)?[7] Moreover, how can inquiry proceed that seeks to expose theoretical production to the popular practices that already engage such issues of literal space, ground, and location?

Choosing an approach of critical ethnography, I have tried to open scholarly discourse to the full grain of what I call lowrider space. Lowrider space is an assemblage of bodies, cars, and landscapes, and their sounds, colors, textures, and movements—a formation that emerges on some scale whenever lowrider style is on display. To open scholarship to being affected by lowrider space is to seek an analysis that remains attentive to the rich, polysemous, and at times contradictory ways that lowriders as objects, the performances of lowrider style, and the "backstage" practices of lowriding all register as significant and how, in doing so, they characterize space. A priority here is to track how the presence and existence of things come to be felt in the world, becoming events to be reckoned with. It is exactly in these processes that I locate the identifying "power," or significance, of lowriding: in the capacity of a particular material aesthetics to generate impacts upon a perceiver, what could be called its affectivity. I argue that as this affective power joins and intervenes in the production of space, it works on the material configuration of the social. This is what constitutes its emergent politics, more than the development of a particular form or content of consciousness.[8] Lowriders moved my thinking in this direction in two ways: first, by maintaining an aesthetics that values significance beyond words; and second, by engaging the affective politics of space.

Excess Significance

I had been told by lowriders at a couple of car shows that the best place to encounter the Austin lowrider scene was Chicano Park on a Sunday night. To get there from downtown, go east on Cesar Chavez, which some people still call First Street. After crossing the elevated lanes of IH-35, and leaving behind the big hotels and convention center of downtown, pass the pawnshop and the Terrazas Branch Library, then the old house that is now Austin Spoilers and Tint Shop, advertising *"Polarizado de Autos."* This strip has changed considerably since I began fieldwork; now you might see an upscale boutique and a continuum of real estate operations: to the left, a very hip office with new-economy décor promising the "good life" through condos, then close by on the right, a thrown-up poster-board sign offering "fast cash" for your home.

Eventually, turn south on a street such as Comal or Chicon and head toward the dammed section of the Colorado River once known as Town Lake. A sign names this space Fiesta Gardens, subject to the administration of the Austin Parks and Recreation Department. But where is Chicano Park? Perhaps you should stop in the nearly empty parking lot by a middle school and ask the young Latino man who stands alone by his 1980s Buick Regal, gleaming with deep maroon lacquer. As you pull into the space beside him, he is reaching down to spray some foam on the tires and meticulously wipe them so they look shiny and brand new. If you get out of your car and ask him where Chicano Park is, he might give you a strange look, since you are standing in it and anyone who would call it that would know.

Before he has time to explain, a boom of electronic bass makes you both turn your heads as a Lincoln Continental, colored the brilliant tangerine orange of a soft drink, rolls slowly into the lot and backs into a parking space, facing the center. Other cars arrive from all directions, announcing themselves with amplified sound, cruising in tight formations of two or three, or solo. Drivers and passengers pile out of cars to talk and watch the traffic casually as the parking lot fills. In the late 1990s, there might have been headlights that turned into flashing blue-white strobes, or neon colors glowing underneath the cars. A few years later, there might have been SUVs with free-spinning rims, or youngsters driving noncustom cars with the doors open, swerving like bats in slow-motion flight. Next summer, who knows? The crowd is almost exclusively Latino: men and women, some kids and babies; also a handful of black folks and a couple of whites, one of whom holds a camera.

Figure I.2. 1964 Impala in Chicano Park.

Figure I.3. "Bombs" in Chicano Park.

So it went most Sunday evenings when the weather was pleasant and gas prices not too high during the time of my fieldwork. What seemed from a perspective centered on the University of Texas to be a journey into a very different Austin, to lowriders was an everyday or every-week event: going to "the park." In the local cruising scene that converged on Chicano Park, custom cars added visual, aural, and tactile textures to the sensorial urban landscape, or what could be called the emergent sensorium. If you get to know a neighborhood like the one that Austin lowriders call the Eastside, which includes Chicano Park, as something more than a focal point of suburban fear, it quickly becomes clear that the identity of such places results from ongoing, highly political processes, including the everyday productions of particular kinds of space. Is this Fiesta Gardens or Chicano Park? It depends on whom you ask, who is using the space when you do, what they are doing there, and to some extent, what the sensorium of that site is at that passing moment.

Back at the park, cars in various states of repair, a range of vintages, customized and stock, slowly follow a circuit through the parking lot. An SUV rolls past with three young women inside, stereo bumping, windows down. Now it is a Nissan truck, a man and woman in the cab, wearing matching white T-shirts with a logo printed over the heart. A classic Chevy Impala convertible shows up, the interior all original except for the LCD video screen poking out of the open trunk. A handful of people are setting up folding lawn chairs near the curb—parents settle down to enjoy the view while children play chase in the grass behind them.

Soon the air in the park is thick with vibration as multiple stereos create an aural palimpsest, different tracks on different systems overlapping. One driver, standing with friends in the lot, climbs into his Cutlass and fires up the stereo first, then the motor. He touches a toggle switch mounted on his dash, just enough so that the hydraulic pumps make their characteristic zipping sound as the car leaps a little, as if it has been startled awake. He pulls slowly out of the lot, turns a corner onto a residential side street, and disappears momentarily—backstage. Then he returns to view, heading in the opposite direction, but as he takes a corner, he cranks the steering wheel and guns the motor; now he is on three wheels, one front fender of his car cocked high in the air. The front end drops, and he drives slowly past the other parked cars while onlookers pause in their conversation to look. His face is a mask of smug nonchalance. Halfway past the parking lot, he hits the switches again. The front wheels leap, drop, and bounce off the ground, clearing a foot or two of air, repeatedly slamming back to pavement—two times, then three. The Cutlass pulls back into place, and the driver casually gets out to rejoin the conversation. The stereo on the

Figure I.4. Monte Carlo in Chicano Park.

Figure I.5. Cruising in Chicano Park.

Monte Carlo in the next spot is playing "chopped and screwed" hip-hop out of Houston. The Cutlass's driver cuts a couple of dance steps along with the music, mimicking the slow-tempo stutter of the DJ's "chop." But then an engine revs, and the onlookers turn to look at the next car making a promenade around the park.

《 》

Why has it proved so enduring for a particular group of people to decorate cars in ways that enhance the semiotics of these industrial objects, and drive them as a kind of performance on the stage of the everyday streetscape? Scholars have come up with interpretations that are plausible enough, though often in relation only to selected lowriders. For instance, lowrider aesthetics has been likened to colonial-era cathedrals (Chavoya 2000; Griffith 1989), the practice of cruising to traditional *paseos* around the *zócalos* of Mexican towns (Penland 2003; Rojas 1995), and a general lowrider attitude of ineffable cool to the traditional *charro* masculinity of Mexican cattle culture (Trillin and Koren 1978; Vigil 1991). Yet all these takes seem to fall short of accounting for the range and diversity of lowrider aesthetics and practice. Furthermore, such interpretations generally proceed on the assumption that a lowrider car carries significance primarily because of something else that it represents or expresses. This follows a habit of validating popular practices as "cultural" by linking them to some older or larger frame, such as the Mexican past.[9] But fixing such a secure, historical root as the key to analysis seems to reduce participation in lowrider style to being an instinctive expression of that essential point of cultural origin or, alternately, of basic psychophysiological drives. Interpretations more attentive to politics and to social structure situate lowriding within a conflicted history of Mexican Americans, but still tend to characterize lowriding as a whole: either as an effect of culture-industry marketing (Plascencia 1983) or as resistance, whether or not this is an explicit motivation of lowiders themselves.

As Joe Schloss has observed about hip-hop, lowriding has rarely been studied "in its own terms," even though this is a classic aim of anthropological *verstehen* (2009, 3–4; see also Schloss 2004, 20). By "terms," I mean not only the literal lowrider vocabulary, but also the terms of its practice. For example, Schloss argues that the focus of his own ethnography, B-boying or break dancing, maintains a vernacular set of priorities around face-to-face "battles," dancing competitions that occur across a scale of formality from impromptu street showdowns to highly organized events. Not only are these local-scale, participatory interactions and the contexts they generate exactly what B-boys and B-girls find significant about this cultural form, according to Schloss, they also happen to be a component of hip-hop, unlike produced music, that is less amenable to recorded mediation and hence to both mass marketing and desktop research. All this provides Schloss with the rationale for his ethnographic approach, locating his study in the vernacular practice of battles.

Lowriding also has its own terms, parallel to the ways that B-boys and B-girls prioritize battles. The lowriders I met during my fieldwork maintained a preference for the car itself as the focus of activity and reception, which is to say, as the site of significance, rather than assuming that a more basic stratum of reference lies behind or beneath it and defines what it is "really" about. Further, lowriders largely seemed to share a consensus that to be part of lowriding is to participate in it. While not all lowriders lived up to the ideal of building a ride solely with their own labor from a bare frame to the final coat of paint, few would have disputed that such a project is worthy of respect. Likewise, few would ascribe prestige to purchasing a lowrider already entirely customized. As expressed in club names like Custom Creations, lowriding was understood not only as adherence to or appreciation of lowrider aesthetics—a form of "fandom"—but also as a mode of innovation and production. A lowrider is someone who practices these things, who takes part in customizing, cruising, and showing cars.

Like scholarly interpreters, the lowriders whom I met in my fieldwork offered legitimating arguments, but often in the form of either generalities or denials: lowriding is about pride and culture, for instance; or counter to stereotypes, lowriding is not about gangs. Lowriders were eager to describe lowriding as "positive" and to tell me about how "it's a family thing," often going to great lengths to characterize the style as entailing a depth of commitment that made it something more substantial than a "fad" or a consumption trend, representing instead a distinctive subjectivity or "lifestyle." In our conversations, lowriders were often happy to endorse an abstract idea such as that the style "expresses our culture," but as I grew familiar with the space of everyday lowriding, it became apparent that such elaborating explanations about cultural values were not a high priority there. Looking back on the interviews, it seems that statements of the motivation behind the practice could easily have been made for the benefit of the visitor in the formalized space of an interview.

More telling were the gaps in conversation, pregnant pauses, and comments like from Roman: "I don't know if there's a word or a term for that . . ." and "I don't want to say it's in our genes, but . . ." Lowriders consistently expressed and enacted a preference for material cars as sources and objects of feeling over abstract explanations about why they mattered. At a Catholic church dinner, I met a man who was nearly overcome with emotion during our first conversation as he explained that he no longer could afford the Buick Regal he once had customized and cruised. Someone else choked up when telling me about an accident that had totaled his finished ride. Lowriders' investment of identity through time, money, sweat, and the deferral of other priorities was intense, motivating some to work overtime during the week to accumulate extra funds, then go home to work right through a weekend with no sleep to prepare a car for a Sunday show. I learned that people identify with their vehicles; indeed, they identify each other by them, so that it was commonplace to hear a reference like "You know Anthony? With the Stratus?" or simply to refer to "that guy with the champagne '66."

These moments among others gestured toward a significance that our talk about lowriding failed to contain, but that rendered the aestheticized cars "feelingful," as numerous semioticians have put it (see, for example, Feld 1990, 219; Samuels 2004). The power of lowriding to enlist affinity and prompt identification was not evidently dependent upon a relation to any one specific, larger, or more important entity (McCarthy 2006). Indeed, an excess significance in lowriding seemed to generate a refrain that recurred across numerous mediations of lowrider discourse, namely, that the style is "more than" one might assume: "more than a hobby" as a journalist (and probably more than one) put it (Hawk 2006). Lowrider scholar Denise Sandoval describes lowriding as "more than just customized cars," as, in fact, an ethos: "Family, honor, and respect, those are more than just words" (2003a).

The efforts to portray lowriding as "more than" runs specifically counter to the tenor of social-scientific explanations or treatments of cultural practice as examples of theoretical propositions. What causes lowriding? Isn't it just compensatory consumption? Out of a context of deprivation, don't lowriders secure nice cars because they can't afford mansions? Or isn't it just a way for a male population that has been historically marginalized as a feminized subaltern to seize the chance to take part in an utterly mainstream means of masculinity (S. Jain 2005)? Or isn't it just another iteration of automobility as the quintessential and compulsory ritual of modern U.S. nationalism (Seiler 2008)? Yes, lowriding probably is all of these things, at certain times, in certain ways, but not "just." The following chapters will speak to some of these threads, but I will resist embracing any one of them as the definitive "final answer" to a cultural analysis of lowriding. In this, I share the view that a distinctive contribution of ethnography can be a suspicion toward "the order of grand summarizing traits that claim to capture the 'gist' of 'things'" (K. Stewart 1996, 3). The gist signaled by "just" offers a security of knowing, having solved the excess significance of lowriding within an explanatory framework that attenuates the energy of an aesthetic object. Yet it is exactly this affective energy that allows such an object to spark a response. That happens in a malleable, material configuration—a site.

In relation to scholarly and otherwise "official" attempts to pin them down, then, lowriders demonstrate a kind of identity practice that Michel Foucault commented on as proliferating in the later twentieth century: "Maybe the target nowadays," he argues, "is not to discover what we are, but to *refuse* what we are" (1982, 216). The "what we are" being refused here is the social position into which lowriders have been interpellated, stereotyped, and constricted— that which they claim to be "more than." What is at stake in research on such reidentifications is not so much finding the absolute criteria of authenticity as it is a political question of cultural authority, which is a spatial question. An authority claim is implicit when a scholar apprehends lowriders by fitting them into a definitive "bigger picture." I attempt to practice ethnography, in contrast, as an effort to attend closely to the ways that social actors themselves claim authority and establish the zone of its relevance through an ethos and practice of cultural production. In doing so, they strive to be bigger than the picture.

To take lowriders' emphases on participation and on cars themselves as authoritative is to locate the significance of lowriding in an emergent materiality. Both parts of this term are crucial. In my field experiences, the prioritization of what a car is—its materiality—rather than what it represents was embedded in an understanding of a car being always a work in progress. Ongoing efforts to develop and elaborate the customization of a particular vehicle were spurred by the perpetual challenge to "come out" with something new as each car show or cruising season rolled around. This temporal aspect of lowrider practice gives the style an improvisatory character in which it is less a matter of seeking to conform to some preordained aesthetic ideal than of exploring what kinds of vehicles are possible or imaginable. As much as anything else, this dynamic puts me in mind of a jazz musician's "versioning." According to this analogy, a Chevy of a certain model year becomes like the "standard" song that gets carved up and refunctioned by a performer, like John Coltrane playing "My Favorite Things." Thus, I view lowriding as working more in an experimental and innovative mode than in one simply reproductive of memory and tradition. That is not to imply that lowriders' versioning of Mexican American identity is free-form: it takes place against the backdrop of a particular cultural context, but one that shares the dynamism of lowriding itself.

The aesthetic boundaries that define the limits of what counts as a lowrider change and are subject to debate. For example, I was once present at a car club meeting for a discussion of what constituted "rims." Owning a custom car was the basic qualification for membership in the club, and the minimal standard for "custom" was that the car had "rims." This became controversial when a relative of one of the club officers applied for membership—he had a relatively new car that another member found to be too "factory," or unadorned. Those advocating for the candidate argued that the rims he had put on the car, though not the traditional lowrider wire spokes, were still chrome plated and larger than the factory wheels. The debate, then, was whether these were custom enough.

"He don't even have rims," protested one member.

"Sixteens is rims," said the club officer, referencing the diameter measurement of the custom wheels.

This typified how "lowrider style" did not define a consensual set of criteria or a static list of visual or mechanical devices so much as it constituted a space of aesthetic experimentation, evaluation, and debate. While the "classic" lowrider look would likely be smaller-than-factory rims, rides on the street could show up with either smaller or bigger wheels. What mattered was that someone had intervened in the car's aesthetics, leaving a mark of innovation. While plenty of lowriders traffic in familiar iconographies of Mexican American identity, lowrider aesthetics also tends to place a value on the element of surprise. The challenge was to stay within the unspecified boundaries that would earn a custom car recognition as a lowrider while pushing the limits to make observers "trip out" with surprise. To generate such a surprise effect while also being deemed tasteful according to lowrider standards was to advance the state of the art.

This negotiation of lowrider aesthetics ran parallel with a negotiation of identity, which called into question the relevance of trying to understand lowriding as an expression of a unitary, cohesive a priori culture. Such an instrumental formulation of expressive culture does not begin to account for the complex social maneuvers of a lowrider like the person I call "Thomas." Thomas shares the surname of a successful Latino boxer. He drove a Chevy with rims, though it was a model made after Chevys started to look more like Toyotas, not a big-body GM classic lowrider. Because Thomas's car looked like an import, some other lowriders called it a "Euro." When I knew him, Thomas spoke only English and, in fact, was beginning to master the jargon of the bourgeoisie. Talking about his job once after a car club meeting, he said, "I'm management, dog! I've got like seven people under me." It mattered that this act of identification occurred not in an office but in the parking lot of a car wash on a summer Saturday night.

Thomas the middle manager claimed eligibility for the Rotary, but at other times he also claimed something else. He wore elaborately decorated nonmagnifying eyeglasses, a kind that I have since seen displayed in stores with the label "urban fashion." He participated in an Internet bulletin board devoted to lowriding, and in response to the popular slogan "Keep Austin Weird," he once posted "You keep Austin weird; we'll keep it Gangsta." Still, when a contingent of the car club was about to leave a meeting and discussed stopping by a particular store in one of Austin's poorer neighborhoods on the way to a night of cruising, Thomas demurred: "I'm not going to the ghetto Wal-Mart." Another time, some other lowriders teased Thomas about not liking Mexican food.

Despite occupying an overdetermined middle ground between race, class, and cultural identities, Thomas was a lowrider because he participated in a lowrider scene, which was also true of other participants. This did not mean that a particular sense of authentic identity was required before joining the scene, nor did it mean that "coming out" as a lowrider secured any guarantees about the legitimacy of one's identity. The participatory definition, that lowriders are those who do it, meant that if and when certain kinds of ambivalence, contradiction, or complexity regarding identity turned up, they would not be sufficient to exclude someone outright from the scene.

This is why the "just" interpretations fail to satisfy when they draw arguments toward either-or questions such as where lowriding falls within a U.S.-Anglo/Chicano-Mexican dichotomy. Do lowriders share in the commitments of mainstream U.S. liberalism to individualism, private property, and others? Or do they maintain a position of difference defined by legacies from the past: survivals from alternative social forms such as collectivism or familialism that can be traced to a deep indigenous heritage (sometimes described as so deep that the forms can be conceived only as mystical or genetic, which may amount to the same thing)? Or are they faint, narrated memories of revolutionary collectivism, or more recent habits of *mutualista* neighborliness, or class solidarity, or something else? Again, the answer is yes to all these as potentialities, for lowriding directly negotiates these boundaries. As ethnographers recognized more than twenty years ago, "actors construct this meaningful order in the process of being constructed in its terms" (Munn 1986, 6).

If the project is not to locate the authentic gist of lowriding, where then should we look to understand why it matters? Other ethnographers of lowriding have told me they share the impression that the significance of lowriding is not reducible to any simple act of representation or expression, but that it consists of a kind of experience.[10] To speak of "experience" is a dangerous game, since the term has the potential to invoke a mystified transcendence or an escape from mediation. In prioritizing lowrider materiality as experience, I am specifically not arguing that lowriding is somehow more "real" than discourse, which has its own materiality and experiences, or that it is ever unmediated. Indeed, I treat lowriding as something that operates like a "discourse" made of objects as much as statements (Hall 1997, 44). Even less would I invoke experience to signal a realm of signification more primitive than text, an expression suited to those who lack words. That idea could easily slide into the notion that practices like lowriding fill a gap left by linguistic deficits due to lowriders' edu-

good engagement w/ lit

cational deprivation, a proposition that I reject. In fact, lowriders as a whole are quite active in their own textual self-representation. The issue is more that the specific mediations at work in lowrider space are not always identical with the historically particular experiences of writing, speaking, and reading, which make up the "natural discourse" of scholarship. The processes of academic text making (including those I am practicing right now, and those that a formal re- search interview implicitly invites others to join) are equally "experiential," but generally produce and take place in a specific kind of context that can be easily distinguished from lowrider space. So the experience of lowriding in this text will serve as a heuristic for material, processual, and sensorial details, some of which resist capture or even notice by the self-conscious, precise, and abstracting registers of a scholarly text.

A concern with experience is nothing new in ethnography, a field based on scholars placing their own textual practice in contact with situations that matter to people in various ways. This reflects the importance that ethnographers have ascribed to contextual specificity, the historically particular ways in which social relations are "realized" (Ferguson and Gupta 2002). Ethnographers conduct research through embodied coparticipation with other people in social space. What they are after, then, includes the "full force" of "being there," being actively present in sites shot through with memory and varying political impacts (Flores 2002, 20). In this sense, the material of ethnography is the affectivity of particular sociospatial, sensory configurations. As phenomenological and embodiment-focused ethnographers have argued, researching this is a matter of activating diverse "modes of attention" (Csordas 1993), an anti-Platonic stance that treats embodied situations as events worthy of contemplation in and of themselves, rather than viewing them as principally symbolic or symptomatic.[11] I likewise orient my study toward particular forms and instances of embodied practice, for this is what lowriders engage in, and if I did not respect what participants view as the source of integrity of their vernacular practice, I would be dismissing their cultural authority, even explaining it away.

The effects generated by lowrider style, however, are not uniformly or necessarily positive and affirming. Lowrider significance describes the potential of a car to generate not only affinity but also alarm, or to provoke reaction. When, by chance, I met the president of the Hispanic Chamber of Commerce of a South Texas town, he asked what I was studying and met my answer with clear disapproval. "Why don't you study people who are *doing* something for their community?" he asked. Even as lowriders themselves deliver a coherent narrative of "positivity" and its aliases—pride, culture, and so on—lowrider style has often sparked reaction on the part of authorities, who read its semiotic excess as a symptom of debased character and a signal of criminality. This feeds the long history of police subjecting lowriders to heightened levels of surveillance and control through traffic stops. In part, the policing of lowriders responds to a stereotype that gangbangers love lowriders—perhaps a kernel of truth that is then reversed and extended into the assumption that all lowriders are gangbangers.

But it is also framed by the identification of lowriders with sociospatial contexts in which violence is undeniably a presence. In popular accounts, the unequal spatial and social distribution of everyday violence in the United States tends to get read in essentialist terms of character, psychology, race, and cultures of poverty, or through a general narrative of moral decline. More plausibly, violence as a characteristic of urban everyday life articulates quite mainstream notions of masculinity with the circumstances of a specific, racialized class position. The gender component of this includes mandates to possess things and territory and to protect possessions through destructive force. The historical positioning of minoritized urban communities, however, has complicated these gendered imperatives by making people particularly subject to the structural violence of racism, criminalization, and impeded social mobility while also being relatively deprived of what is embodied in middle-class suburbia: the means to control territory on a sufficient scale to form enclaves and keep violence at a distance.

All these social relations resonate in the aesthetics of identity, which is why to speak of lowrider aesthetics is by no means a flight from the political. On the contrary, I suggest that social relations are intensified by and draw force from the affectivity of semiotic distinctiveness (style identity). It was reactions to lowriding and efforts to regulate urban space that often brought this to the fore during my fieldwork. At that time, I attended town-hall meetings about what was then Austin's new "community policing" agenda, with its emphasis on what were called "quality-of-life issues." It was immediately clear that such language would have implications for lowriders. After all, consider some of the modes of automobility that could be expected to raise alarm about the quality of life of an area: the sounds of high-powered subwoofer stereo systems on a public street, or the presence of aging, undrivable vehicles in a front yard. These are exactly what lowriders would take to be signs of the good life. What landlords, middle-class aspirants, and code enforcers would see as "a junk car problem," lowriders would identify as a precious and rare resource, the parts car. Thus, new governmental strategies oriented toward a semiotics of security and risk politicized the diversity of spatial and material aesthetics in Austin, and lowriders along with it. This is one reason that lowriders can simultaneously represent positivity and stigma: lowrider style is situated squarely within the conflicts and contradictions of contemporary life in the United States. More than representing them, lowriders are shaped by these contradictions, and embody and respond to them.

The Affective Politics of Space

The excess significance of a customized ride lies in its capacity to deliver impacts, including moments of "aesthetic experience" (Sheriff 1994, 67). Aesthetic experience, as distinct from aesthetic judgment, consists of moments of perception that first produce an embodied response in a perceiver, and that later get processed as feelings, anxiety, evaluation, identification, or some other recognizable category. As Roland Barthes writes about the difference between engaging with a photograph as an aesthetic or familiar image rather than as a datum of scientific consideration, the intellectual quest for ideological or symbolic explanation may tend to make the force of an image "less acute" (1981, 36). Such a blunting effect goes a long way toward showing why lowriders may be less excited by metacommentary on their work than by the cars—the work—themselves. Yet a growing literature in theory and cultural criticism both calls for and provides "equipment" (Rabinow 2003) for modes of attention to the affective dimension, and to events on the scale of the ordinary that are infused with affectivity. Kathleen Stewart describes the object of such work:

> Ordinary affects are the varied, surging capacities to affect and to be affected that give everyday life the quality of a continual motion of relations, scenes, contingencies, and emergences. They're things that happen. They happen in impulses, sensations, expectations, daydreams, encounters, and habits of relating, in strategies and their failures, in forms of persuasion, contagion, and compulsion, in modes of attention, attachment, and agency, and in publics and social worlds of all kinds that catch people up in something that feels like something. . . . At once abstract and concrete, ordinary affects are more directly compelling than ideologies, as well as more fractious, multiplicitous, and unpredictable than symbolic meanings. (2007, 1–3)

Attuning scholarship to affectivity requires projects that are concerned not only with history in the sense of what happened, but with what Lauren Berlant calls "the conditions of an historical moment's production as a visceral moment" (2008, 846; see also Benjamin 1968a). I propose that lowriding, as a spatial and aesthetic practice that works on the sensorium of specific sites, produces "new visceral imaginaries for what the present could be" (Berlant 2008, 847). Visceral imaginaries occur not only in the domain of ideas but also in material formations. This book is largely concerned with visceral imaginaries that take the form of spatial fields, something like what Nancy Munn describes as a way to understand complex and layered affectivities associated with ritually marked travel. In her work with aboriginal people in Australia, Munn develops a notion of spatial fields as carrying a certain ritual status that may at times render the space around a marked person as forbidden to others:

> It is space defined by reference to an actor, its organizing center. Since a spatial field extends from the actor, it can also be understood as a culturally defined, corporeal-sensual field of significant distances stretching out from the body in a particular stance or action at a given locale or as it moves through locales. . . . The body is thus understood as a spatial field (and the spatial field as a bodily field). (1996, 93)

As the body moves, the center of this spatial field is temporary and shifting, its boundaries are "quasi-perimetric," and its significance is "concrete if transient" (Munn 1996, 95). Besides being mobile, such a spatial field not only emerges with reference to particular bodies, but also is realized affectively as a palpable bodily experience. This is what renders distance and proximity "significant." In similar ways, lowrider space forms a temporary zone within and around a lowrider car as it moves through traffic and as it is customized, occupied, driven, and in these ways "animated" by the person who thus identifies as a lowrider.

Affectivity is inherently spatial, operating on scales of event, force, perception or proprioception, and impact. This is another reminder of how lowriding engages with urban politics, for, as Nigel Thrift puts it, "Cities may be seen as roiling maelstroms of affect" (2004b, 57). Whether or not such affectivity is a unique property of cities, Thrift demonstrates in several of his theoretical works that affect is universally salient in the spatial productions, political assemblages, and everyday social processes of cities. Moreover, Thrift presents this as a kind of subjugated knowledge, in that urbanist scholarship has been far from open to affect as a relevant source of data. As part of the long history of urbanity, that heterogeneous category of experience in which people share or contest space in relatively concentrated circumstances (Copjec and Sorkin 1999), affectivity has emerged not only as an epiphenomenal feature of dense population, but also as a dimension of all relations and processes of politics, understood in the broadest sense as the shifting lines of confrontation and solidarity by which people encounter, understand, and engage with relations of authority and governmentality.

What Thrift notes is that people involved in the government of cities, as well as in their representational identification and marketing, have come to recognize that any historical assemblage of power depends and relies not only on rational discourse and official political process, but also upon people being moved in various ways. Affectivity is thus marshaled for diverse projects: for instance, measures designed to produce an effect of comfort in people's spatial semiconsciousness make them feel safe and at home. This is obviously a concern for real-estate interests. It also matters to those whose positions of authority depend on the support of constituencies. Thus, a range of "cultural" or aesthetic concerns contribute to an affective politics of urban space: historic preservation; neighborhood, street, and park names; the characteristic details of the built urban landscape and the managed ecosystem; and economic projects such as "renewal" and "development" (see Zukin 2009). Affective politics frame such issues as who has access to and is welcomed in the public (Davis 2000; Deutsche 1996), how various scales of allegiance and citizenship are negotiated (Ramos-Zayas 2003), and who can claim identification as "the community" (Dávila 2004). Such issues intensify and locate historical constructions and hierarchies of race, class, gender, legal status, and others. Perhaps most generally, these are versions of the Lefebvrian question of the "right to the city" (Lefebvre 1996; see also Harvey 1998b).[12]

When a lowrider cruises down a street, its spatial field, an aura of identified spatiality, goes with it. The emotional and political charge that seems to infuse encounters with this mobile zone of lowrider space reveals that lowrider style is not a simple or neutral kind of picturesque "difference." In this way, it is never "just culture." Rather, to perform lowrider style in any site carries a strong and immanent rhetorical argument: that *this* is lowrider space. Yet this is a visceral more than a textual argument. As a mobile, material medium, rich with signs that are not always referential ones, lowrider style engages in iconic, metonymic, and other kinds of semiotic relations with other objects, genres, spaces, and imaginaries. A manifestation of lowrider space ties the immediate context of a lowrider car to the barrio spaces of Latino urbanity in the United States, both material and imagined. The impact of this varies depending on how that immediate context has been spatially produced so far—a lowrider in the Eastside barrio produces different effects than one cruising Congress Avenue, the center of official and "mainstream" Austin; it generates others yet on the upscale suburban boulevard of Bee Cave Road.

The effects-cum-affects of such an event, as well as the interpreted responses that follow its initial impact, depend on whether one wants or expects to be standing in a barrio. What does that term signal? Is the barrio home? A repository of memory and a source of authenticity? Is it a bad area? A property-value vortex? A lowrider not only raises but also weighs in on these questions in an assemblage of allusions and possibilities that are rendered precise by their material form, but nevertheless at times maintain a certain ambivalence. A lowrider car intervenes in the emergent character of social space not necessarily to resolve such contradictions—the car itself is, after all, a place-identified means of mobility—but primarily to assert its material presence. Such a presence can pose a challenge to a public that tends to expect encounters with the Mexican American part of Texas to come in more consumable forms, like music, food, fiction, and mispronounced place names. Thus, regardless of whether the stated motivation of lowrider cruising is to get noticed, to show off, to court romance, or to take in the spectacle of a weekend night in the city, there is an immanent politics to the ways that a lowrider moving about in public affects the production of city space and spatial imaginaries. It is a politics that is not necessarily an expression of consciousness or a reasoned-out position within some debate with clear-cut sides and stakes. It is a politics of presence.

The sites of lowrider space are places where a performance of lowrider style lays the contested political-cultural landscape bare, or makes this fluid landscape momentarily "snap into place" as a condensed structure of feeling (K. Stewart 2005, 1015). For Mexican Americans in U.S. cities, moments of such clarity or intensification engage a historical tension, as outlined by Raúl Homero Villa, between spatial practices of "barrioization" and a collective cultural memory of "barriology." Lowriders embody the relation between local, "barriological" cultural practices that affirm an identification with barrio communities on one hand, and on the other, "barrioizing" social processes that relegate Mexican Americans to designated spaces, erase them from the public sphere, and subject them to repressive patterns of social control (Villa 2000).[13]

As a cultural form that both creates and refers to barriological memory, while simultaneously becoming a target for police practices that make up part of barrioization, lowriding embraces the ambivalence of urban Mexican American experience. Louis Mendoza elaborates on Villa:

> The barrio, too, has often been a source of ambivalence for Chicanos, because it is both isolating as well as insulating. It signifies Chicanos' social status (economic and political subordination), but it is also their refuge, a safe-house from a harsh world wherein Raza can escape their "minority" status and be surrounded by that which is familiar and comforting. (Mendoza 2001, 334)

Again, the politics of a barriological form like lowriding lies not in transcending such ambivalence, but in refusing to repress it. Occurring at this ambivalent intersection, lowrider space is both material and metaphorical. It refers to the production of actual, spatial configurations of bodies, things, and environments so that the whole assemblage takes on a particular character, a "geographical identity" (Villa 2000, 5). To the extent that this spatial production always occurs in relation to an imagined and constructed mainstream public sphere, lowrider space also constitutes a metaphorical "space" within the social: room to be "Mexican" within "America." Exemplary of this, Villa points out the barriological production of an alternate city within the metropolis of Los Angeles:

> If not always with the producer's awareness of their collective effect, these practices cumulatively produce and reproduce a mexopolis within the metropolis . . . This Raza second city—contrary to the rigid laws of physics but consonant with the fluid arts of urbanity—exists in the same space of the putative Anglo-American first city (signs of its diminution are everywhere to be seen), yet in a significantly other place from its dominant cultural milieu. (2000, 234–235)

Thus lowriding draws upon and materializes social imaginaries, or what I would call "imagined cities" (see Gregory 1994; Lynch 1960; Pile 2005). Both official and alternative versions of geographical identity are imagined, in the sense developed by Benedict Anderson (1991), Arjun Appadurai (1996), and

Charles Taylor (2004): they are collectively imaged and put into practice. The question is not which city is real as opposed to imaginary, but rather what imaginaries will be brought into visceral materiality through ongoing and repetitive performance, becoming part of the "second nature" of urban space (Buck-Morss 1991) that frames and partially determines future practice and spatial formation.

Directions

This book recounts lowrider space as I found it in Austin, Texas, among mostly English-speaking, nonimmigrant Mexican Americans. The social position of Austin lowriders is both locally specific and generally significant. Locally, it marks the history of one sector of Mexican American Austin: those of at least the second generation in the United States, many of whose parents had Spanish beaten out of them at school in the bad old days. As one former resident of the Eastside barrio, a publically employed physician in his sixties when I met him, told me, his kids grew up with the clear instruction that English was the way and the means to social mobility. This was one of multiple factors that distinguished some Austin Mexican Americans from immigrants recently arrived from Mexico, who were a driving force behind Austin's revived Spanish-language cultural scene (providing a market for newspapers, radio and TV stations, nightclubs, and other Spanish-dominant arenas). By the same token, Mexican American Austin is also set apart from the storied and studied region of South Texas, which stands in the folkloric and anthropological literature as an area of concentration of *lo mexicano* in the United States. The lowriders I met were of a generation that is subject to a kind of reverse stigma of presumed culture loss. From a Mexican national point of view, they could be construed as being mired in *pocho* inauthenticity, culturally denuded by a migrant past; from a Chicano/a one, they could be seen as victims of continued colonization. Yet in occupying this fraught position, Austin lowriders represent an enormous population of Mexican Americans around the United States who have experienced a measure of integration into the mainstreams of American life. This was certainly not an unproblematic integration that proceeded according to the classic immigrant "ethnic model" that promises social mobility in exchange for assimilation to unmarked (hence Anglo) norms. In any event, while Austin lowriders showed themselves in many ways to be well acculturated to consumer

Segmented assimilation idea

society and fluent in the public culture of the United States, the sociological notion of assimilation as a waning of ethnic difference was not in evidence (Alba
and Nee 2003; Jiménez 2010)—and given their racialization, not an option.

Casual talk in Austin's lowrider scene frequently expressed participants'
profound knowledge of the limits of the bootstraps-and-melting-pot narrative.
While lowriders indicated a sense of being entitled to inclusion in the U.S. public sphere—as often as not by participating in consumerism—they also seemed
to have few if any illusions about the limits to social mobility posed by the enduring salience of race and their own racialization, or of the class position determined by their relations to higher education and employment. The specific
historical situation of Austin Mexican Americans whom I met in lowriding was
that of being too "American" to be identified within certain essentialist or nationalist notions of "Mexican," yet being by no means "white."[14] This is one
sight line along which the current project, while referring to a very specific time
and place, may offer more general resonance.

To pursue and represent this articulation of contested identities with emergent materiality, I required an improvisatory bricolage of methods. Though I
conducted some recorded interviews, I generally found that participation in
everyday lowrider activities yielded more of the "poetic wisdom" I sought (Fernandez and Herzfeld 1998). Perhaps less sentimental than it sounds, poetic
wisdom describes an embodied knowledge of the means of productive cultural
action: the practices of making, understood through participation. Establishing a relationship with a car club, I was able to travel with club members to car
shows elsewhere, including in San Antonio and Houston; view film and music
video representations of lowrider style with them; and engage in some of the
same print and Internet discourses that they did. Most importantly, during the
longest period devoted to fieldwork in 1999–2001, I participated in the everyday
life of the local lowrider scene, including not only car shows, but also car club
meetings, fund-raising car washes, and "taco plate" sales. I engaged in negotiation and exchange on the informal market of used cars and custom parts, and
cruised streets and parking lots on weekends. After my graduate studies, I returned to Austin for intensive stints of fieldwork in 2002, 2003, 2005, and 2006.
My field experiences are documented in written field notes, photographs, and
recordings of soundscapes and audio notes made while I was driving.

From that collection of stories, documents, and souvenirs, I offer the chapters that follow. The first three begin with what is perhaps the most obvious
scale of "urban space," the city streetscape, and then "zoom in" on progres-

sively smaller scales in order to draw closer. Chapter One, "Cruising Spaces," deals with the everyday politics of occupying and moving through urban space in lowrider cruising and related practices. Sketching out a partial "identity map" of Austin, I relate how lowriding as an identity-marked version of auto-mobility contributes to the inscription of barrio space. Considering the subtle negotiations of space and identity that go on when lowriders cross neighbor-hood boundary lines, I interpret lowrider cruising as a counter-cartography that unmaps certain "imagined cities" and renders others as visceral impacts on the sensorium.

In Chapter Two, "Inside Out," I shift scales to consider the aesthetics of a lowrider car as a mobile, interior space. I view the establishment and adorn-ment of car interior "rooms" as a process of self-definition and public presenta-tion in a larger social context that creates a scarcity of personal space. I note how, in the process of customizing interiors, lowriders depart from or exceed the norms of bourgeois interiority in specific ways, instead manifesting a nonauto-nomous yet heterotopic space that resists foreclosing on diverse possibilities.

Chapter Three, "Auto Bodies" draws closer yet to address the embodied practices of lowriding. Following Lefebvre's rejoinder that social space begins with the body (1991, 40), I take note of the contrasts between lowrider embodi-ment and the way bodies are represented in lowrider media. This requires that I confront the use of women's bodies as objects to decorate cars in lowrider pho-tography, which reveals gender to be a point of contact that connects lowrid-ing with two much larger social formations: media culture and automobility in general. I argue that lowriding is neither immune to the ideological baggage of these associations nor fully defined by them, proposing that it is the emphasis on embodied practice that opens possibilities to practice a nondismissive cri-tique of lowriding and to imagine a less gender-restrictive future for it.

The next two chapters spin out some of the implications of considering lowriding as a material practice. Chapter Four, "Work," engages the material-ity of lowriding as a working-class pursuit as I narrate my own efforts to par-ticipate in the economic context of Austin lowriding. I endeavor to give flesh to some of the arguments from the previous chapters, namely, that a lowrider manifests personal histories of work and struggle in material form, and that the importance of this materialization is what makes participation in lowriding a cultural priority. In describing my experiences in attempting to earn the funds for my own lowrider in the at-will service sector of the "new economy," and to secure the car and parts necessary in the secondhand market of barrio automobility, I elaborate on the point that cars themselves are what matters about lowriding to participants.

Chapter Five, "Neither Gangsters nor *Santitos*," returns to the scale of the city streetscape to address the ascribed criminality of lowriders as part of a general stigmatizing of Mexican Americans, enacted in the mundane space of traffic. This is part of a broader set of minoritizing cartographies with which difference has been managed in U.S. cities. Thus, lowriders are implicated in larger social debates about the nature of "security," the limits of the public sphere, and the categories of political subjects who can claim protection from the police. I note that this web of implications can imbue everyday aesthetics with life-or-death consequences.

Finally, in the Conclusion I pull together strands from the previous chapters to elaborate on the intersections of aesthetics and politics that they suggest. This calls for methodological attention to material practices in everyday life, a dynamic notion of culture as a mode of performance that engages imaginaries in order to produce contexts, and most generally, a politics based on opening up future possibilities rather than shoring up past positions. While this work cannot define any such politics exhaustively, I argue that it becomes more possible when one takes vernacular subjugated knowledges seriously.

Cruising Spaces

I sat with members of the Custom Kings lowrider car club in Long John Silver's, eating after the weekly club meeting at a car wash. It was February, and I was surprised when the discussion turned to plans for cruising later that night, which I thought was mostly a summer activity. Before I met the Kings, I had gone in search of the cruising scene a couple of times, driving around East Riverside Drive to look for lowriders. Usually by around 10:30 I gave up and went home, apparently about an hour too early. At midnight on a Friday or Saturday, Riverside was crowded with cruisers, even in February.

Smiley took a call on his cell phone. "Where you at? Yeah? Is it packed?" He hung up and reported that the caller was at Best Buy, an electronics chain store in a large area of malls and shopping centers on the north side of Austin. The parking lot there, he said, was "packed" with custom cars, though not likely lowriders. That particular scene was known for the import street racers that would later be made famous by the *Fast and the Furious* Hollywood movies. The Best Buy was also close to mostly white suburbs and a long haul from the usual Eastside cruising sites. "Should we check it out later?" Smiley suggested.

"I don't want to go all the way up there—it's too far," said Eddie, the club president. "Plus, my water pump is leaking."

Steve, the only Anglo member of the club at that time, added, "Yeah, anyway you know what happens when you cross Airport." Eddie and Steve simultaneously imitated a police siren: "Weeeeeew." Running diagonally from the Eastside to the northwest, Airport Boulevard is an efficient way to drive from one end of town to the other. As it approaches the parking lot in question, however, it also parallels the boundary, usually marked by IH-35, between East and West Austin. Eddie continued the enactment of an imaginary encounter with the police: "What are you, lost? What are you doing in this neighborhood?" "Nah," he said. "We're not wanted over there." Elaborating for my benefit, Eddie pointed out that such encounters with police happen not only when lowriders cross a boundary line, but also sometimes when officers do. "You can always tell when the cops switch shifts," he said. "If they're from the west side and they're covering somebody's shift on the Eastside, they'll come and run us off."

In any city with a substantial lowrider community, the cruising scene is its everyday manifestation. As lowriders choose sites in which to gather or "post up," they consider where they can be seen by rivals or admirers and meet up with friends, calculate where they are "not wanted," and engage in the cat-and-mouse game of getting "run off" from public parking lots by police. In the midst of this, they affect the spatial formation of their city. In Austin during my fieldwork, there was regular cruising on East Riverside on Friday and Saturday nights, and on Sundays in the early evening in the park known officially as Fiesta Gardens but colloquially as Chicano Park. Driving around these areas was part of cruising, but so was standing near parked cars in a parking lot, scanning traffic for familiar rides, and noting the latest custom part or modification that a driver was "coming out with" that weekend. Owners of cars with hydraulics would "hit on" one another, briefly demonstrating the relative power of their suspension setups as they drove past, or sometimes a pair of them would stop to "hop on" each other in a longer, head-to-head duel to see whose hydraulics could bounce higher. More than anything else, the parking lots on Riverside were a scene for socializing, catching up on the latest word on the street, making plans for upcoming car shows, asking for and giving mechanical advice, or trying to "talk to" a potential courting partner. Crowds that gathered alongside dramatically customized cars made the situation highly noticeable to all passersby.

The zones of activity and attention that form around groups of lowriders in a cruising scene are perhaps the most obvious instance of a performance of lowrider space. In Austin, as in many U.S. cities, the urban landscape against which such performances take place could be mapped according to areas of concentration for particular racial and class identities. The eclipse of legal segregation after the mid-twentieth-century civil rights movement did not shift American cities from being enclave patchworks into hybrid melting pots. Rather, lines of ethnicity, class, and color mark out a kind of "identity map" for many U.S. cities, reflecting the de facto or virtual segregation that is part of an urban, spatial common sense.[1] According to market-based ideology, which presumes agency in such matters as where to live, the clumping of identities is simply an instance of old segregated residential patterns being reproduced because people choose freely to settle close to others like themselves. Yet attention to the production of the bounded spaces within cities suggests that the ordinary practices of organizing and regulating urban space are a means by which "difference" is managed and social stratification reproduced.

Identity maps do not reflect only an aggregate of individual decisions—in any event, they are by no means simply that. Regardless of the stated intentions or level of consciousness involved in producing identity maps in practice or representation, they are part of a collective struggle with privilege at stake. The racial legacy of urbanity in the United States suggests that these mappings are battlegrounds in what George Lipsitz has termed the "possessive investment in whiteness," by which white people have made use of public policy and cultural politics to establish and preserve their advantages. Spatial issues such as housing and the formation of neighborhood communities intersect with this both as advantages in themselves and as determinants of other positioning factors (1998, 33).

Lowriders play a dynamic role in these processes of spatial production, carrying an association with the barrio and its specific ethnoracial identity even as they move throughout cities. Their presence can reinforce the spatial identity of an area as a barrio, or they can assert their barriological aesthetics in the public sphere beyond those boundaries. This dual potentiality lends force to the affectivity of visual, aural, and kinetic signs that make up lowrider style. By making themselves difficult to miss, lowriders concentrate and locate the capacity to affect and be affected, making their presence and the occupation of a site an event. Differently conditioned subjects encountering the same lowrider may alternately interpret it as a comforting sign of home or as a social indicator of marginality. At the same time, while lowriders do not represent all barrio communities in their entirety, they do offer a convenient, racialized, and place-identified target for regulation. Thus, when police close down popular cruising sites, the most famous of which, LA's Whittier Boulevard,

Figure 1.1. Cruising downtown Austin.

was closed in 1979 (R. Rodríguez 1997), lowriders provide a focal point not only for police control of public space, but also for the symbolic exercise of state power over an entire community. Intentionally or not, and regardless of official policy, the logic of identity maps, according to which certain aesthetics and certain people "belong" in designated places, is enacted in the low-intensity policing of public space and its use: traffic stops, park curfews, and other means of regulation.

Everyday lowrider cruising offers a view of how such spatial management takes place, and of how lowriders at once draw on and contest the spatial identification of imagined identity maps. Looking at these processes from the vantage of lowrider space not only reveals how they function, but also suggests what might be at stake. Participating in cruising with lowriders and talking with them about their experiences in traffic allowed me to see how the production of space combines with popular aesthetics to define a particular relation to the city and its authorities. As a mobile, marked presence generating spatial fields that evoke and embody certain imaginaries, lowriders contest the political strategies and material configurations with which difference has been produced and managed in modern cities. The way that city authorities, notably police in traffic, respond to this contestation shows that lowriding carries a measure of political force, regardless of whether intervening in spatial politics is the motivation behind lowriding in the first place, or whether a particular lowrider carries an overtly resistant slogan or iconography.

In what follows, I attempt to render the spatial politics of cruising on the scale of city streets, first by introducing some of the contours of an identity map of Austin at the turn of the millennium, which emerged from larger histories of barrioization and spatial minoritization. Against this background, I will further narrate and describe how lowriders appropriate space and inscribe the barrio on the Austin streetscape through everyday cruising, as well as the converse: how the mapping of barrio space gets reinforced in the regulation of traffic by police. Finally, I discuss how lowriders effect a transversal counter-cartography (see Reynolds and Fitzpatrick 1999) when they cruise across conventional neighborhood boundary lines.

Identity Maps

In contemporary U.S. cities, cultural and racial diversity is overlaid with spatial arrangements and social stratification, so identity-linked ("identified") popular aesthetic practices like lowriding become part of a struggle over territory (Zukin 1995, 41–42). Such performances respond to the historical containment of those populations and communities that have been "territorially subjugated by the workings of hegemonic power" (Soja 1996, 87). Among the processes of "territorial subjugation" at work in this history is the designation and enforcement of particular distributions of identity, a cartography that proceeds through what anthropologist Michel Laguerre calls the "minoritization" of space (1999). The notion of "minority" here is best understood as a social position in relation to various forms of capital and public recognition rather than as a value-neutral demographic descriptor (Laguerre 1999, 31). To be "minoritized" is to be positioned as marginal according to dominant discourses and imaginaries—being in an actual, statistical minority is not always required. This sense of "minority" became particularly relevant for my field site as Texas became the fourth "majority-minority" state in the United States (U.S. Census Bureau 2005). Laguerre's term "minoritized" is particularly useful in such situations, in which demographic preponderance does not equate with political dominance. Regarding minoritized space, Laguerre's central, Lefebvrian point is that the spatial ramifications of social struggle are not epiphenomenal to actual politics, but figure into the very construction of patterns of domination: in a stratified, culturally diverse society, as concentrated in a stratified, culturally diverse city, difference is produced and managed spatially. Thus, there can be no minoritized population without minoritized space (Laguerre 1999, 95).

In minoritized space, location comes to stand as both reflective and constitutive of the subjects that occupy it: where residents are seems to offer both a causal explanation and a justification for their social marginality (Laguerre 1999, 96). Minoritized space also exceeds actual, material location to take on a metaphorical power that travels. A common example of this in everyday discourse is the use of "ghetto" as a pejorative adjective, which might be (offensively) used to describe a person as well as a place: "He's so ghetto." This usage assumes that people who "belong" in minoritized space will eventually show their true colors in stigmatized behavior. Those, on the other hand, who are entitled to a greater share of privilege will make it apparent that they are not from minoritized space, or at least not of it—they are not "ghetto," and hence know how to act.

Everyday practices accompany these conceptual maps and contribute to the "senses of place"—or, more broadly, the imagined cities—that are either produced and challenged depending on who occupies a site and how. Identified aesthetic practices join this fray in the production of space. Lowriders do so as part of the particular history of urban Mexican Americans, in which the processes of urban planning and zoning, real estate practices, financial redlining, and other "representations of space" (Lefebvre 1991, 33), have been the means of barrioization (Camarillo 1979; Villa 2000, 15). Everyday practices, including police surveillance, selective law enforcement, and collective punishment, reinforce these designations. Yet as Villa notes, barrioization is not purely repressive. The production of identified space nurtures both the deployment of that local identity as a resource and the valuation of local knowledge, what he calls, borrowing from the underground magazine *Con Safos*, "barriology" (2000, 9).

This schema might seem in accord with a distinction, described by the prominent spatial anthropologist Setha Low, between the "production of space" in the planning and execution of the built environment and the "construction of space" through everyday use, including cultural ascriptions of significance (1999b). Yet Lefebvre's insistence on the importance of everyday dialectics suggests that both of these are aspects of the same process. While representations of space such as policy, land use law, real estate ownership, and maps may chart or represent a frozen moment in spatial production, they do not "fix" spatial form itself. That form is an arrangement of things, bodies, surfaces, and contents, many of which exist in motion, so it must be constantly produced and reproduced. For the dominant map to take hold, the spatial imaginaries of planners and governments must be brought into material being and reinforced, and deviant bodies and things must be put in their place or simply "moved on." Meanwhile the spatial processes of everyday life open chances for divergent spatialities to alter or undo the map. This is what it means to argue that everyday practices produce social space.

In the early 2000s, Austin was undergoing rapid change, which has since continued enough to alter the built landscape and circuits of transportation considerably from how they looked during my initial field research. New toll roads, a light-rail line, and rapid gentrification of neighborhoods in the central city have affected Austin's streetscape and the spatial identities of the areas that it outlines. This clarifies a problem with the "ethnographic present" noted by critics of anthropology, and should serve as a reminder that this book constructs an image of Austin and its spatial formations at a particular historical moment. These have by no means remained static. Yet I suspect that the ongoing production of space in Austin is likely to have intensified, rather than superseded, the spatial-political relations that I glimpsed from lowrider space. Boundaries may have shifted, but they still matter, and those who experience and construct them now will no doubt have something to say about my arguments here.

Maps 1.1 and 1.2 provide a rough sketch of the field site and outlines some of the roadway infrastructure that determined flows of traffic during my research. This streetscape also marked out the boundaries of an identity map of Austin. The heavy line representing IH-35 reflects the principal identifying divide among Austin neighborhoods. At least six lanes wide and in some places two levels high, the interstate separates the majority-minority area generally known as East Austin from the rest of the city. The neighborhoods to the east were products of a long and complex history of segregation, and according to the 2000 census, remained around 15 percent or less white/Anglo, with African Americans and Latino/as, in different proportions, combining to make the population 90 percent residents of color in some areas.[2] On the other side of the highway are some obvious centers of cultural and political authority. The downtown area, anchored by Congress Avenue, includes the state Capitol, Governor's Mansion, office buildings, and the Sixth Street entertainment district,

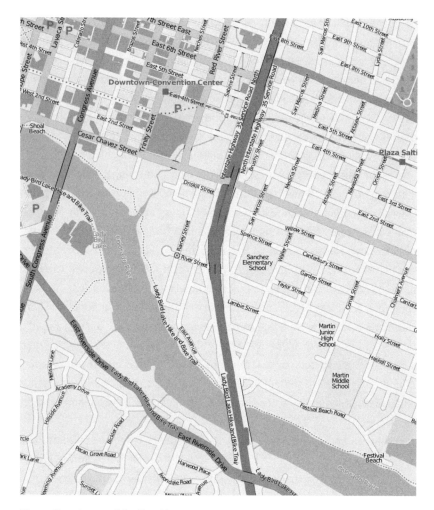

Map 1.1 Downtown and the Eastside.
© OpenStreetMap contributors, CC-BY-SA, http://www.openstreetmap.org.

which is an important part of Austin's consumption landscape as a "lifestyle" city. Just north of downtown is the University of Texas, which also sits mostly west of the highway, but has gradually expanded eastward with university buildings, a baseball stadium, and housing and restaurants oriented to a student-and-intellectual market.[3]

The other most important geographic component that, along with IH-35, divides central Austin into rough quadrants is the Colorado River. Dams mark off a series of reservoirs on the river, including, on the west side of town, Lake

Austin between Mansfield Dam and Tom Miller Dam; from downtown east-ward, Town Lake (now known as Lady Bird Lake) sits between Tom Miller Dam and Longhorn Dam. South of the river, Congress Avenue was formerly a qui-eter and, people often said, funkier extension of downtown. Lowriders spoke of cruising South Congress "back in the day," but during my fieldwork, that street and the surrounding area were beginning a dramatic transformation that would, in ensuing years, make it a high-dollar, trendy residential and commer-cial area now promoted to tourists and shoppers as "SoCo." West and south of this relatively privileged corridor were working-class neighborhoods in an area known as South Austin. The areas closest to the river were about evenly divided between Anglo and Latino residents, with fewer Anglos to the south. More af-fluent suburbs lay farther to the southwest, some of these with white popula-tions exceeding 90 percent.

Map 1.2 East Riverside cruising area.
© OpenStreetMap contributors, CC-BY-SA, http://www.openstreetmap.org.

Most but not all the lowriders I got to know lived in or identified in some way with South and East Austin barrios. South Austin had a working-class and "alternative" identity that in some ways reflected its racial and economic diversity and was celebrated in bits of public culture like the popular bumper sticker that reads: "South Austin: We're all here because we're not all there."[4] A blue-collar relationship to cars was part of the South Austin vibe in general, and classic custom vehicles were permanent fixtures outside the hip Continental Club live-music venue on South Congress. Among lowriders, a specific South Austin identity was also evident in car club names like South Side Life, and in their celebration of the area's zip code, 78704, as an emblem of pride. Lowriders joined other South Austinites in this: another bumper sticker easy to spot around town read: "78704: It's not just a zip code, it's a way of life." Though bumper stickers were not lowriders' preferred medium of communication, recently a lowrider with whom I keep in touch via social media shared a photo from a friend, a close-up shot of a car odometer turning over to 78704. An Anglo lowrider whom I call Chris told me in an interview about how he embraced a south side identity for the benefit of police helicopters in the decoration of his lowrider van:

> It was a unfinished work, but I had about, probably 70 percent of it covered in graffiti in thirteen different colors, I was—this is when I was living over here in, uh, 78704? And I was going to do the uh, the zip code on the roof, so the cops could . . . Dude, I got pulled over *so* much . . . I haven't got pulled over since I got it back, but they still mess with me.

Several of the lowriders I knew lived in South Austin in a neighborhood anchored by the large San José Catholic Church, established in 1939, which today runs four services every Sunday, alternating in English and Spanish. Some lowriders I met from South Austin had parents who grew up in the neighborhoods known collectively to lowriders as the Eastside, just across the highway from downtown, but had since moved away. One advantage of South Austin was an abundance of relatively affordable and decent housing—the Eastside offered historic residential neighborhoods of single-family homes and several public housing projects, so much of what was considered desirable housing stock was not likely within the financial reach of relatively young blue-collar workers. In contrast, by moving away from the downtown core southward, it was possible to find condos and newer housing developments that avoided the stigma of "the projects," but required lower entry-level costs than a freestanding house. I learned that the relationship between east and south is not always smooth. A break-dancer active in the local hip-hop scene who grew up in a low-income neighborhood on the southeast side told me: "Eastside don't like the South Side because we got out, got a little more money." In this discourse, "South Side" tended to index areas west of the IH-35 boundary and their relatively stable, working-class reputation. In contrast, southeast areas such as Dove Springs were known—perhaps stereotypically—for greater levels of deprivation and crime.

The Custom Kings held their weekly meetings west of the highway and about five miles south of downtown at a car wash on William Cannon Drive. Some time after I connected with the Kings, I was in a pizza restaurant with a handful of club members, and Eddie asked me where I lived. When I said East Second, he laughed heartily. "I thought you were going to say South Fifth or something. You live on the Eastside!" He called down the table to another member to tell him about it. Thomas replied, "Hell, we all want to move out of the Eastside and you want to move in." Eddie himself lived at that time in Del Valle, an exurban town just east of Austin, near the airport, and he had family in Montopolis, an East Austin neighborhood that was farther out from the central neighborhoods that were usually called the Eastside. I had eaten at home before going out that night, and when Eddie offered me a piece of his pizza, I said no thanks. He insisted. "Come on, I know what you eat there on the Eastside. Nothing but beans. You must be hungry."

Despite the fact that lowriders lived all over Austin and in several suburbs (in varying concentrations), the Eastside remained an important focus for cruising. Each weekend, lowriders returned to the cruising strip of East Riverside Drive, on the south side of Town Lake, and to Chicano Park. The Eastside barrio that includes "the park," with its proximity to downtown, was becoming a likely target for gentrification and "urban removal" during the time of my research.[5] This made for competing ideas about what the neighborhood represented. A community activist who showed me around the Holly Street area of the Eastside wanted me to notice how peaceful the residential blocks were, in contrast with the heavy traffic in other parts of Austin. At another time, I talked about the same area with a young professional in a high-tech field who knew someone who had moved to Holly. She described it as dangerous, telling me that her friend had "sacrificed" several car CD players to local thieves and cautioned me against choosing to live there.

The dissonant mappings of the Eastside became more evident when my wife, Marike Janzen, and I moved there and rented a house during my fieldwork. Our landlady was a white bohemian character who held some investment properties—not an uncommon identity in Austin at that time. She made a selling point of the "Mexican-style" aesthetic of her rental house, which was finished in brightly colored paint and ceramic tile, but in the next breath also cautioned us about "neighborhood types" and expressly forbade what she called any "Appalachian" neglect of the front porch. "Think property values!" she said as we moved in, "That's the key!" Despite our efforts to maintain the landlady's asset, I soon learned that certain pizza places located west of the highway would not deliver to our street. Yet twice Latino candidates for public office personally came to our door—an influential state senator seeking reelection and a community activist running for the city council. Another time, a young Anglo woman rang our doorbell, apparently having seen us around the yard, to ask whether we felt safe living in the neighborhood. When I introduced myself to the Latina proprietor of a neighborhood restaurant, she observed, "Oh, yeah, a lot of Americans have been moving into this neighborhood."

These were all signs that the Eastside was in transition, as the activist sticker that showed up on a stop sign on our block noted: "Warning: This neighborhood is being gentrified." As I got to know a couple of elderly neighbors, I was privileged to hear their family memories of the previous transition, which established these neighborhoods as "the Eastside." Mrs. Díaz, a couple of doors down from us, who was always out watering her lawn, invited us in one afternoon for a piece of pineapple cake. Mrs. Díaz told me her family had lived in the country on Lake Austin until her parents sold their place and moved into town, to the area once known as "Mexico" or "Little Mexico" on the south end of downtown, west of what is now the highway. Mrs. Díaz went to work cleaning house for the previous owner of her Eastside home, a woman of German descent named Kohl. When Mrs. Kohl's husband died, Mrs. Díaz bought the house and offered to rent a room back to her former employer, but Mrs. Kohl's children thought better of it. Mrs. Díaz had lived there for fifty-five years. When I visited, the house was a bustling hub of great-grandchildren, to whom she was trying to teach Spanish.

Across the street was ninety-year-old Mrs. Alonso, who could still manage her own lawn mower and invited me to look at some photos of herself as a young woman sporting a pompadour. Mrs. Alonso had also lived downtown in the Third Street area, a few blocks west of Congress, where a barrio had formed around a chile-canning factory. She invited me to dinner with her son-in-law Leyton, who grew up speaking Spanish in Corpus Christi and had met Mrs. Alonso's daughter when he came to study at the University of Texas. Now a psychiatrist, he regaled me with tales of political activism during his student days, before the Chicano/a movement was in full swing. He told me, "Of course, in those days, when we went to protest, we wore coats and ties." Despite his references to political activity, Leyton's account of how the Eastside became a barrio was matter-of-fact: "Well, it always was, because the city was all on the other side of the *calle ancha*—the wide street." As people settled west of Congress to work in the chile cannery, he said, that area got crowded. People started looking for other places to live, and they could afford land east of *la calle ancha*, which was East Avenue, a boulevard that ran where IH-35 eventually would. "So, the street decided—well, the street didn't decide, but the people on the street decided to live here. And then the blacks decided to live a little north."

Leyton's account is not unlike that offered by Our Lady of Guadalupe Catholic Church, which itself made the move from west to east in 1926. The parish history echoes Leyton's reference to crowding as the spur to move east, recounting the arrival of a new pastor a year earlier:

> He began by preaching a two week's mission, and so great was the attendance and the consequent fruit of the mission that it immediately became necessary to seek a more ample site for the church and the school. On the other hand, the new families which were coming in, were located mostly to the east of the city. (Our Lady of Guadalupe Catholic Church, n.d.)

Hence land for the parish was purchased in East Austin, the Our Lady of Guadalupe Church on West Fifth Street torn down, and a new building constructed at East Ninth.

The Eastside poet Raúl R. Salinas offers a different view of all this deciding and choosing in his poem "Via Crucis 150," which inserts into the 150-year history of Austin (when the poem was written in 1986) glimpses of communities like Little Mexico, which were subject to displacement and erasure in the interest of progress planned elsewhere:

[handwritten annotation: moved because y Jim Crow?]

In the roarin' of the 20s
city fathers (who else)
map OUT/Speck you late
Westside colonia
Soon be cumming DOWN town!

"Move their church
and the natives will follow,
it's an old trick."

They moved the church
To a "rocky hill"
On the Eastern edge of
Town.
And soon El Barrio
Mejicano was no more
(1995, 66–67)

The displacement of Little Mexico and the barrioization of the Eastside incorporated Mexicans arriving in Austin into a scheme of segregation designed to separate African Americans and white Anglos. The arrival of Mexicans in the 1920s, to a city on land that once had been part of Mexico, can be construed as new only because of the forced expulsion of most Mexicans from Austin in 1854. After Texas independence, proximity to Mexico posed a threat to the institution of slavery by offering a possible avenue of escape. Indeed, a series of resolutions adopted by white citizens' meetings at the time raised the alarm that in associating with slaves, Mexicans could instill "false notions of freedom," making the enslaved "discontented and insubordinate" (Lack 1981, 9). Spurred by these fears, the press called for "a little timely exertion in clearing our country of rascally peons" (5), which came to fruition when vigilantes drove some twenty Mexican families out of town. Further actions kept Austin hostile to Mexicans, leaving only twenty people with Spanish surnames in Travis County in 1860, all vouched for in one way or another by Anglos (11).

When, following the Mexican Revolution, migration began to rebuild Austin's Mexican community, this coincided with the production of East Austin as a minoritized space, a milestone of which was the 1928 city master plan for Austin (Koch and Fowler 1928). That plan included a designation of the east end of town, rather than several noncontiguous "freedom towns" where former slaves had settled, as the "Negro" district. The policy was explicitly aimed at solving "the problem of segregation," which, to white Austinites in the 1920s, was a problem of how to segregate races effectively and efficiently. As the Our Lady of Guadalupe parish history recounts, Latinos were already settling to the east. But the same period presents recognizable signs of barrioization, including the establishment of segregated institutions such as a "Mexican ward" in the municipal hospital, a "Mexican park" in East Austin, and the continuation of segregated education (McDonald 2005, 4). Desegregation in Austin, as in many places, lagged behind its official mandate: the Austin Independent School District refused to desegregate even after being sued by the federal government in 1970 for not complying with the *Brown v. Board of Education* decision (Almanza and Alvarez 1997, 112). It took nearly thirty years for Austin schools to be recognized as "unitary," and only after extensive legal action and attempts by the city to describe schools as "integrated" if they included both African Americans and Mexican Americans but were almost completely devoid of whites.

As was typical elsewhere, the spatial containment of communities of color allowed them to nurture sites of identity or barriological memory, such as Anderson High School and the A. B. Cantu Pan American Recreation Center. The legacies of segregation thus include senses of attachment to places and institutions that may have originated in quite overt systems of oppression. Conversely, in the postsegregation era, the production of identity-based boundaries is not as official or overt as the 1928 plan for Austin or the signs that historically designated other places as "sundown towns" (Loewen 2005). The feeling of being "not wanted," as Steve suggested the Kings would be at Best Buy, now plays a larger role than official segregation, but this experience itself is a complex production. The dominant, neoliberal perspective on spatial formation, based on an ontology of freely acting individuals in a competitive marketplace, presumes that people settle and spend time in places where they feel at home. This feeling of being in place or, in an affirming sense, "wanted" can be understood as a kind of commodified affect, part of what is purchased with home ownership. That was the perspective represented by a developer quoted in a news story I read during my fieldwork. The reporter was covering rising home values and rents on the Eastside and raised the possibility that such increases might have a dislocating effect on current residents. The real estate developer being interviewed shrugged off that possibility by saying, "That's the price you pay to live in Austin."

Such a perspective requires a level of indifference to the people and relationships—what is sometimes called the community—that exist in any given area, and takes dislocation to be a neutral effect of normal market function. It clearly does not take into account the individual and collective meanings that get layered onto a place—the spatial memory—over time and through repeated, routine activities like lowrider cruising. Spatial memory is a resource not strictly tied to spending power, but one that amasses from time spent, copresence, survival, and discourses of remembering. It does not convert easily to cash value and cannot be quickly or conveniently created. Yet because real estate markets and spatial planning schemes trade on "senses of place," sites of collective spatial memory may become prime targets for consumption in the process known ironically or pejoratively as "gentrification" (Aoki 1993). Ultimately, the free-market image propagated by neoliberal accounts of spatial production obscures the divergent interests that are set in conflicting relation: the urban renewal of one class is the urban removal of another. By the same token, it obscures how spatial affects, the material-perceptual events that lead to feelings such as being "at home" or "not wanted," are produced through specific patterns of relations to authority and law enforcement, and their performance.

Figure 1.2. *Día de la Raza* celebration on the Eastside.

The history of the Eastside barrio is a rich vein for many research projects in its own right. Here, suffice it to say that the character of the Eastside as a barrio presents a collective archive of spatial memory that lowriders work with and contribute to. Indeed, by their regular presence, most noticeably on weekends, but also throughout the week in ordinary traffic, lowriders reinscribe the Eastside as a barrio space.

Cruising the Eastside

When we had finished eating at Long John Silver's, the Custom Kings agreed to "hit up Riverside" and drove in caravan from the restaurant to a Pizza Hut situated on one of the busiest blocks of the divided boulevard. We arrived around 11:30, and the cruising scene was just getting started. Although that stretch of Riverside is lined with hills and embankments, the Pizza Hut parking lot is at street level, with only a narrow sidewalk separating it from the traffic. It is on a corner with a stoplight, making it a prime location for watching the cruising action and interacting with people in cars stopped at the intersection. The parking places close to the street are often taken first, but that night they were clear, and we pulled in. Eddie engaged his hydraulic suspension and lifted his 1973 Monte Carlo onto three wheels so it loomed in the air, seeming frozen in the act of lunging toward the cars that passed. We hung out in the parking lot and watched traffic go by, commenting on other custom cars as they passed, the metal plaques in their windows claiming rival or friendly club allegiances. A couple of cars from the Stylistic Syndicate came into the lot and pulled in next to us. Members of the two clubs greeted each other with handshakes and stood around chatting.

I noticed a car parked on the opposite side of the lot, slightly uphill from the street—a 1980s GM sedan that I had not seen before, relatively uncustomized apart from its shiny chrome rims. The logo covering the rear window identified the car as belonging to Just Cruzin, a relatively new car club in town whose members were quickly acquiring a reputation among the Kings and the Syndicate as "troublemakers." A lone Cruzer stood leaning against his car and watching the traffic and the rest of us warily.

A car passing in the westbound lanes on the other side of the street gunned its motor and sounded its horn in a rhythm something like that of "Shave and a Haircut," the signature of the Cruzers. A few minutes later, a caravan of several more cars rolled by in the opposite direction, all honking the cadence. One car did the first section, "Shave and a Haircut," and the others responded with three honks, as if to articulate the syllables of "Just Cruzin" instead of "two bits." The Kings observed, nonplussed—the tune didn't carry quite the aggressive connotation it would on some streets in Mexico—but the encounter was not without tension.[6] Whether or not they deserved the reputation for making trouble, the Cruzers were a rival club. The Cruzer caravan pulled onto the side street, and the cars began to make their way into the lot, pulling up beside their lone comrade.

Someone beside me said softly, "*Chota*" (police), and I turned around to see an Austin Police Department car entering by the opposite driveway. The red and blue strobe lights on the roof came on. The officer did not leave the car, but spoke over his loudspeaker: "All right. Everybody clear the parking lot." We all walked to our cars, calling over our shoulders to one another to establish the next meeting place.

"Want to go to the pawnshop?"

"What about the bingo?"

"All right, the bingo."

We got into our cars and pulled out of the Pizza Hut parking lot in caravan: Eddie first, as president; then Smiley, the vice president; then Joseph, the secretary; and Thomas, the sergeant at arms. Theirs were the custom cars. Then came Raymond in his mom's Taurus, since his 1970 Monte Carlo was not running that night; Aaron in his new PT Cruiser with chrome alloy rims; and me in the rear in my white Toyota, nondescript except for aluminum wheels that had seen better days and sections of paint where the glossy clear coat was flaking. At the corner, everyone got through on a green light up to Aaron, who raced through the intersection as it changed from yellow to red. I stopped for the light, and soon the other cars were out of sight. I did not carry a cell phone, so I was out of touch. They had said we were going to the bingo hall, which I thought was to the west, but they were headed east on Riverside, perhaps to take a cruise around the circuit of the strip.

The light changed, and I headed east as well. There was no sign of the others. I turned north on Pleasant Valley Road, which runs toward the river and crosses at Longhorn Dam into the heart of the Eastside. I checked another cruising spot known as "The Logs," but it was dark and empty. I continued north on Pleasant Valley, turning around at the next intersection. As I crossed the river, I noticed a police car sitting in a small park on the north shore, all its lights out.

By the time I turned around and headed back toward Riverside, the patrol car was pulling out of the lot onto Pleasant Valley.

Driving down Riverside now from east to west, I caught a glimpse of the sign marking the closed bingo parlor on the north side of the street, scarcely a quarter of a mile from the Pizza Hut where we had first posted up. I saw the Kings and a handful of others gathered in one corner of the large parking lot. It was otherwise empty on that side, but the other half, adjoining a pawnshop, taco stands, and a nightclub I will call "Club Latino," was packed with cars and trucks. By the time I managed to turn into the lot, I was in front of the pawnshop in the crowded section near Club Latino. I fell into a long line of cars moving slowly through the packed lot while patrons, many wearing *ropa norteña* western clothes—boots, belt buckles, and hats—walked toward the nightclub, where amplified cumbias rolled out the open door.[7] A county sheriff's car was near the entrance, and a deputy in uniform was leaning against it, talking to some people casually. I inched my car forward along with the others who were looking for a spot close to Club Latino's entrance. Ahead on a side street, I saw an SUV stretch limousine moving toward Riverside. All around me were pickup trucks, some customized with spoilers or pinstripes, definitely a different scene from when the Kings get their GM sedans together. Finally, I reached the last of the parked cars, leaving the club goers behind, and drove across the emptier side of the lot to where the Kings were gathered.

"There you are—we thought we lost you!" said Smiley, explaining that they had stopped at a gas station to use the restroom. It crossed my mind that I could have used the opportunity, too, since we had been out for several hours by then. I explained that I had lost them at the light, and joked that I was driving around for a while because I got used to the warm car. It was cold for Texas, even though I was wearing a hooded sweatshirt and a lined flannel shirt over it. One of the slighter Kings shivered and said, "Man, I'm too *flaco*"—thin—"I'm getting cold." But why was I slightly embarrassed not to have known where the bingo parlor was? It was an obvious gap in my knowledge, a mark of my novice incompetence in cruising. But then again, why would I have known? Although a thin, misty rain had started, the street remained busy with cruisers. Smiley pulled out his cell phone and switched on the display light to check the time: 1:40 a.m. Soon the last call would be issued at "Club InSane," just across the street. Smiley announced that he was going to get home before the drunks started leaving the clubs in their cars. It seemed like a good idea, so I joined him and a few others in saying good-bye and driving home.

In these ordinary movements when out cruising on Riverside, lowriders appropriated the streetscape and remapped it through use according to their own geographies of preferred cruising spots and anticipated hazards—including the police, thoughtless street racers, crowds of partiers, gangbangers, or drunk drivers. The lowriders' presence alone did not determine the spatial identity of East Riverside: the barrioization of the Eastside and the political economy of real estate and urban development had their own parts to play in producing the conditions under which lowriders effected their remappings (Bright 1995; Thrift 2004a). Riverside was lined with retail businesses, several nightclubs, and relatively affordable apartments, so students, immigrants, and young working families were among those who joined lowriders in the public space along the broad boulevard on weekend nights. The resulting "barrio" landscape, to which the noticeable presence of lowriders contributed, was affectionately mocked in a sketch by a local performing group called the Latino Comedy Project. Parodying the traffic report of a mainstream radio or TV station as a representation of the city, the LCP imagined an Eastside version featuring "Chuy in the sky":

> **ANCHOR:** Chuy could you tell us your position?
>
> **CHUY:** I am presently at the intersection of East Riverside and Burton Drive overlooking the Club Carnival parking lot.
>
> **ANCHOR:** And where are you located?
>
> **CHUY:** Across the street on the roof of the Taco Bell.
>
> **ANCHOR:** Okay, and what is the traffic situation there?
>
> **CHUY:** Aw, man, lowriders are backed up for blocks, güey. Congestion is real heavy near the Taqueria stand and also, if you're traveling east, we strongly suggest that you find an alternate route around the group of about a dozen drunken mojados now moving westbound through the club parking lot. You can't miss 'em, holmes, they're all dressed alike. Just keep an eye out for a large, weaving mass of hot pink and aqua. We estimate that they may be bien borrachos for the next several hours or so, so take the proper precautions.
>
> **ANCHOR:** Uh-huh. And what about the cops?
>
> **CHUY:** Oh, you mean the Five-O?
>
> **ANCHOR:** Um, yeah.
>
> **CHUY:** Yes, beware the unmarked cop vehicle circling the area. He doesn't think that anybody knows he's a cop, but you don't see too many "Re-Elect Bush" bumper stickers on the Eastside, know what I'm sayin'?

ANCHOR: An unmarked cop vehicle . . . and what do you recommend for that, Chuy?

CHUY: Uh, invisibility. That'd be good.

(Latino Comedy Project 2002)

Cruising on the Eastside reinforced lowriders' imagined placement within Austin barrio space, even though some of the participants actually lived in other parts of town. But lowriders also appropriated this "given" social space by occupying it performatively, that is, through repeated outward presentations of their rides as identifiable acts of signification. Thus, the presence of lowriders was a persistent performance of barrio space, and an embrace of certain affects related to it.

Regulating Lowrider Space

The light poles at the bingo hall held No Parking signs indicating that the lot was a tow-away zone after business hours—that was why that half of the parking lot was so empty on Saturdays. Every now and then, a car would pull into the far corner of the lot, which was across the street from Club InSane, presumably because the club's lot was full. At least once I saw a tow truck arrive and start to pull a car away just as the driver came out of the club, ran over, and pleaded to be allowed to move the car himself. When I was in the bingo lot with the Kings, we stayed close to our cars, ready to leave if the tow truck came our way or a police officer arrived to clear the area. One night when a police car did pull into the bingo lot, Smiley put one finger in the air and whirled it to indicate "we're rolling.'" Several people had gotten in their cars and started them up when the officer, an African American woman, got out of the car. "Where y'all going?" she said. A couple of people laughed nervously and paused in the process of leaving, still unsure whether we were being run off as the officer struck up a conversation.

"How much do those lights cost?" she asked, pointing to Smiley's blue strobes. She looked around pleasantly. "Y'all aren't doing nothing. Just hanging out here. That's cool."

Her manner was calm and friendly, almost obscuring the subtle one-way negotiation she was carrying on: by stating what we were doing—just hanging out, having a good time—she made it clear that was what we needed to do to stay out of trouble. After a bit of small talk, she said, "Y'all be careful now," an idiomatic farewell that I heard often in East Austin, and climbed back into her car. As she pulled away, someone behind me called, "Couldn't she give us a letter that says we're allowed to be here?" A few people laughed.

After the nice cop had gone, I went to my car to move it closer to the group. Earlier, I had parked some distance away from where the lowriders ultimately gathered, and I was still wary of the tow trucks. I chose not to risk it, having had my share of interactions with the Austin "land sharks" over parking places at apartment complexes in the past. When I got into my car and started the engine, I noticed headlights approaching in my rearview mirror as a late-model car—was it a Crown Victoria?—pulled in behind me. I stayed put. No one got out of the car. I waited for what seemed like a long time until the Crown Vic slowly backed out and drove off to another section of the parking lot. Most likely it was an unmarked police car, and the officers had been "running my plates" to check for any record in their computer. I had sat there for only a few minutes, but it seemed much longer.

By the time I rejoined the group, everyone was watching a large white van with blacked-out windows drive slowly down the side street between the bingo hall and Club InSane. Smiley said, "This doesn't feel right. I don't like the way this feels at all." He turned to me. "You see that van? That's the jump-out boys. SWAT team." Suddenly, the van accelerated to the corner and took off onto Riverside, eastbound. A police car pulled in behind it. At about the same time, three or four other police cars appeared on the side street and, along with the unmarked car that had sat behind me, slowly cruised into the InSane parking lot, around the building, and out of sight. Watching them, I noticed a couple more cops standing by the doorway to the nightclub, checking IDs.

A guy I didn't know pulled up in a Nissan compact with custom chrome rims, but not lowered. "Man," he said as he greeted the Kings one by one, "I just came from homeboy's party, and the laws was looking for me 'cause I was racing." He fell silent when another police car pulled down the street beside the parking lot where we were posted up and suddenly lit up its strobes, causing most people in our group again to instinctively put their hands on door handles or take a couple of steps toward their cars. But the patrol car was headed past us. An import with a custom spoiler affixed to its rear end raced through the intersection, and the cop sounded his siren, peeling out and turning east in pursuit. People started joking about their own jumpiness. Lito, a gregarious lowrider friendly with the Kings who often turned the conversation at cruising sites into a standup comedy routine, singled out one young lowrider who had moved quickly to his car at the sound of the siren: "Cop's like, 'weeew!' and he just starts running. Shit, dog, that's the Mexican in you! See a cop and buuuuu-um!" Lito pumped his arms to pantomime running while he imitated the sound of an accelerating motor with his voice. He acted out a dialogue between two fleeing lowriders. "It's like: 'What's going on?' 'I don't know, dog, just run! I'll call you later on the cell phone!'"

Lito's comment on "the Mexican in you" as accounting for a young low-rider's jumpiness testifies to the constant state of being under surveillance in a barrio space. Traffic stops by police were a ubiquitous means of this spatial reg-ulation, one familiar to all lowriders I met. Roman, who was unaffiliated with a car club but well known locally for his 1964 Impala lowrider, spoke in an in-terview about being pulled over as his only negative experience with lowriding. Without privileging one dimension of identity over others, Roman portrayed these situations as an articulation of race, class, and style—it was never clear that either his identity as a Mexican American or the distinctive look of his car was the "real" reason for his being pulled over. The heavy implication of stories like Roman's was that the given reasons were just pretexts.

> **BEN:** You said that there were lots and lots of, uh, positive experiences. Were there any experiences where you thought, "Aw, man, it would be a lot easier if I, uh, if I weren't driving a lowrider right now," or . . .
>
> **ROMAN:** I think that the only part that I had, that came to my mind was, when I would get pulled over driving my car. That was the only time that I would think, "God, man, what the hell am I doing in this car?" I think of, man, just the easiest way to get out of it. But then, uh, I had nothing to fear, 'cause I didn't violate anything. I would just get pulled over 'cause, uh, let me see . . . I got pulled over because, uh, one time a cop said that I had too much gold on my car and that it would distract people. I'm like, "Come on, man." Another time I got pulled over 'cause we went to HEB [a local grocery store]. We were going to have a barbecue at my friend's house who lives over on the other side of Airport. Well, we had four—I remember we had four grocery bags. Of course I was driving, my friend was on this side, Steve, and my friend Robbie was in the backseat. And we had two bags of groceries in the front, two bags in the back, and we got—we just hadn't been paying attention, and we—I told Steve "Hey, man, put those groceries in the back, I don't want 'em up here." So he

grabs the bags and he turns around and he gives them to my friend Robbie. Right there those lights came on. "Oh, my God." Looked over and said, "God dang . . ." We pulled over where—you know where the tank farm is at? [. . .] We got pulled over there and another thing, we got taken out, they got us out of the car, we got searched, wanted to know what we were doing, what we were doing in the neighborhood, "Are you from this area?"

"Man, I live right here, right in front of Govalle Elementary."

"Where y'all going?"

The whole time I asked him why had he pulled me over. He goes, "Well . . ." He wouldn't answer me. After a good while, after more officers show up, he said, "Under suspicion," 'cause I was handing bags to the back.

I said, "Man, they're grocery bags. Man, why don't you look?" I said, "I got some ribs, I got some hamburger meat."

"Well, you were passing something. That's not all I saw." He goes, "I saw you pass something else." And all we passed was two bags of, uh, of groceries to the back. Well, uh, in one of the bags was a bottle. It was a Budweiser bottle that big. It was for my friend's mom, and she asked for it. He wanted to know what we were doing with that bottle, and I said, "I bought it." I said, "I bought it for my friend's mom, and that's who we're taking it to." Well, he couldn't do nothing about it, 'cause it wasn't open or anything. Well, to make a long story short, we got pulled out, after that he just—I guess he was angry 'cause he couldn't find anything. Without asking, he started searching my car.

The low-intensity harassment that Roman described was part of a wider controversy over racial profiling, or "driving while Mexican" (see Gilroy's [2001] comments on "driving while black").[8] But lowriders also noticed that car club affiliation could draw attention, suggesting that a deliberate performance of lowrider identity could fuse with race, class, and location in the interpretive logic of such encounters. Indeed, if the police interpreted club membership as referring to a specific social position, they were not alone. Chris, who was one of a handful of white lowriders I met, was a member of the predominately Mexican American club Nuestra Manera. Chris was well aware that lowrider style privileged a Mexican American identity and thus publicly compromised his whiteness to an extent. Specifically, displaying lowrider style and club affiliation in traffic marked him as a target in ways from which white privilege did not make him entirely immune. Indeed, identifying as a lowrider also introduced a degree of racial suspicion from whites, which a friend of Chris's reproduced comically in the background of a recorded interview.

BEN: The first time I met you, you said—I asked you about being pulled over, and you said, yeah, it's part of being in a club.

CHRIS: Yeah, you know, when I had those [club] stickers on there, that was a long time ago—when I had those stickers on there, I got pulled over a lot.

BEN: Really?

CHRIS: Yeah, when I had [Nuestra Manera] on the, on the back window?

BEN: So what you think it—do you think it's mostly—what makes you, what makes you a target for getting pulled over?

CHRIS: You know, it's a combination of the accessories, but it's the stereotype. It's the perception of the people who are involved in lowriding. I mean, it's negative. I encounter it everywhere. Everybody's like—I mean even some racism within, like, you know, 'cause I'm white, within, uh, my own race. 'Cause they're like—what do they say, they're like . . . "What race are you?" You know, just—you know, like . . .

BEN: Like you don't know who you are? Is that what they—is that the idea?

CHRIS: No, not necessarily implying that, but they're just like, are you—are you Hispanic? You know what I'm saying? Because they know, you know, they know I'm white, but they're just implying like, "Do you know who you are?" Exactly. It's, it's . . .

BEN: Even at work?

CHRIS: Everywhere. Yeah. Everywhere.

BEN: When you get pulled over, how do the police respond to the fact that you're white? [. . .] Do you ever notice surprise or anything like that, or do you think it's just . . .

CHRIS: Um, yeah. Well I've heard it from them, too. I've, I've heard it somewhat. But most of all they pull you over not necessarily because of your race, but more of the car. But, I mean, they just assume that you're going to be Hispanic.

BEN: Yeah.

CHRIS'S FRIEND: [Chris]'s a Mexican wannabe.

CHRIS: [*ironically*] Yeah, something like that. No, I don't look at it that way. A lot of people say that.

BEN: Yeah?

CHRIS: I mean, I love the culture, so . . . I mean, I don't care, you know, they can—you know, I have a clean driving record and I keep all my stuff straight, I have insurance, you know.

CHRIS'S FRIEND: Got a membership to a tanning salon.

While lowriders accepted as common knowledge that performing lowrider style and spending time in a barrio space meant being subject to heightened scrutiny from the police, they often maintained that this was a matter of mistaken identity. Such misinformation could be mitigated somewhat by community connections, though being pulled over in your own neighborhood could also bring a particular humiliation:

BEN: Seems like everybody has, um, an experience with getting pulled over by the police. Have you had any trouble with that at all?

SMILEY: Oh, yeah, when I first started I did. I would get pulled over about, probably once every week.

BEN: Wow.

SMILEY: Um, one time I got, um . . . charged for a false license plate. Actually it was—the plate numbers were reading back for another car [. . .] Course, it was a mistake that they did at, um, at the title place when they gave me the plates. [. . .] It was fat-fingered in or something in the system. But I think that was my worst experience, because they got me out of the car, they searched me, the car, me and a friend of mine. We were just down the street from his house. The police officer—of course, his [Smiley's friend's] mom came out and asked what was going on. The police officer just started rambling, saying that we had drugs, we had guns, we had this, we had that. [. . .] I took it to court for that and, um, I got the ticket dismissed. [. . .] I've gotten stopped before, saying, "Hey, you know, your license plate light isn't working."

"Oh, really?" Park it, get out of the car, let me see myself, and it is working.

"Well, let me just check your, uh, let me just check your license, see if you got any warrants." So, I mean, already—my record's always been clean, and it's—I mean, I'm going to keep it clean, but. You know that's the whole thing, they want to—they see a lowrider, they say, "Oh, I know he's got warrants" or "I know that he's got something up, he probably has some kind of drugs in his car." But yeah, I've gotten hassled by a lot of police. At the same time, there's a lot of police officers out there that know who we are and know who I am, so I don't really get hassled.

Despite the overwhelming body of narrative about profiling and stereotyping, nearly everyone I talked to freely admitted that not all lowriders were innocent, and some went so far as to say that lowriders must share some of the blame for their antagonistic relationship with the police.

> **BEN:** So what do you think it is that, uh, makes police target lowriders in particular?
>
> **ROMAN:** Partly because the reputation our own people's giving our cars, really, which I can't blame them for. But also, a lot of it has to do with color. Um-hm. A lot of it has to do with color. 'Cause, uh, I have encountered good officers, I really have. I've encountered some that are just nice, I've encountered some that—they have, even just at a gas station they'll walk up and tell me something like, "Hey, just to let you know, you have a nice car and everything, but your inspection sticker's getting ready to expire in about five days." Now that's a good officer. You know, somebody who compliments you, you know, give you a warning on your car, you know, you're getting ready to—I've encountered a lot of good cops, but let me tell you, there's a lot of bad ones out there, lot of bad ones. Un—very, not too professional, and have no respect. Because they use that badge as authority. A lot of us encounter that, but then again, there's a lot of bad lowriders out there too. Lot of bad guys.

《 》

On another Saturday, at the Kings' regular club meeting at the car wash, we decided that we would meet later for cruising in the parking lot of a large grocery store near the end of the commercial section of Riverside. When I arrived at the store, Eddie and Joseph were there; Smiley was at a gas station across the parking lot, filling up. We again talked over the idea of going up to check out the Best Buy on the north side, and hung out to wait for the others. I saw a black 1978 Monte Carlo that looked as long as a town car pull into the lot. "There's Locomoco," said Eddie. As the immense car approached, I could make out the large frame of a man whom I had seen around town. Beside him in the passenger seat was a woman who looked a couple of heads shorter than he, and very thin.

The black MC pulled even with the parked cars of the Kings and stopped in the parking lot driveway. Locomoco got out, picked up his switch box, pulled it through the window, and shut the door, drawing the slack cable toward him.

The woman got out on the other side and moved a couple of steps away from the car. Locomoco hit a switch and the front of the MC jumped slightly. "That all you got?" yelled Eddie, with mock bravado. He walked to his own car, also an MC but a '73, and got in. He started it, racing the motor, then pulled slowly out of his parking space and turned into the driveway so that his car was facing Locomoco's. Eddie also got out with his switch box. Both drivers started rhythmically throwing the switches on their boxes, and the front ends of the two lowriders began to bounce until gradually the front tires cleared the ground and hopped into the air. The bottom of Locomoco's car began to strike the pavement on each bounce with an alarming (to me) metallic thunk. The hopping battle was short-lived: neither Eddie nor Locomoco had fully charged all his batteries, and the hops were not on a level with those at a car show competition. Finally, they stopped without a clear winner, grinning, and shook hands.

While we stood around the two Monte Carlos, Joseph walked casually over to his dropped Chevy S-10 sport pickup nearby and switched on his sound system—now it was his turn to show off his technology. A bass-heavy hip-hop jam rolled out the open windows of the truck. Joseph reached inside and fine-tuned the equalizer so that the two eighteen–inch subwoofers behind the seats started to hit, and the lot was filled with a steady, low hum, punctuated rhythmically by an electronic kick drum. Before the song was over, someone shouted, "Joseph!" and pointed across the lot toward the street, where a police car was cruising by. Joseph reached again through the open window for the stereo controls and lowered the volume.

A beat-up, rusty 1980 Monte Carlo pulled up behind Eddie's car, and a fair-skinned man with light brown hair got out. The Kings greeted him: "What's up, Güero?"

"Hey, I got that amp, dog." Güero walked around his car and opened the trunk. Installed amid the rust spots and dents was a shiny metallic-blue metal box with several wires running from its side to the car's interior.

"How much?"

"800."

"Does it hit pretty good?"

"I don't got it tuned yet." Joseph switched off his system to allow Güero to play his. When he raised the bass on the equalizer, the music's rhythm was drowned out by an uninterrupted blast of low-frequency sound that caused the MC's trunk to vibrate. The beat was indistinguishable. Güero said, "I ain't adjusted it just right yet."

"Wadn't you locked up?" someone asked him abruptly.

"Yeah, they got me on a warrant. Now I'm suspended. You can't work for [Timberview] and get locked up." "Timberview" was a private, for-profit prison a couple of hours from Austin. Güero said that he regretted being suspended because the work had its perks—overtime, for example, which was how he raised the cash for the sub amp. He then told disturbing stories from his job as a guard at the facility, talking about spying on female inmates via closed-circuit security cameras.

As Güero turned off his system, a high-powered engine roared from across the lot, and I saw a red 1950s Chevy pickup coming our way. The truck pulled up, and I could see that its body was exquisitely restored: fresh paint, no rust, a deep shine from plenty of waxing and buffing. The driver was a Latino man in his twenties, I guessed. He called out a greeting, and Eddie stepped over to the open passenger-side window, leaning in to talk. The driver held a Budweiser longneck in one hand, down below the dashboard and in front of the seat so it was not in plain view.

"What's up?" said Eddie. "We're getting ready to go up north to the Best Buy. You should come on up and race."

"Nah," said the truck driver. "I got to break this motor in. It's only got a thousand miles on it." He took a swig from the bottle, draining it, and climbed out of the cab, leaving the motor running. Stepping to the rear of the truck, he carefully laid the empty bottle in the bed. Güero in his beat-up Monte Carlo and the driver of the hot-rod truck moved along—they had just wanted to say hello. Those of us headed north said good-bye to the others and pulled into a caravan of five or six cars.

Counter-cartography

Riverside was no utopia—besides the police, encounters with a rival club or an unpredictable person could raise the collective tension when I was out with the Kings. This could be a matter of a club member getting involved in a specific beef or conflict with someone in another club. In the case of the Cruzers, there was general tension or drama, since the Kings felt they were troublemakers. Lowriders competed for space with those heading out to the clubs, or with car customizers working in other genres, like the import tuners. While lowriders might at any time join one of these populations—going to a club or getting into a race—being out for a cruise with their rides put them on the defensive against drunk or reckless drivers. Lowriders sometimes pointed out to me that their investment of money and labor in their cars gave them an incentive to avoid trouble. But like a suit of clothes, a nice car offered no guarantees about its occupant. At least once when I was posted up with the club, a young man who was not a member but was well known to the Kings showed up after a bout of drinking, still driving his Cadillac even though he could barely stand. Eddie stepped in and confiscated the guy's keys, asking a club member to drive the inebriated neighbor to Eddie's house and put him to sleep on the couch.

To say that lowriders assert a barriological presence should not be understood as a romantic claim, nor does it imply a uniform posture of resistance. Some clubs—the Kings among them—sought a reputation for being "positive" and forbade their members to drink, use drugs, or become involved in gangs, at least at club events, when they were actively representing the group. That such expectations are even worth mentioning, however, indicates that there was not perfect uniformity on such issues in the cruising scene. Policies like the Kings' alcohol ban appealed to some lowriders seeking to give their pastime a better name or public image; they also might just as easily have appealed to those who simply wanted to encounter less drama on the weekend streets and be able to relax. But some measure of drama was also part of the appeal of lowriding.

Even though lowrider cars reinforced the spatial identity of Riverside, their mobility introduced the possibility of contesting dominant identity maps. Indeed, when cruising took lowriders across recognized lines, it effected a counter-cartography, unmapping the boundaries between minoritized and dominant space. In between stretches of time spent posted up in the parking lot at the Pizza Hut, the bingo hall, or the Albertson's on Riverside, lowriders would sometimes "drive around" on a circuit that took them from barrio space to the center of downtown Austin and back. Taking Riverside west across IH-35 led to the Congress Avenue Bridge (now called the Ann W. Richards Congress Avenue Bridge), a multilane crossing of Town Lake that, by design, offers a picturesque view of downtown centered on the state Capitol. From there, a typical cruise might go up Congress Avenue to the vicinity of the nightlife district on Sixth Street, circumventing the few blocks designated as pedestrian-only on weekend nights, and back to Riverside via the southbound frontage road along IH-35. On that route, lowriders traversed boundaries between spatial designations that were not entirely legislated, but were actively produced and reinforced in ordinary life. Thus, lowriders worked both within and against the circulation of public-cultural discourses and rationales about what kind of people and practices "belong" in particular places.

《 》

We drove up Pleasant Valley through the Eastside and turned onto U.S. 183, a divided highway. Traffic was moderately heavy, and it was soon difficult for me to distinguish the other club cars in the stream of white headlights and red tail-lights. Once on the multilane road, though, the lowriders ahead of me turned on their hazard blinkers, making it easier to keep track of them in the traffic. I was behind Albert's truck, with a Suburban behind me driven by Joe, a friend of some club members. At first, I wasn't sure whether I should turn on my haz-ards—would it be presumptuous to act as though I were part of the club? Beto had his on; Joe did not. Eventually, I turned mine on as well so as not to break the caravan of blinking cars.

We arrived at the Best Buy parking lot, a sprawling expanse of asphalt that abutted the intersection of several highways on the north side of the city. We slowly made a circuit around the parking lot, which was full of custom cars and people standing around them. I saw mostly imports, street racers, and mini-trucks.[9] We passed three Toyota Supras customized with identical rear spoilers and decal stickers, painted white, yellow, and baby blue and parked together in a row so they looked like an advertisement—a complete collection. I heard some stereo systems in the distance and rolled down my window. Right be-side me there was a loud hiss, and a parked minitruck suddenly dropped to the pavement—the owner had released his air bag suspension. We parked to-gether near the edge of the crowds, got out, and walked toward a couple of cars from Nuestra Manera, the only other lowriders there. Locomoco kept cruising around in his monstrous black MC.

Chris was one of the Nuestra Manera drivers. His Buick Skylark convert-ible sat on old-school lowrider rims—they were the small-scale 5.20 size with wire spokes—and was parked with the hood open to show off the immaculately detailed engine. Eddie asked him what he had done lately, and Chris pointed out the custom metal brake lines he had installed. Eddie asked whether he had seen any hydraulics, or "hydros," in the lot that night, and Chris said no, it was mostly "airbags." Airbag suspensions were the mark of the minitruck-customizing genre, as distinct from lowriders. Minitrucks equipped with air-bags could suddenly drop all the way to the pavement when the pressure was released, but then the suspension had to be refilled with an air compressor, and the truck would rise slowly compared to those with hydraulic lifts. Gener-ally, that meant no hopping, which recently built sport trucks were unfit for anyway. Crash-test-mandated crumple zones in the body would not stand up to the structural stress of hydraulic hopping the way the hard-metal frames did on classic lowriders. Chris speculated about the application of airbags for low-riding: "Man, I bet those things are the future. There's no fluid to lose, they're reliable, and it rides like a Cadillac, man. The only thing is they don't lift fast. But you know, as they come up with the new technology, man it's going to get better and better. Already there's people who hop them."

Down the line of parked cars, Locomoco was hitting his hydraulics and hopping the MC as he drove around. A white high school kid in baggy denim shorts ran up and started filming Locomoco with his video camera. Locomoco drove in a tight circle and hit the switches for three-wheel motion, cocking one corner of the car in the air. Raymond walked to his mom's Taurus, opened the trunk, and got out his own video camera. Suddenly, some way off I heard motors revving and the squeal of burning rubber, and people all around us started to run in that direction. Several in our group grabbed for their car door handles again and looked around for the police. Lito said, "Shit! I didn't hear any shots! What, they got silencers up here?" Somebody else said that two cars were racing on the lane that divided two parking lots. Eddie walked toward the drag racers—he had been a hot-rodder in high school and used to race his MC in the street. Meanwhile, Albert, who was sometimes called Big Beto, got in his truck and performed a little parody of the scene, peeling out while looking at the rest of us through the window with an ironic, deadpan expression. Big Beto pulled in behind Locomoco, and they both drove around an empty area, peeling out, pulling tight U-turns, and otherwise playing around.

A big 1980s station wagon came by us. Its decidedly uncustomized appearance was an anomaly in the lot, but the driver still gunned the motor and peeled out as he approached the intersection of the parking lot lanes. Another car was passing, and the wagon had to stop short. Lito commented with mock concern, "Good thing he didn't wreck. He's not even supposed to be out in his Mama's station wagon. He told her he was just going to get a loaf of bread," and we all laughed. Thomas cruised by and opened his remote-control trunk, showing the neon lights inside shaped to spell out "Don't Hate." From another group nearby, I heard a young voice say, "Look at that trunk!" and laughter.

Eddie had come back from the racing strip and was talking to Chris again. He mentioned that the Kings didn't come up that way much, saying that they had thought they "weren't wanted" in the Euro scene, which dominated up north. Chris was diplomatic: "It's just different styles. It goes the same way with other things. I've heard people say, I hate those fuckin' Euros."

Eddie said, "I don't mind Euros. It's just that they drive crazy."

Chris said, "You know, I kind of get some shit, too, in the hot-rod scene when I show up in my lowrider."

They fell silent and pondered this a moment. Eddie asked Chris, "How long they let you stay out here?" Chris replied that the scene went until the police showed up about midnight, but that it was legal over at a Harley-Davidson shop by the highway. The owners had made it clear that they didn't mind cruising in the parking lot, so the police were unable to run people off. Eddie said that the lowriders had once had a place like that on Riverside, but after "too many beer bottles, too many knives," and a fistfight that had resulted in a broken window, the owners changed their minds and refused to sanction the cruising.

Some of the people who had come with the Kings started talking about heading back south to Riverside. Joe from the Stylistic Syndicate pulled in front of our cars in his Suburban and leaned out his window. "Do you guys have to follow me to get back to Austin?" We all laughed—it did almost feel as if we were in a different city. Eventually, everyone I had come with was gathered in the same place, and we decided to head back.

After another caravan down the highway with hazard lights blinking, we ended up at the Pizza Hut where we had been run off the previous week. Some spaces by the street were vacant, and we took them. The Stylistic Syndicate was already there. A white man with a full gray beard and a baseball cap on walked over and asked Lito whether he would mind moving his Cadillac, which was blocking a vacant parking spot. With a wide-eyed, innocent face, Lito said, "Sure, bro, but just be careful when you pull in, 'cause my Mama don't know I got her Cadillac out here. Just don't hit my Mama's Cadillac." He said it all deadpan while the rest of us cracked up at the sudden shift in his register and manner. His humor was all the more inside to those of us who had heard the joke in an earlier stage of development up north. Lito kept us entertained with his stories, doing his standup routine on everyday vignettes. "Yeah, dog, last night I wanted some Ding Dongs. Like, 'Man, we got all this milk in the fridge, all we need is some fuckin' Ding Dongs.' So I go in the store. 'You got any fuckin' Ding Dongs?' Lady's like 'Fuck you talkin' about?'" The carnivalesque profanity seemed to reintroduce a bit of grit, as if we had come down to earth from the slick, bright big-box stores around Best Buy, and it helped everyone relax after venturing into another cruising scene. For the few minutes before the police ran us off, the lowriders were at home.

Inside Out
The Ambivalent Aesthetics of Lowrider Interiors

The car, it seems to me, acquires importance in the imagination precisely because it can move through public space generating images that might camouflage private space. The car, obviously, is a practical tool as well, but its practicality can never fully explain, as we will see, the use of a car as a site for self-display. The car, if the owner wishes, can be a mobile display of an artfully constructed self. This self can safely cruise public space because it knows that there is not enough knowledge out there to unveil the camouflage. The car, then, is a particularly useful site for the creation of hyperbole.

Ralph Cintron, *Angel's Town*

Lowriding as a version of Mexican American identity became possible when Mexican Americans joined the U.S. car culture, a convergence of two developments: on one hand, the rise of Mexican Americans as a consumer market, and on the other, the expansion of the automobile class. The mid-twentieth century was a significant moment in this conjuncture, corresponding with the rise of a nascent Chicano/a identity among the grown children of those who had migrated to the United States from Mexico to escape the revolutionary upheaval of 1910–1920, as well as the visibility of *mexicanos* who had asserted their Americanness by serving in the U.S. military in World War II. This was the time that postwar surpluses in production and measures such as the G.I. Bill were building the U.S. middle class: the expanding availability of used cars spurred the development of customization and the hot rod and cruising scenes that are now iconically associated with the 1950s. Not coincidentally, the same midcentury historical context was formative for the politics of popular culture, since consumption became the focus of economic activity (Hebdige 1988), even, as one of the leading scholars of consumption puts it, "the vanguard of history" (Miller 1995, 1). Thus, lowriding emerged as part of a family of practices through which people exercise agency and appropriation in acts of consumption, and its version of Mexican American identity was in part a consumer identity.

People continue to engage consumption as a field of everyday "second nature" (Benjamin 2002b; Buck-Morss 1991) that offers opportunities to appropriate and recombine objects and elements of the semiosphere never intended for one another, such as decorating clothing with safety pins, or walls with spray paint. Such bricolage in the use and reinvention of everyday things became a master trope of popular culture with the ascendance of the "cut and mix" poetics of hip-hop, and continues to develop in the concept of a "mashup." The ubiquity of this agentive consumption and the centrality of the consuming subject in contemporary capitalism render the category of "subcultures," under which these practices appeared in the academic field of vision, a bit dated (Hebdige 1979). While the pathbreaking studies of subculture found a political charge in the "semioclasm" (Barthes 1972) that deviant modes of consumption effected, subsequent critiques have demonstrated that modern capitalism readily reincorporates such deviations as niche markets of taste. Indeed, sodalities of taste are widely viewed as one of the typical social forms of the present age (Bennett 1999). And agentive consumption is not only a matter of making certain choices from what the culture industries offer or mapping unscripted meanings onto purchased commodities—it can also blur any boundary separating it from production. Lowriding, for instance, emphasizes material modification and the physical reconstruction of an industrial object more than the collage aesthetic enabled by digital media.

This material reconstruction, or customization, functions within and against habits of consumption and the contemporary cultural-political "system of objects" (Baudrillard 1996). Customization represents the excorporation of materials and time from the ordinary process of capitalist circulation for some purpose other than their prescribed function for the interests of capital (Certeau 1984; Limón 1983). It exists as a dynamic between mainstream commodity culture, which is one of the second-nature circumstances "not of their choosing" within which people make history (Marx 1994), and acts undertaken to challenge, alter, or reappropriate that consumerism in some way. For lowriders, this second nature includes the social system of automobility and, in a larger sense, transport as a factor in the modern political economy. In a society in which public transportation has been more or less decimated outside the most densely populated urban centers, some relationship to cars is, for most people, economically necessary. But lowriders also demonstrate that cars are not just transport. This chapter, by considering lowrider spatiality on the scale of the car as space rather than only in space, also situates lowrider style in relation to another domain of second nature, that of interior material aesthetics, the domestic space of the normative bourgeois home.

As I have emphasized, it is not my purpose or project to assert that lowriding, or any customization, conforms to a consistent revolutionary or resistant line. Close attention to interiority in this chapter will continue my efforts to show how lowrider aesthetics is nonetheless political in its relation to space. Customization in fact bears more than a passing resemblance to the "oppositionality" that Ross Chambers identifies as a potential within narrative (1991). Joining the perennial debate on where to locate the politics of cultural work, Chambers advocates for a tempered sense of the political: rather than equating the politics of narrative with resistance, Chambers nonetheless "excavates the political" (Conquergood 1991) in the capacity of narrative to establish "room to maneuver" through the construction of authority. The point is not that such "room" can itself generate wide-ranging social change, but that in claiming authority through narrative, authors may momentarily displace existing social authority and create virtual space for resistant imaginaries.

As for narrative, so for customization in material aesthetics. A customizer— without conspiring or plotting any intentional revolutionary purpose—seeks to manifest a difference in things from the way they are offered by producers, that is, from their designed, intended, or marketed commercial forms. Observers who hope to find in customization a wholesale rejection of the consumer culture and social relations that maintain it as an engine of capital accumulation will be disappointed. But for people whose received identities situate them outside the driver's seat of the cultural economy, customization serves, on an attenuated scale, to assert a measure of authority, and one that matters.

To trace these dynamics of customization as the production of significant difference in a sector of consumer culture, I turn here to how lowrider aesthetics produces space on a scale smaller than streets and neighborhoods—in particular, the scale of a car interior. For this analysis, I rely on Susan Stewart's prior work to unearth the "narratives" bound up in material practices of the

Western bourgeoisie (1993). To speak of this class, not to mention a historical "mainstream" of American consumer culture that is challenged by lowrider aesthetics, is to aim at moving targets, themselves riven with contradiction. On one hand, there is a principle of cultural capital expressed as tasteful restraint, exemplified by the notion that old money need not show itself (Bourdieu 1984, 1999). In their excess significance, lowriders show little concern for this standard: they are generally not worried about being taken for parvenus. Indeed, lowrider aesthetics specifically rejects the subdued "tints and nuances" that Baudrillard finds in "bourgeois objects" (1996, 31), what Stewart characterizes as "the moral refusal of color" (1993, 29).

The relativity of the boundaries of "taste" highlights the racial, class, and cultural specificity of any definition of excess. Yet conspicuous consumption has a particular resonance in American society: after all, the bourgeoisie is not an upstart threat to the nobles here, but has been central, even dominant in the United States from the founding of the republic and before. To say the least, this complicates a Bourdieu-style analysis that locates class identities in A/B choices. It can be equally difficult to apply theories of transgression to modes of consumption (Bakhtin 1984; Bourdieu 1984; A. Jain 2002; Stallabrass 1996; Stallybrass and White 1986). What, after all, can out-excess American consumer culture?

However shifting and adaptable the mainstream of American consumption may be, I argue nonetheless that lowriding diverges from it in several specific ways. First is what prior scholars have recognized as a popular baroque sensibility, an excessive style of lowrider aesthetics that causes the practice to appear to some outsiders as gaudy. The lowrider baroque represents an elaboration of a move by midcentury "kustom kar" fans to reject austere and ascetic modernism (Wolfe 1971). This acquired a distinct resonance when practiced by Mexican Americans, who have historically been constructed by Anglo discourse as irresponsible, ruled by passion, and, in other floridly expressive ways, less than modern. The connotation of the lowrider baroque, then, could be interpreted as "This is my aesthetics—¿y que?" ("and what are you going to do about it?"). While ascetic restraint may have lost its cachet as the singular mark of responsible consumption (though it has by no means disappeared, as I explain below), an emphasis on functionality remains in the marketing of industrial commodities, carrying on the "utilitarian values" embodied in early modern automobility by the Ford Model T and the process of its production (Seiler 2008, 38). Lowriding's full-on embrace of aesthetics rejects the priority of functional utility.

Figure 2.1. Model lowrider on José's table.

Second, I show how lowriding refuses the legacies of romanticism and of bourgeois aesthetics that seek to separate the domain of the beautiful from the taint of mundane labor and commodity exchange. Bringing aesthetic priorities together with a social identity tied to labor, working-class lowriders embody a kind of opulence out of place. This complicates class-based interpretations of the lowrider aesthetic as "cheap" or illicit luxury, which I unpack through its material resonance with other kinds of interiors, notably those associated with commodified sex and death.

Finally, tying these threads together will show how lowriding explodes the very notion of interiority itself: cars and other spaces occupied by lowriders are not constructed to be closed off and protected from the outside. In this sense, lowrider aesthetics violates the core principle of bourgeois interiority: closure. In contrast, lowrider interiority is porous and multifunctional, providing a space for subjects to exercise agency in configuring the ties between private and public spheres, and between individual and collective identities.

Before elaborating on these themes of a counterbourgeois baroque, a non-autonomous yet immanently political aesthetic, and an interiority that reaches to the outside, it will help to consider why lowrider interiority matters in the way it does, and to situate Austin lowriders in relation to interiors as such.

I found opportunities to do so when encountering lowrider style in the quintessential interior, a home.

(A) Room to Maneuver (In)

After we met at a neighborhood car show, José invited me to his apartment to work on model cars. I followed his directions out east on Riverside past the cruising strip, then turned on a side street and into a maze of apartment-building parking lots. I pulled into one and got out of my car. The sun was setting, and the numbers weren't easy to see from the street in the dim light. I glimpsed a group of three people sitting on the steps of one of the apartment buildings. Hearing them speaking Spanish as I approached, I asked for "*trece-cero-dos*" (1302) and was directed around the corner to the next building.

José answered my knock and invited me in. The apartment was a small two-bedroom, with a main room comprising the carpeted living area and linoleum kitchen, divided by a couch facing the television on the living-room side. A small table in the kitchen was covered with plastic parts for lowrider model cars, modeling tools, tubes of cement, and jars of paint. The kitchen window held an air-conditioner unit, and underneath it was a cardboard box placed open on its side. The inside of the box and the floor around it was nearly black with accumulated layers of spray paint—the kitchen was also a workshop. José gestured toward this corner. "I know you're not supposed to shoot paint inside, but I tell the kids to leave the room. I can't do it outside because the overspray would get on somebody's car."

He gave me a brief tour, pointing out his older daughter Maria's room, but leaving the door closed. His younger son Steve, about fourteen, was home and excited to show me his room. One wall was covered with a large Mexican flag, and beneath it was the DJ equipment and stereo system that José bought Steve for his last birthday. Steve showed me some of the choice records he had acquired from a local vinyl shop that supplied DJs. Another wall had lowrider posters, pictures cut from magazines, and shelves loaded with lowrider model cars and "collectible" Hot Wheels cars. Referring to an earlier conversation we had had about lowriders and hip-hop, José said to me, "See, it's just like you said. The music and cars all together." We moved on to the living room, and José told me that he slept on the couch.

We sat down at the kitchen table to start working on cars, cutting parts from the plastic frames, trimming pieces off first with X-Acto knives, then smoothing

Figure 2.2. 1964 Impala model lowrider painted in blue metal flake by the author.

them with fine sandpaper. It was detailed work. The knives could cut the soft plastic too easily at times; José showed me how to score the material with the dull side of a blade, then snap it off with my fingers. I prepared the body of the '64 Impala model from a kit I had bought at the hobby store. I had decided to go with blue, and José suggested that I shoot a gold base coat followed by blue metal flake. We placed the plastic car body in the cardboard painting chamber, and I aimed a steady stream from the aerosol can of gold model paint in its general direction. The paint went on thick and dripped in unsightly globs. José took the can from me and said, "You have to do it like this." Touching the nozzle lightly in brief bursts, he swept the can across the car, laying on fine coats of paint. He suggested we strip the car to start over. He placed it in a sealable plastic food container, sprayed it with chemical oven cleaner from another can, and quickly closed the lid. By now, the air was thick and sweet in the small kitchen.

José's brother-in-law arrived. We were introduced, and he walked to the pantry closet in the kitchen. When he opened the door, I could see boxes of model-car kits stacked floor to ceiling. He turned to me: "Can I get you something to eat? A '58? Maybe a '72? How about a Buick?"

José laughed, "Man?" We went on building the models.

《 》

Austin lowriders generally moved between small living spaces and large cars. The constrained space in which José lived and practiced his craft of model-car customization was a condition that many Austin lowriders shared—one of many indications that in the urban United States, access to space is a class issue, joined with race, gender, sexuality, and other lines of identification. Lowriders' position in relation to interiority is ambivalent. On one hand, their class position and the political economy of real estate make interior space scarce, while the importance of constructing individuated interiors remains undiminished as part of the consumption that is central to cultural citizenship in the United States (Norton 1993). Given this tension between the limited resource of "private" space and a mandate to have and distinguish a "room of one's own," it is small wonder that car interiors are the focus of intensive customization.

The perennial saturation of available housing in Austin's real estate market, coupled with the gentrification mentioned in the last chapter, resulted in some of the highest rents in Texas. This made living space all the more scarce for people who worked for an hourly wage. It is not uncommon in the United States for housing costs to be far disproportionate to earning power. Barbara Ehrenreich, in her undercover journalism on the low-wage working life (2001), argues that this is partly because poverty levels, which are the basis for statistical indicators of the welfare of the nation as well as for state interventions on behalf of the poor, are calculated using food expenditures as a benchmark. The problem with this is that food costs have been among the most stable of household expenses since they were identified, fifty years ago, as the basis for calculating poverty.[1]

Thus a principal hurdle to "getting by" during Ehrenreich's experiment as a wageworker was to find and keep housing. Personal-finance gurus may instruct us to spend no more than one-fourth to one-third of our incomes on housing, but Ehrenreich found that for low-wage workers, putting together a deposit or down payment for stable housing was sometimes impossible. For those who did find a place, keeping it was a constant struggle, often leading people to work overtime, take on second or third jobs, or go without other things normally considered necessities in order to pay the rent. This permanent crisis of housing is compounded in urban markets where central cities have been "revitalized," "gentrified," and otherwise reclaimed in a process of "reurbanization" by consumers with a taste for "authenticity," "character," and good investments, not to mention the means to pay higher prices than the urban residents who preceded them. In "lifestyle" cities, which trade on such tastes in the consumption of space, the "hotter" the town, the more difficult it becomes to live there on a limited budget. Yet limited means, ironically, are all that are usually afforded to a great many who work in the service industries that support the very "quality of life" consumption opportunities that characterize such places. The disconnect produces depressing and depressed urban landscapes like the trailer park where Ehrenreich lived for a short while, and which she began to think of as a social machine that rendered its residents "not exactly people . . . but what amounts to canned labor, being preserved between shifts from the heat" (2001, 40).

In the southeast-side areas of Austin around Riverside and Oltorf, there were plenty of warehouses for human material, sprawling cinder-block apartment complexes, some of which resembled rabbit warrens. This area, which I once heard someone refer to as "Legoland" for its architectural landscape, represents a marked contrast with both the single-family housing stock of the traditional barrio neighborhoods like the Eastside and the newer "smart-growth, mixed-use" blocks of ground-floor retail space with upstairs apartments that have sprung up more recently in the gentrification of East Austin. In other words, mass housing has managed to avoid the charms of both historical buildings and innovative development. But such apartment complexes were where wage earners, students, and young families, including some of the lowriders in Austin, could afford to live. Other lowriders lived with parents or other relatives, squeezing themselves and sometimes their immediate families into bedrooms and apartments in a larger house.

The visit to José's apartment demonstrates how a scarcity of space impedes the ability to practice lowriding, even the miniaturized version of customizing model cars. Yet this situation was certainly more the norm than the exception. Contrasting with their restricted living space, many lowriders in Austin, particularly those who were recognized as or aspired to be "old school," preferred their cars on the big side—in order to qualify as "traditionals," lowriders generally must be made from "big body" American cars. When talking with me about his '64 Impala, Roman conceded the practicality of smaller cars, like the imports that lowriders called "Euros" regardless of their geographic origin: "They're cheap to work on because the parts are everywhere. They're easy to get around in, but . . ." He paused. I thought of an earlier point in our conversation, when he had approvingly mentioned that when he first saw lowriders in town, everyone was into older models, "hard metal cars . . . nothing up-to-date." Roman seemed to consider how best to put his reservations about small cars tactfully. Finally, he summed it up thus: "I drive an American classic, not foreign plastic."

In this phrase, Roman conjoins a claim to consumer citizenship with the particular advantages for lowrider customization of old-fashioned thick-gauge steel. Such material is able to sustain stresses for which it was not designed, brought on by "radical" body modifications or the jarring punishment of hydraulic hopping. As cars have been engineered with greater precision and lighter, more flexible materials, fuel economy and crash safety have improved, but the range of possible improvisations for a customizer has been restricted. Big Beto told me about his attempt to equip a late-model Nissan sport pickup with hydraulics—the first time he hopped it, the truck nearly bent in half due to the "crumple zones" built into the body to absorb the impact of a crash.

Plenty of others joined Roman in his preference: the standard lowriders for at least twenty-five years have been built from 1960s-model Chevy Impalas.[2] Later generations have added such full-sized, affordable luxury rides as Regals, Monte Carlos, Cutlasses, and Grand Ams to the repertoire. Lately, Cadillacs, or "'lacs," and Lincolns (which are rare exceptions to a general preference for General Motors vehicles) have made serious inroads, and may well have been the most popular choice as a cruising ride at the time of my fieldwork. One of the biggest and most well-known national lowrider car clubs was establishing an Austin chapter as I concluded my research, and in a bid to further boost its prestige, the national organization had amended the club rules to accept only owners of big-body cars, no Euros or compacts. Apart from aesthetic and functional reasons, the politics of presence enacted in lowrider cruising depends on size as one of its resources: if you are big, you occupy more space, establishing more of a presence that must be dealt with. While not necessarily an intentional motivation for bodily self-construction, this amplified presence showed in both the big bodies and the big cars of lowriders. For various reasons, then, lowrider cars tended to be on the large side of the automotive scale.

The interior space of a car the size of Eddie's 1973 Monte Carlo feels almost comparable in size to a room, at least the room that Eddie, Elisa, and their three children shared in Elisa's grandparents' house east of Austin in the town of Del Valle. Elisa's grandparents had built the house for their retirement. Gradually, members of the extended family moved in, and Elisa's uncle, sister, and their families and children had all joined the household. The grandparents retreated into their bedroom, eventually outfitting it with carpet, air-conditioning, and their own private refrigerator while the rest of the house stayed in a semifinished state. By the time of my postdoctoral field trips, Eddie and Elisa had moved to Eddie's grandmother's house in the East Austin barrio of Montopolis, though by then, Eddie's brother and other relatives also needed a place and had joined them. When I visited him at home in Montopolis, Eddie described how the Del Valle house had finally gotten too cramped, saying, "Seventeen in one house is too many."

"Yeah, a lot of those kids are getting big, too," I said.

"Now I got seven in one house. Five are mine, two are [Mike] and our cousin."

In the new space, new trials emerged. The cousin had aspirations to be a dog breeder, and kept puppies in the back room without, as Eddie put it, "cleaning up the piss or the shit." When Mike and the cousin, along with various children, moved in, they did some limited renovations to the house to make it ready for the crowd. They put up new Sheetrock walls, but had not yet painted them. Eddie told me their room was still grey with white dots of mud over the screws, "like a garage." Eddie's brother Mike, himself a lowrider and a mechanic, apparently paid the gas bill for the house as his contribution toward expenses. Such arrangements enabled intricate exchanges of work and money within the already complex economy of customizing. When Eddie quit his job at a tire shop to become a delivery driver, he could no longer do side work on his ride in the garage after hours. So Mike, who worked at another repair shop, would occasionally do a job for him after work, and Eddie picked up the responsibility for the gas bill in exchange. Eddie explained the deal to another lowrider, Arturo, who was looking to get Mike to do some work. Arturo said, "Tell him I'll pay for the parts and get the labor later!"

Eddie said, "No, what he does is he just does the labor, then next time the gas bill comes, he just gives it to me. That's all he pays is the gas. I pay electric. I can go home and the AC's going full blast. 'Why's the door open?' Go in, all the lights are on. 'Why you got to leave the light on? There's nobody in there.' The TV's on, the video game's on pause, kids running around. 'You playing that or what?' [. . .] I go back there, [Mike's] asleep! I wake him up. 'How come the AC's on? You're not even out in the living room! Plus the door's open!'" Eddie had fun describing the domestic mayhem of so many people sharing a house and its bills; there was status, after all, in being in a position to be annoyed by it.

The image of a lot of people living in the same house, or traveling in the same car for that matter, is a stereotype of Latino/as that can be a comical reference to familialism, the cultural prioritization of family relationships (Del Castillo 1996), as well as a knowing parody of working-class economic standing. As with all stereotypes, the comedy in this image depends on who is using it.

The specter of suburban homes becoming rooming houses for many single men in an *"encargado"* (subletting) situation has been the source of anti-immigrant panics.[3] Both of these constructions of Mexican homes in the United States— as comedy and as threat—tend to portray crowded space as a cultural trait or shared preference rather than an economic necessity. Lowriders were well aware of the stereotype and, as Eddie demonstrated, were able to deploy it in a joke, but they also know intimately the economic reality that produced it.

A situation that finds adults sharing living space beyond the nuclear family alters the meaning of the clichéd "family car." In situations of shared space, cars can easily become important as individual units of property, comparable to the rooms of a shared house: a spatial zone one step more expansive than the body, an environment big enough to occupy, and thus to be constructed as "personal space." A room is potentially an autotopographical spatial field (González 1995), a medium for the material performance of versions of the self. Popular aesthetics have provided a means for producing "my space" long before that phrase was a brand of social-networking software. One's own room at "home" or "the house" is not the only site of these autotopographies. José told me about the difficult negotiation required of him when he got a stable job with the county government, a move that placed him in a social context that contrasted with that of his home community. José's coworkers sometimes stereotyped his urban aesthetic as being indicative of gang membership:

> One lady even told me, goes, "Well, don't you think 'cause you're working here you should get rid of the earring, 'cause you're not in a gang anymore?" I'm like [*laughs*]—I'm not wearing a earring 'cause I was in a gang, I just wear it, you know . . . I just had a earring 'cause I wanted a earring.

This suspicion was matched by José's neighbors when he first got the office job. He said:

> And you know, I was wearing a suit and stuff, and I would go to the neighborhood to pick up my son, and my friends are like, "Damn, you know what? You ain't hanging around us no more, 'cause you're all—uptown?" So I was like, "No, it ain't nothing about that." You know, you go to my office, and people trip out. You know, I got lowrider pictures, I got homies, the little homie figures on my computer, I got all the lowrider Hot

Wheels, you know, on my desk. I got pictures of, of zoot-suiters, of Aztec pictures, and everything, you know, on my desk. And I tell people who I—what I'm about. You know people come in, they're like, "Damn, man, you know, check this dude out." [. . .] But after a while, it's like, man, you know what? [*laughs*] You know, this is who I am.

José negotiated home and work identities in part by altering the space of his "room" at work—his desk—bringing barriological "accents" (Bakhtin 1981) to the workplace. His desk then became a site of conjuncture between spaces otherwise produced and hence expected to be private (home) and public (work) (Harris 1992). A car interior is no less a conjunctural space. Customized and personalized as an individuated space of identification, the car becomes something more than a mode of transportation. It becomes a mobile room, one's "place" that can be taken places, and a mode of self-representation in public.

Outside the Inside: An Extra-bourgeois Baroque

In this social context in which space is scarce, and yet personal space is an important locus for negotiating personal and community identities, cars appear as portable, inhabitable sites. Cars are expensive, especially if you carry insurance (required by Texas law but not necessarily by lowrider ethics) or do a little customizing. Nevertheless, they are not houses or land. People who do not realistically hope to own their own downtown loft apartment, vintage bungalow, or little ranch out in the hills, as many new Austinites did during the high-tech boom of the late 1990s, can nonetheless aspire to owning a car, thanks in part to two features of the late-modern American economy: credit and depreciation.

The ready availability of automobiles because of the ability to buy them on credit became central to modern American automobility in the second half of the twentieth century, and it is what drives the enduring market for new cars, despite rising prices. As Sarah Mahler notes in her ethnography of mostly Central American immigrants, this is one of the economic advantages that draws people to the United States, even though it is a national market in which housing and other costs can cut into any wage advantage (1995; see also Massey, Durand, and Malone 2003, 145–146). The availability of credit opens possibilities for consumption—such as automobile ownership—that remain out of reach in countries where the credit industry has not expanded as it did in the United States; this directly contributes to the production of a "republic of drivers"

(Seiler 2008). Beyond the mainstream practice of purchasing an automobile on credit, many lowriders take advantage of the rapid decline in value of a used car, compensating for a shortage of funds with the mechanical acumen to make something out of a $500 vehicle, perhaps wrecked or engineless, and by drawing on personal social networks to barter and trade.

All this investment of limited funds, along with extensive work and social connections with those who have the right skills or tools, goes into a production of opulence. Lowrider interiors often have lush, custom upholstery: crushed velvet is a favorite material (Figure 2.3). Cars are appointed with luxury accessories miniaturized to their scale: fountains, chandeliers, and increasingly, audio and video equipment come together to suggest a moveable mansion (see Chappell 2008) as much as a "cathedral on wheels" (Ortíz-Torres 2000; see Figure 2.4). The sensibility that values such opulence was not lost on earlier lowrider ethnographers. James Griffith found a baroque sensibility "in the opulence of materials and appointments, in their interest in miniaturization, and especially in their concentration and accumulation of independently significant details" (1989, 55). A specifically baroque aesthetic in the U.S. Southwest signified to Griffith an allusion to Spanish missions and eighteenth-century chapels, a historical Mexican-ness of the territories lost to the United States through what Mexicans call "the intervention" and the following Treaty of Guadalupe Hidalgo (58).

Figure 2.3. Lowrider with velvet upholstery.

Figure 2.4. Lowrider with running fountain.

The historical resonance that Griffith identifies as tying lowrider baroque to the aesthetics of greater Mexico's Spanish colonial history is no doubt present or implicit in many lowriders, but this reading of the baroque as "belonging" to a specific historical epoch and territorial region does not exhaust the significance of the baroque in lowriding. More than formal homologies with Spanish colonial architecture and religious art, lowrider baroque aesthetics situates car-interior customization in a particular relation to modern bourgeois norms of interiority.[4]

《 》

When I was riding with Albert in his Nissan truck to see about some used rims rumored to be for sale, we discussed his plans for customizing his vehicle. Like most lowriders I met, Albert had elaborate steps laid out, most of which were as yet unrealized. There was some bodywork that the truck needed, and then it was to be the paint job. Albert's partner, Gloria, had picked out the color: something called "plum passion," which he described as "kind of a fuchsia . . . with a pearl." It was important that the color be distinctive enough to stand out in competition at car shows. He planned to do the graphics "California style—

which I ain't seen much down here." I gathered that meant a lot of multicolored nonfigurative designs. He wanted to put a stripe around the side that would seem to shift color in the light, and then "patterns" on the roof. There would not be much room on top, since he also had plans to cut a moonroof in, but from the sides there would be a lot of visible detail.

The conversation stood out to me because of the extensive and detailed thought Albert was putting into color, design, and texture. Though Albert may not have claimed any special status, such as "artist," his imaginative work and the execution to come was not typical of car ownership as I knew it. It was also noticeable that although it is safe to say that most lowriding represents a means of performing masculinity, the specific choices of color and visual effect were not necessarily typical of a hegemonic version of manly automobility. This highlighted the contextual and contingent nature of the gendering of visual aesthetics, and specifically pointed to an important way in which gender and other identity formations are bound up with forms of visuality. Indeed, the idea that restraint and the negation of "color as such" (Baudrillard 1996, 31) indicate distinction and a cultivated taste presumes a subject that gazes and consumes others visually. This, rather than being the object of such a gaze, is the conventional subject-position of hegemonic masculinity.

Such principles do not hold absolutely true, since forms of conspicuous consumption have mutated and become mainstream enough to be widely salient across the class spectrum as part of a modern, commonsense relation to things. Still, when what makes an object like a car desirable is its utility, as opposed to its flash, this locates subjectivity in a seeing driver, not the seen. The fact that Albert's plans for his truck were oriented toward visual impact offered a contrast to consumers' mainstream obsession with utility. He imagined the ride as a performance.

Utility as a value in commodities is a trend that has not yet run its course: homeowners outfit their kitchens as if they were chefs and cruise immaculate streets in purportedly off-road vehicles. The irony is that utility is also a performance. Moreover, the distinction between visual performance and utility does not map exactly onto different models of vehicles—sport-utility vehicles were, in fact, popular among lowriders. The point is more a matter of prioritization. While lowriders certainly can be interested in utility—the big-body cars that make classic lowriders often are driven by a v-8 engine that puts plenty of speed at the driver's disposal—this is not the top priority in lowrider customization, and in fact may be sacrificed for aesthetic effect.

Prioritization of the visual and of ornamentation can be seen in lowrider interior effects like ornate candelabras or gruesomely suffering Christ images. These might, as Griffith argues, specifically suggest a Spanish colonial baroque, but the opulence of lowrider interiors could at times equally suggest a barriological version of "ghetto fabulous," the "peripheral consumption" (Norton 1993, 56) of luxury goods as part of an assertion of urban minority subjectivity. It was common during my research for show cars to feature minibars with brandy or cognac bottles and ornate stemware. This was the era in which the vast marketability of hip-hop seemed to offer instant celebrity and limitless cash to performers who could portray a plausible urban "bling" persona, and high-class brand names such as Hennessy and Bentley acquired new "street" resonance. One of the latest trends on the street then was to install liquid-crystal-display (LCD) video monitors or "screens" on surfaces like sun visors or the backs of seats. Video screens were integrated with the stereo system to make a multimedia entertainment system capable of playing back DVDs as well as audio CDs.

The automotive industry followed customizers in the integration of screens, which in hindsight makes lowriders appear to be avant-garde tech consumers rather than class rebels. Indeed, the luxury accessorization of lowriders is just as likely to call to mind the bourgeois den as Spanish colonial cathedrals. Norms for this space of private leisure have evolved from the cigarette-lighter statuary and spirit decanters that accessorized the domestic pleasure zones of postwar suburban homes to home theaters tricked out with entertainment technology or "man caves" accessorized to enable and enhance the consumption of various kinds of commodified and mediatized masculinity. Home media now promise unlimited diversion in the private sphere. With the advent of high-speed Internet, this promise is intensified, and the much-heralded "information superhighway" is detoured through the living room of the suburban family. In this mediatization of the home lies the ultimate bourgeois aim of information consumption: the ready availability of "everything" entertaining or informative that the world has to offer, deliverable in a perfectly sheltered form, eliminating the need to drive by marginal neighborhoods or deal with undesirable persons en route to the stadium or movie palace. The elaboration of sound and image technology for car interiors has effected a similar mediatization that renders the term "car stereo" quaint.

With such trends in mind, it is admittedly difficult to define a style of consumption as "excessive" in the historical context of the turn of the twenty-first century, a time when there appeared to be no horizon limiting the capacity of the U.S. market to consume. Automobiles were thoroughly integrated in this system. As a commodity, the automobile is a quintessential fetish. Not only do the material forms of cars conceal their social production, but they also ultimately prove unable to live up to the promises of autonomy they represent. Cars are the stuff of massive ideological campaigns, pervasive myths, and volumes of commonsense knowledge: the open road, speed and power, individual liberty, boundless mobility (Seiler 2008). The consumption of automotive commodities (and these myths) also represents the massive consumption of resources and the global imbalance of power it requires (Stallabrass 1996), the ecological insanity and imperial imperatives of petroleum-based social formations, and some of the "most destructive and seductive commodities around us" (Gilroy 2001, 82).[5]

On this stage of extractive and resource-intensive consumption, the buying behaviors of marginal and mainstream consumers often converge, suggesting that contrary to the tidy rubrics of Pierre Bourdieu's landmark study *Distinction* (1984), distinct classes in fact participate in the same singular and multiply-centered market of both things and cultural values (Frow 1995). Yet as Paul Gilroy notes in his essay "Driving While Black" (2001; see also Seiler 2006), the experience of automobility is not entirely uniform, even if participants in American society are commonly driven to take part in it. Unlike Marcuse in his observations about the "Negro and his Cadillac" (1991, 8), I propose that capitalist consumption is not without difference: as members of a collective consumer "market," we are not all created equal, and this is significant even for social practices that fall short of absolute or pure refusal (though I will explore this possibility as well below). Most tellingly, the "lives" of bought things diverge after the moment of commodity exchange. Customization in particular holds the capacity to make some consumption otherwise.

Social identities inflect commodities through contexts of consumption and display, juxtaposition with other objects, such as ornately designed athletic clothing, and material modification. This becomes a matter of customization, since it contrasts with the significance scripted onto a product as part of carefully plotted marketing. Customized excess is different from the excess "utility" desired by the suburbanite who uses a massively inefficient, military-designed vehicle for navigating the paved wilds of big-box stores. Such excess conforms in an orderly fashion to the bundled narratives that are sold along with a Hummer, which are also as amenable to lowriders as anyone. Yet the aesthetics of bling suggests that the same products must be understood differently if consumed and used by differently situated social actors. For those who enjoy social privilege, to desire a high-end luxury car is to seek the satisfaction of entitlement—for others, it may represent exceeding limits posed by access to resources, including not only money but also, and just as saliently, time (Borhek 1989). Consumption can be not only the conspicuous underwriting of achieved status (Weber 2003), but also a rebellion against a prescribed or assumed position of deprivation.

In this way, any customization of consumption begins as part of an utterly mainstream process through which American subjectivity is constituted. Yet the performative consumption habits of those whose marked identities are overdetermined as different from Anglocentric, bourgeois, hetero-male normativity, whom political theorist Anne Norton calls "peripheral consumers," do not fail to meet with ridicule or hostility from the dominant classes (1993, 56). This is why lowriding in the media culture, for instance, when it is not put to use as a representation of threats related to minoritized urban space, is often a comic device. It is as such that lowriders appeared in a commercial featuring Pepsi delivery trucks "lifted" with hydraulics, or in films like *Napoleon Dynamite* (2004) and *Cars* (2006).[6] In these represented contexts, lowriders are exoticized, the humor deriving from their distance from "normal" automobility. Lowriders themselves are not always trying to be funny with a baroque aesthetic. Rather, their acts of consumption claim entry to the club of luxury consumers without leaving behind distinctive marks of barriological memory.

Figure 2.5. Tucked velvet upholstery and bar accessories on a show car.

Death, Sex, and the Nonautonomy of the Reverse Image

After Albert described his vision for the custom paint work on his truck, he told me about his new job at a custom upholstery shop. He had just started as the lowrider upholstery guy, "doing nothing but biscuits and wrinkles." That was good, he said, because he didn't get bored—every car was a different challenge. Albert's comment on "biscuits and wrinkles" refers to the velvet upholstery that often covers all available surfaces in a completely customized lowrider, and is arranged by the upholsterer in a variety of different "tucks" (see Figure 2.5). The most famous of these is the "tuck and roll," and a favorite is the heavily padded "biscuit tuck." At a different time, I had heard Albert discussing a tuck job with another lowrider, and he called the style he was describing "coffin."

The notion of a style of car upholstery called coffin gestures toward ways in which lowrider opulence is luxury with a difference—these are not merely imitations of what the automotive industry offers as luxury for sale. Perhaps not intentionally, material references to funereal spaces circle around a structure of feeling about how and why lowrider opulence fits within a particular aesthetic and yet, to a larger audience, represents opulence out of place (Douglas 1966). The very language of mortuary space—funeral "home"; funeral "parlor"—suggests an anachronistic, hyperrespectable domesticity. Lowrider style is associated explicitly with the aesthetics of a funeral parlor in the terminology of the coffin tuck, but also in the form of the sculpted metal plaques with which lowriders declare their club or neighborhood identity (Figure 2.6). The closest material cognate I have seen to plaques outside lowriding are on a hearse, where they declare the name of the funeral service.

Other material resonances with funerary space are less specific but can be traced. The liquor presented on a tray as if waiting for visitors may still represent the fulfillment of a fantasy of luxury life, of "living large," but surrounded by the textures of a coffin, it just as easily suggests a libation to the dead. This is underscored in cars that serve a memorial function (see Figure 2.7). Perhaps the most famous lowrider car outside lowrider circles is "Dave's Dream," a memorial car that was installed in the National Museum of American History as part of an exhibit on New Mexico. The owner of the Ford LTD, David Jaramillo, died before he could finish it. His family and friends completed the car as a tribute to him, and had it blessed by a priest before it was taken to Washington (Smithsonian Institution n.d.).

"Dave's Dream" is hardly unique. I saw numerous cars and bikes at lowrider shows that were in some way dedicated to a deceased friend or family member.

Figure 2.6. Cadillac with Crager-style wheels and a plaque,
Montopolis neighborhood, East Austin.

Figure 2.7. Memorial truck on display at a San Antonio car show.

As a public repository of memory and a means of expression, memorial cars function like "RIP" graffiti murals (Kim 1995; Phillips 2000; Sánchez-Tranquilino 1995; see Figure 2.8). Lowriders also serve as focal points for individual or collective grieving, as seen in the numerous show cars that depict celebrities who met with untimely or tragic deaths and with whom the lowriders identify: in my work, Selena, Tupac Shakur, and Biggie Smalls were all memorialized in this way.[7] When confronting the passing of a human life, lowriders turn to the relative permanence of metal and paint as a public and personal medium for memory.

But it is not only a general relationship with death and memory that is at work in the coffin upholstery style and the implied funereal association. It matters that a funeral parlor is also a site of the baroque in contemporary life. A funeral can become the occasion for gaudy or excessive decoration by the standards of dominant aesthetics. In this, it represents the last chance by friends and family members to show love and respect, indeed to perform the importance of their relationship to the deceased. This can be more pronounced in communities where death is more widely distributed than wealth.

Figure 2.8. "RIP" graffiti mural, East Austin.

When Eazy-E, a founding member of the seminal West Coast rap group NWA, met an untimely death from HIV, he was buried in a gold-plated coffin, a supreme rejection of utility in favor of bling. The luxury of a coffin may represent the comfort of one who is "at rest," but it also speaks to the unclaimed balance of physical pleasures that the deceased will never be able to experience. Like a funeral, a lowrider car carries a certain "now or never" aesthetic urgency. The opulent interior is not a foretaste of the wealth that will follow deferred gratification, but a substitute for the bourgeois interior that may be permanently out of reach.

Lowriders and hearses are not the only sites of baroque opulence to be found on the American cultural landscape. Another point of material resonance is signaled by the urban trope of a "pimped out" ride and the more generally circulating design concept of a "brothel interior." Like the imagined spaces of commodified sex or lore about the dandyism of the urban pimp, the luxury of a lowrider interior promises fulfilled fantasy and desire, intensified and contaminated by illicit associations. The air of illicitness is neither a matter of fact nor only a misguided stereotype, in the sense that nobody really thinks that a car described as "pimping" functions like the actual "brothel bus" that made headlines in Miami (Sutton 2008). Lowrider interiors are usually devoid of explicit references to the illegality or violence of prostitution, though it could be argued that when lowrider mural images draw on sexualized and objectified iconographies of the female body, they also conscript women to the role of pleasure providers for male subjects.

More than the actual sex trade, though, the connection signaled by the term "pimped" lies in a common aesthetic of degraded opulence. Like a house of ill repute, a lowrider is rendered profane in the literal sense: that which is socially sacred (sex, ownership of property) is brought down to earth by its inextricable connection to commodity exchange. As Walter Benjamin noted, not without problematic gender assumptions of his own, prostitutes in the Paris arcades represented the truest image of human beings' relationship to commodities (2002a, 10; see also Buck-Morss 1991, 345): in fact, we are all commodities in a way, and while most of us sell our time and labor, prostitutes cut to the chase by selling access to their bodies.[8] Like the last-chance aesthetic of a funeral, a brothel aesthetic connotes that anything goes, but this license is tempered by the constant awareness that the pleasure den is a limited, inscribed space, and one ultimately defined by desire for one party and by commerce or even bondage for the other(s).

The notion of a brothel aesthetic unrelated to actual sex work also connotes anachronism or secondhand luxury—"brothel interior" style speaks of the lush materials and ornamentation of Victorian décor, which is not so much indicative of privilege in the present as it is of faded or ironic luxury. Lowriders may very well struggle against this kind of association in building their cars—their interior opulence is certainly not ironic in a detached or distancing sense—but inasmuch as the car is a dialogical meeting point between the imagination of its builder and a broader circulation of discourses and material aesthetics, lowrider opulence remains an encounter between a fantastical desire to transcend limits and real social boundaries that hobble it.

All these material narratives—of freedom, of limitless possibility, of going "all out," of fantasy, of one last chance, and so on—look very different from the perspective of the producer than they do from that of the consumer. Indeed, the sense of absolute license or transcendence of temporal actuality in funerary spaces or those of commodified sexuality are produced carefully for consumers. Producers, knowing all the backstage work that is concealed from the consumer, never lose sight of the fact that the whole thing is a production. In customization, the two come together. The point is not deception and concealment, but the creation of a realm of relative freedom that has been forcibly wrenched from the realm of necessity. Thus, while lowrider practice is motivated by the pursuit of beauty, innovation, and the like, its aesthetics do not conform entirely to the traditional bourgeois notion of authentic beauty as autonomous from necessity (Marcuse 1978). This is reiterated in the precarious economics of lowriding, in which owners frequently have to buy, sell, or trade accessories or whole cars because of their vulnerability to large-scale swings in the economy. The lowrider's role as a consumer is also more precarious than that of someone from the middle class. The luxury of a lowrider interior is often dearly bought, not with sterile, interest-deferred credit cards, but with literal sweat, blood, and, most of all, time. The lowriders I met during my research financed their luxury rides through overtime hours, "side work," layaways, other schemes for making payments, and various other strategies. With this in mind, it is possible to see a lowrider car as the objectification of its owner's labor. Thus, what appears excessive or illicit from the perspective of bourgeois interiors can offer a lowrider the affect of being "right."

Roman brought this sense of aesthetic satisfaction back to the connection between one's ride and one's home space. I had asked him to define what lowriding was, mentioning that I had heard people refer to it as culture, as a sport, as an art, as a lifestyle, and in other ways. These terms seemed to circulate in an elliptical orbit around a deep, personal identification with and investment in a car on the order of a house or home. Roman responded to my question:

> **ROMAN:** Those are basically it.
>
> **BEN:** All those things?
>
> **ROMAN:** A deep culture that—I think it's, it's . . . [*laughs*] I don't want to say it's in our genes. I want to say it's more something that, I guess . . . being, being minority, uh, growing up—to automatically just own a house is not going to happen. You got to start from the beginning. And, I think, just owning the vehicle itself [. . .] that's a big accomplishment. Uh, I figure—that's the way how—that's how I felt, that's how I saw my friends feel, to earn your first vehicle, and not just to own it, but to make it look nice. 'Cause you're coming out in public and you want people to realize what you've accomplished, and not only have you owned that, but you've made it look a little bit better than what it originally looked. That's . . . that's how I feel. I don't know there's a word or a term for that.

The fetishism of the automobile as commodity both instructs us to take it as a sign of something more than the use value it represents, and conceals the relations of production that made it possible. Yet through the labor of customization and use over time, a car also comes to signify something else, to have a symbolic value beyond the cultural capital ascribed to cars by their design and advertising ideology. Rather than Thorstein Veblen's conspicuous consumption, or better, in addition to this, a lowrider displays conspicuous production. Thus, as Bright found:

> In his personal network of labor and recreation, the low rider seeks to forge his synthesis. His car presents a style of leisure and opposition, unique in its movement and finishes. The handcrafting of details serves to identify the car with its owner. All marks of the industry which produced the car are removed. All of this work is intended to remove the marks of institutions and invest the car with an image pertinent to its owner's experience. His desire is replaced with pleasure. His leisure becomes invested with signs of his work. (1986, 11)

Though Austin lowriders I met did not reject brand markers and, hence, consumerism itself, cars were emblematic of experiences, not only representing but also embodying them. Customization is only a more conscious and overt version of the signification that occurs in the social life of things generally (Kopytoff 1986), with or without our help, as the marks and scars of history accumulate and are read as memory. I asked Roman why older cars had more prestige. He said, "A lot of that comes from respect. Because those were the things that our fathers rode around in. Those are the things that provided us with what we have today." Roman showed me an old, beat-up blue Chevrolet pickup parked in the yard behind his house. "This is worth more than any of our other vehicles. My father worked very hard to get it." Without the work truck, he couldn't have made the money that he eventually used to buy some property, a home. Roman's grandfather also used the truck to get around while he worked in fields outside town and sold watermelons on his days off. Roman said, "A lot of people go toward older vehicles, not only 'cause they got the cool look, but these cars have been more than just around the block."

Thus, even as lowriders are fetishized, they acquire the characteristics of a reverse fetish. I mean "reverse" not as the opposite of a fetish, but like Lefebvre's notion of the "reverse image," in which the products of the culture industry take its ideological claims to their logical extremes, becoming parodies that reveal, rather than obfuscate, social embeddedness (1992, 12). For Lefebvre, Charlie Chaplin performed this image in the character of the Little Tramp, whose body became the hyperbolic extension of a capitalist logic of everyday life, turning a funhouse mirror on social reality (see Kracauer 1995). Lefebvre argues that "by its false and illusory and euphoric and presumptuous insistence upon the self, the 'free world' immediately creates its pure negative image" (1992, 12). Thus, the reverse image becomes the site of an immanent critique of the society that produces it. The promise of commodity fetishism is agency and deliverance through consumption. Lowriders do not explode this relation entirely, but shift it: rather than delivering agency, consumption becomes the ground for building it.

Inside the Outside: Distance and Heterotopias

The plan was to meet at midnight and go down to Chicano Park to stake out the only shelter house. It was Saturday night before Easter, and several car clubs were getting together for a barbecue. Originally, the Kings had planned their own event in the park, then someone heard that Jimmy Castro, an old-school *veterano* in the scene, was also planning to throw one and invite all the car clubs he was friendly with. It was agreed that the two parties should merge. The park was going to be packed on Easter Sunday, and the Kings decided that in order to reserve the shelter house, someone would have to spend the night out there. So we would allow ourselves a measure of cruising on Saturday night, then meet at midnight to get the spot.

I was standing with a handful of the Kings in the parking lot of the Pizza Hut on Riverside at about 10:30 when Thomas rolled up in his Euro-style Chevy, with his subwoofers issuing a muddy boom from the trunk. He pulled over and rolled down his window. I felt a blast of air-conditioning and heard the treble tones of his system join the bass that pounded in the trunk.

He leaned out. "There's already somebody down there, dog. At the park. They got the grill going, playing music and everything."

Everyone looked to Eddie, the president, for the next call. At one point, Zilker Park, southwest of downtown, had been considered an alternative picnic site, since it is one of the largest and most central parks in Austin, but it was unlikely that there would be tables available without a reservation. Eddie decided that we should go with the next-best option: stick with Chicano Park, but give up on the shelter house and save some shaded tables near the water. The decision made, everyone moved to their cars to go to the park while Eddie pulled out his cell phone and started dialing people who were just getting off work or had gone nightclubbing.

We drove in a caravan of five cars down Riverside, then turned north along the highway, away from the cruising action and into the sleeping residential area of the Eastside. There was a small parking lot a few steps from a row of concrete picnic tables that stood near Town Lake. Thomas and Big Beto both skillfully navigated their vehicles through the wheelchair-access cutout to get over the curb without bottoming out—they rode on rims, but their rides were not lowered too dramatically. They parked on the grass close to the tables. Eddie and Darren opted not to bump over the curb in their lowered rides, but left their vehicles in the lot, backing them into parking spaces. Despite his caution, Darren's tailpipe hit the curb at the back of his parking space and scraped, setting everyone's teeth on edge.

Town Lake provided a buffer from the noise of the streets on the south side. We could just see the lights of the businesses in the Riverside area cast against the night sky, but the park, extending north of us toward the residential area and east toward the dam, was dark and still. Just to the west were the raised lanes of I-35, far enough off for the traffic to sound as a uniform, steady hiss. Beyond that, downtown glowed.

We unloaded the grilling stuff from Darren's truck: a couple of large bags of charcoal, lighter fluid, aluminum foil. Several people sat at the tables and talked quietly. Thomas left his parking lights on and the car running to charge the battery. He had mentioned several times that evening that he had rented some videos, including *Friday*, to help pass the time. A small LCD monitor screen was set in the sun visor on the passenger side of his car, connected to a VHS recorder resting on the floorboards of the passenger side. Thomas sat in his car, every now and then touching the gas pedal and softly revving the engine. No one moved to join him in the car, but soon the sound track of *Friday* could be faintly heard coming from his open windows.

Big Beto's Nissan truck had a soft vinyl bed cover attached to the bed with snaps. The truck bed was a box of wonders: you never knew what he was going to pull out of there. The cover was on whenever I saw the truck, and at various times all manner of things emerged from underneath, just when they were needed: spare bulbs, a soft lead knock-off mallet for changing rims, twist ties, a tire gauge, delicate tools for dismantling a car interior. Beto, whose partner, Gloria, worked at an auto parts store, always seemed to have the tool or small part needed for a particular job at a particular time. After Thomas had retired to his front seat to watch the movie, Beto unfastened a corner of the truck bed cover and pulled out a small futon mattress, which he threw on the grass in front of Thomas's car. "Gaw, make yourself at home," somebody said. "What's this, your bedroom?" Beto dove onto the futon and then flopped onto his back, looking up at the stars. Then he spoke.

"Every time I come in the kitchen, you in the kitchen!"

I was confused for a second by Beto's non sequitur. But then I heard the line repeated faintly inside Thomas's car: "Every time I come in the kitchen, you in the kitchen!"

Then Beto: "In the goddamn refrigerator!"

Then the tape: "In the goddamn refrigerator!"

And so he continued to recite the movie, one line at a time, a second before the videotape, until he tired of it and fell silent.

The movie in Thomas's car played on, only faintly audible and accompanied by the soft buzz of the highway.

《 》

As lowriders make living space of the exterior sites that they occupy, they in some ways imitate bourgeois modes. A car show is an example: the most popular ones offer a plethora of categories and awards, giving participants a good chance to take home a trophy. This in turn makes it more likely that a well-staged car show will include a diversity of makes and models—it seeks the completeness that Susan Stewart identifies with bourgeois interiors and sees apotheosized in "collections" (1993, 155). A good car show thus becomes a collective collection. Each participant displaying a car marks off his or her space with some tangible boundary: a velvet rope, for example (see Chappell 1998). In this way, within the collective space of completion, an individual interior space is marked out. Not only is brand loyalty evident to Chevrolets and GM cars in general, but the bourgeois-commodity ethos that Benjamin noted in the Paris arcades is also reproduced in car show locations, and quite literally: hand-lettered signs on show cars read "Look, but Don't Touch" (see Buck-Morss 1991, 85).

In another congruence with Stewart's subjects, this interiority of lowrider aesthetics is also found in miniature: displays of lowrider model cars at car shows often develop into panorama-like tableaux that use plastic "Homies" figurines as characters in an idealized or nostalgic (even if comic) scene of barrio life (Figure 2.9).[9] Again, although this miniaturization reflects a bourgeois gesture toward completeness and control, it occurs within the temporary, bounded space of a car show rather than in private domestic space, and thus occupies more the status of a wish image than a component in the American dream world. Furthermore, the parodic figures of the Homies differ from exoticizing and romantic bourgeois images of pastoralists (S. Stewart 1993, 56). While pastoral scenes in a decorative context render workers as "picturesque," the Homies are self-parodying. The contrast amounts to a carnivalesque, rather than individualist, laughter: lowriders who laugh at the Homies implicate themselves in the barriological iconographies the Homies both satirize and represent (Bakhtin 1984).

Yet while bourgeois interiors are mimed or modeled to an extent in lowriders, the interiorization is not complete. A connection with the outside remains, since mobility renders the boundaries of the car temporary, even if not entirely permeable, thus marking the social marginalization that cannot be easily erased by participation in the mainstream regime of consumption (see Chappell 2000). The particular marginality to which I refer is not only political-economic and racialized, but also spatial, concerning the terrain covered by the concept of private property (by "my property," do you mean a car or land?) and by relative levels of agency in crossing and controlling borders. It also extends metaphorically to the abstract space that is the referent of discourse. Attempts to stake out a place inside mainstream consumer society are not fully accomplished, and yet lowriders are not fully outside this public, either.

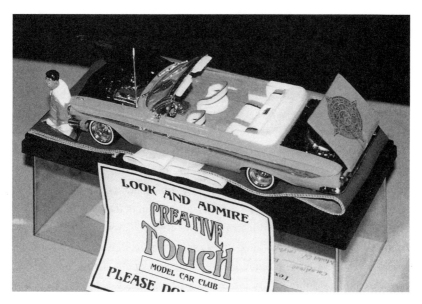

Figure 2.9. Model lowrider with a Homies figure, on display at a car show.

Photographs by Alex Harris that were included in the exhibition *Custom-*
ized: Art Inspired by Hot Rods, Low Riders, and American Car Culture at Boston's
Institute of Contemporary Art capture the dual nature of the car as a site itself
and as something that moves between sites (Donnelly 2000). Each photograph
is taken from the front seat of a car that can be imagined as a lowrider because
of various interior adornments, such as velvet upholstery on the dash or a welded-chain steering wheel. The first-person vantage point creates a field of vision
that includes the front seat of the car as well as the landscape lying before and
beyond the windshield. The titles of the photographs locate this vantage point
precisely according to various coordinates: *Chamisal, New Mexico, looking north*
from Juan Dominguez's 1957 Chevrolet Impala or *Las Vegas, New Mexico, look-*
ing east from Myles Sweeney's 1960 Chevrolet Impala. In one title, Harris adds a
degree of specificity: *Hong Kong Lounge, Las Vegas, New Mexico, looking north*
from Richard Lucero's 1972 Buick Centurion. In another, he adds a temporal dimension so that the scene refers to a chronotope: *Furr's Parking Lot, Saturday*
Night, Española, New Mexico, looking south from J. R. Roybal's 1966 Chevrolet
Caprice. Harris's photos emphasize an aspect of lowriding that is too often over-
looked by outside observers who fixate on the cars as things of beauty: it is a
beautiful thing also to ride in one, to sit behind the wheel, to look in any direction at your town or neighborhood from inside a *firme* ("cool" or "nice") ride.

Besides this perspectivism, Harris's photographs thematize a relation to space that clashes with the bourgeois norm of bounded interiority, a relation that reaches out from the interior of private space into the public. Through carefully composed and accentuated continuities of color and texture between the car interiors and their locations, the photographs depict interiors that do not hold the outside at bay—far from it, in fact.

On the videotaped version of *Friday* that Thomas was playing in the park the night before Easter, the film is followed by a music video of the title song by Ice Cube that illustrates a relationship to interiority that clashes with the classic bounded space of bourgeois property. This is not a completely random connection. *Friday* (1995) was the screenwriting debut of the pivotal West Coast hip-hop MC and lowrider enthusiast Ice Cube. Ice Cube drove a lowrider as the character Doughboy in John Singleton's *Boyz n the Hood*, and hosted lowrider car shows as part of the promotional campaign for *Friday*. Lowriders are portrayed as integral to the urban landscape where *Friday* is set, appreciated by African Americans and Mexican Americans alike.[10]

Ice Cube's music video for the title song is set in a bedroom much like that of Craig, Ice Cube's character and the protagonist of the film. Craig lives as a young adult in his parents' house in inner city Los Angeles. The room is sparsely furnished with a bed, a weight bench, and four car tires on Dayton-style wire wheels stacked on the floor.[11] In the film, Craig can't afford his own car, but the rims in the video show that he has begun the gradual process of accumulating one, even if only part by part. He has started with the most crucial element of a ride by lowrider standards. As long as they fit, or can be traded for ones that do, or if the proper adaptors can be found, these rims can transform any car into a lowrider.

In the music video, the relationship between the interior of a room and the public space outside is fantastically reversed. Everything happens in Craig's bedroom in the course of the song. People come and go, they lift weights, they dance and party. The line between public and private is flouted as visitors make the room their space; more accurately, it remains Craig's room, but they are all invited, benefitting from his largess. The utter marginality of an unemployed, urban teenager of color's bedroom is transformed into a center of authority. From the fictive world of Craig's bedroom, Ice Cube reaches out, drawing "real" places into the picture by naming them and, by implication, including in the party the people associated with those places. In the convention of hip-hop shout-outs or the graffiti roll call, Ice Cube invokes specific neighborhoods: "West side's in the house. East side's in the house." Yet the room isn't sheltered from incursions by unwelcome outsiders. At one point in the video, the police come in and bust everyone, a cogent performance of the public encroaching into the bedroom, the quintessential private space. Throughout, the video enacts a theoretical argument about what is at stake in acquiring and appropriating "a room" in the contentious landscape of property.

When I saw the music video for the song "Friday," it reminded me of a room I had visited. Richard was the longest-standing member of the Kings and became the club president shortly after I concluded my fieldwork. During my involvement with the club, there were occasionally meetings in his house, in a room furnished with a pool table and simple stereo system. That room was Richard's space in the family home. Besides its function as a meeting place for the club, the room stored car parts. His '68 Impala had been in the shop for more than a year, undergoing a gradual transformation that included building suicide doors that open backward as well as a new paint job: a "makeover," in Richard's words. He had stripped off any parts that would interfere with the project or would be subject to damage, and so the pool-table room was full of chrome trim, mirrors, a grille, headlights, a welded-chain steering wheel—quite a bit more than Craig had in the "Friday" video. Richard's room also had a stack of rims, though, and the thirteen-inch wheels with tires looked a lot bigger inside a house than they would have on a big-body car like Richard's '68. Watching pool games or flipping through the large collection of lowrider magazines that he kept close at hand in a foot locker, we took turns sitting in the Impala's velvet-upholstered front seats, which rested on the floor.

I also visited Eddie and Elisa's room one afternoon after interviewing Eddie on the front porch of the Del Valle house. He had mentioned in the interview some videotapes he had of the club, including a music video by a local rapper and a news report taped from television about the club's Christmas charity work, for which they adopted a needy family each year. When we went inside to check out the tape, Elisa was sitting on the bed playing a video game connected to the television while her older son watched. Eddie and Elisa's room was a little bigger than their double bed. The walls were covered with shelves holding model cars, car show trophies, and other lowrider paraphernalia. One shelf was made out of a spare grille for the '73. A few photographs, some of which were of the family standing in front of Eddie's car, were tacked to the wall. Facing the bed was a tall shelf unit holding the TV, VCR, video game machine, and a portable stereo. On the wall was a poster of the cartoon character Tasmanian Devil hopping a lifted lowrider.

Five adults and two children crowded into the room: there was Eddie, his friend Locomoco—a good head taller than my six feet and heavily built—a videographer with an interest in making a lowrider documentary, who had accompanied me to the interview, Elisa, and their two sons. There was enough room for all of us to stand, but barely. Eddie searched through some things on a shelf and came up with a videotape. Elisa slid it into the VCR and started scanning through it on fast-forward with the remote control. "There," said Eddie. Elisa played the tape, and the music video came on. The director had set shots under some of Austin's very few, nonnative palm trees, so by the look of the video, the scene could have been a park in Southern California. But close attention revealed local identifications on the cars' plaques: ATX, Austin Tejas, and so on, and while we watched, Eddie identified his own and others' cars: "That's [Lito's] Cutlass. That's [Anthony], who founded the club. That's my brother." There was Locomoco, whose name I finally learned was actually Ernest and who stood beside me in the bedroom just as he appeared in the video. His shaved head, goatee, tattoos, and baggy Dickies khakis made him appear on the small screen as a recognizable type, the classic cholo gangster like so many others in West Coast "Latin" rap videos. Yet he was standing next to me in a house on the semirural outskirts of Austin; the park in the video was the same one where we had been cruising every Sunday night that summer. From the cramped space of Eddie and Elisa's bedroom in her grandparents' shared house, we reached out across time zones in an imagined geography linking the mediated spaces of fame and notoriety with the remembered spaces of local experience.

Reaching out this way from an intimate home space to connect with the public outside, the interiors of lowrider homes thus do not conform to the prototype of hermetic bourgeois space, epitomized by Robinson Crusoe's island, which, as Stewart notes, sees its perfect individualist idyll ruptured by the appearance of the footprint of the "native" whom Crusoe comes to call Friday. This is the intrusion of the social into Crusoe's sanctum of complete control and autonomous production (S. Stewart 1993, 5). Lowriders' participation in the fantasy of bourgeois space is always incomplete in that they always bear Friday's footprints, the marks of the social and, in particular, racial, class, and cultural markings that, for all the proliferation of "diversity," remain rare in the spaces of privilege. It is certainly not always lowriders' choice to occupy this position. As in the model-builder José's crowded apartment, the social intrudes sometimes unbidden—"people's cars" parked outside his apartment restricted his options for painting models—and the advantages of bounded space are not lost on those who don't happen to enjoy it at the moment. Yet even if the relation to bourgeois space occupied by lowriders is not chosen or constructed as a coherent political strategy, there remains a politics to it, a politics engendered by aesthetic and practical decisions and affects that lead to the construction of a particular kind of space. I suggest that space is a heterotopia.

I have argued that lowrider aesthetics deflects the commodity of a car interior from its promise of manufactured and prepackaged freedom, a concept that is immanently critiqued in the act of customization, which takes the produced, purchased industrial object as raw material for further work. The disruption of the specific teleologies of consumer capitalism interrupts "uniaccentual" materiality, parallel to monological narratives (Volosinov 1986, 23; see also Bakhtin 1981). Such an intervention conjures a limited measure of authority for the customizer within the second-nature landscape of property and automobility. But in a broader sense, this spatial practice is an instance of what Foucault forecast would be a political task of increasing importance: the "desacralization of space" (1986, 23). Foucault argues that modernity's desacralization of time, effected by imposing and then affording a critique of the idea of progress, would be followed by a desacralization of space, which can be understood on one hand as the proliferation of mobilities, and on the other as acts of rebellion against disciplinary measures to reify spaces for particular functions and particular populations.

Lowrider interiors contrast with "sacred," or authorized and meaning-fixed, space and are thus exemplary of "heterotopias," spaces of multiple and perhaps contradictory possibilities. The automobile, traditionally a phallic object, does not cease to function as a blunt instrument of force, but also proliferates a feminized interior space, exercising a seductive as well as a kinetic power. In its excess, this interiority also transgresses the boundaries of the car's skin, opening and overspilling all available "orifices" (Bakhtin 1984). The paradoxically grotesque luxury of a lowrider is thus degraded in Bakhtin's, ultimately positive, sense: that is, it is brought down to earth. It is a material sign of semiotic richness and fertility, not purity. It is not the bourgeois interior that seeks to be kept apart from profane elements of necessity, labor, and the contaminated social world, nor does it allow the continuation of a governmental project of "asepsis" (Foucault 1980, 55).

Foucault specifically locates the historical challenge to sacralized space in the inherent mobility and presumed functionality of a vehicle. In a lecture that treads uncharacteristically close to the programmatic, Foucault briefly discusses boats as exemplifying "a floating piece of space," one that moves between ports and the perceived infinity of the ocean, which is to say, between settled places and a condition of heterotopia. Thus it is that

> the boat has not only been for our civilization, from the sixteenth century until the present, the great instrument of economic development . . . but has been simultaneously the greatest reserve of the imagination. The ship is the heterotopia par excellence. In civilizations without boats, dreams dry up, espionage takes the place of adventure, and the police take the place of pirates. (1986, 27)

There is awesome affectivity in a thing that is large enough to constitute its own occupiable space and yet can be moved so easily. This power resides in cars as well, although internal combustion is a less mystical and dirtier power than wind on sails. American colloquial speech makes the conceptual leap between modes of transport for us, terming the huge gas-guzzling cars of the late '60s and '70s "boats." Such associations of power have never been lost on the U.S. public in its much-noted love affair with automobility. The liberation of mobility posed by the automobile granted youths the means to get out of the house and yet still enjoy a bounded interior space (and in the process, contributed to the invention of "the teenager" as a social category—see Berger 1991, 64; Flink 1988, 159). Classic studies like Paul Willis's ethnography of motorcycle clubs (1978) and Tom Wolfe's new journalism on the California "kustom" scene (1971) reinforced the depiction of the mechanical power of traveling machines as a focal point for Dionysian youth cultures and their claims to agency in automotive pleasure.

Such myths have been recuperated from the domain of rebellion as selling points, but it remains notable that these associations of automobility and freedom continually emerge in social contexts that at some point in their history constituted a threat to the order of things (Packer 2008). My point is not the facile one that where there is pleasure, there is necessarily freedom, but rather that the pleasures that consumer capitalism trades in afford space for explorations into what alternative gestures, what shifting of authority may be possible (O'Malley 1993). This is, in a way, an answer to the question that remains crucial for the study of popular culture and everyday life: "How can one rethink these materials as a Marxist narrative of 'resistance,' especially when they do not nicely lend themselves to such a reading as do peasant rituals of inversion, black spirituals, and English artisans?" (Limón 1994, 130).

It is precisely a reliance on "peasant rituals" as the horizon of authentic popular practice that I want to dispute. But it also seems likely that not even such folksy materials ever offered the unsullied resistance that we critical scholars have ascribed to them. In any event, the appetite of capital for recuperating resistant gestures to the cause of social reproduction has been revealed as nearly boundless. Thus, it is in the assertion of openness as such, not in a seamless narrative of resistance, that customization is political.

The openness of lowrider aesthetics lies in its ambivalence, which in turn is an unsynthesized dialectical image of enduring contradictions. The notion of automotive aesthetics trafficking in a contradictory "dualism" is corroborated by Daniel Miller's (1994) Trinidad ethnography, which considered car upholstery as part of a broader objectification of the experience of modernity. Miller identifies a dialectic between "transcendence" and "transience" in Trinidadian automotive aesthetics, which he suggests echoes a similar tension in holidays (Christmas and Easter) and home interiors, all these being symptomatic of the claims and realities of modernity.

What Miller calls transcendence is security from the historical contingencies of everyday survival, a condition characterized by the qualities of constancy, permanence, and stability. Property ownership represents transcendence in that it provides a rooted location for "home." As a form of property available to those with a certain level of purchasing power, then, an individual's automobile signifies the transcendence afforded to a certain class status. To be modern, subjects are expected to possess and perform this status or to desire it. At the same time, modernity offers "transience" in the mobility exemplified by the automobile and indeed demanded of economic subjects in capitalism. By embodying not one or the other tendency but their dualism, the automobile becomes central to modern cultural life, and the efforts of Trinidadians to elaborate the significance of the automobile through aestheticization underscores and develops this centrality.

Miller emphasizes that this characteristic of the automobile is principally a symptom of modernity. He specifically argues that other factors such as race, gender, and ethnicity follow the class determinations of modernity and reinscribe its lines. Here I part with Miller somewhat, since in the U.S. context, it makes little sense to disarticulate race and gender from class in this fashion. Not every acting subject encounters modernity in the same way, and hence the specific form that its dualistic relations take will vary. Put another way, people and communities engage the contradictions of modernity within a general history, but also while drawing on the cultural resources of specific and local memories, of which barriology is exemplary.

To situate the specific duality of lowrider automobile aesthetics within barriology, a precedent may be found in the pachuco and zoot-suiter culture popular in 1940s Los Angeles and elsewhere—an aesthetic precedent that lowriders embrace and accentuate. The zoot-suiter became a masculine, nationalist symbol through such representations as Luís Valdéz's film *Zoot Suit* (1981), though recent scholarship has questioned whether this singular identity represents the entire zoot phenomenon (Alvarez 2008; Noriega 2001; Ramírez 2008). A more compelling connection between lowriders and their zoot-suiter antecedents is provided not so much by a specific identity or a coherent attitude of resistance as by a dual dynamic of ambivalence and emergence. Marcos Sánchez-Tranquilino and John Tagg offer an emergent reading of the zoot-suiter:

> Pachuco culture was an assemblage, built from machines for which they never read the manuals. It was a cultural affirmation not by nostalgic return to an imaginary original wholeness and past, but by appropriation, transgression, reassemblage, breaking and restructuring the laws of language: in the speech of Caló and pochismos, but also in the languages of the body, gesture, hair, tattoos, dress, and dance; and in the languages of the space, the city, the barrio, the street. [An intellectual like Octavio] Paz was offended and saw only negativity: a grotesque and anarchic language that said nothing and everything: a failure of memory or assimilation. The refusal to choose made no sense. (1992, 559)

Ambivalence makes no sense against the bourgeois norm of property—bounded completeness. But the zoot-suiters were coming from a different social position, and thus manifested and maintained a negative dialectic that is also related to the contradictory social positions and prospects occupied by the people who practice lowriding. By giving form to apparently contradictory meanings and tendencies in the construction of a car interior as a mobile room and home space, lowriding, like zoot-suiting, is a retort to the promises of transcendence and completion that are the enduring classics of commodity fetishism. Within the phantasmagoria of modern consumption, the promise is that owning and possessing the right thing will bring satisfaction, security, completion. It will settle things. Rather than settling things, however, lowrider aesthetics opens them.

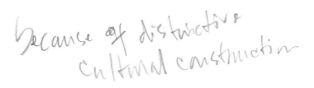

because of distinctive cultural construction

Auto Bodies

I have a heart like a car, you know. My heart is in my wheels.

Dennis Martinez, quoted in Brenda Jo Bright, "'Heart like a Car'"

A "heart that's like a car" suggests the ways in which the car is an embodiment, enhancing both bodily mobility and affectivity. In this vein, the car is
similar to the human body, a site of cultural inscription. . . . Customizing a car
enlarges the possibilities of bodily inscription, exhibition, and, for many lowriders, social relations.

Brenda Jo Bright, "'Heart like a Car'"

Hence the detailing of the cars, the flashing lights around license plates, the
hydraulics, the sometimes tinted windows, and so on expanded the thumpers'
ability to *create respect under conditions of little or no respect.* . . . In short, the
body, car, and thumper sound system were transitions from the biological to
the technological, from the visual to the aural, allowing the ego to occupy ever-
increasing amounts of public space.

Ralph Cintron, *Angel's Town*

Begin, though, not with a continent or a country or a house, but with the geography closest in—the body.

Adrienne Rich, "Notes Toward a Politics of Location"

In the process of being customized and used in everyday cruising, a lowrider car becomes an extension and enlargement of the human body (Cintron 1997; Graves-Brown 2000; Sheller and Urry 2000). This aspect of lowrider poetics, what I call lowrider embodiment, is part of a larger history of human subjects creating and encountering the second nature of automotive technology, and thus displays certain general characteristics of American automobility. But as in the discussion of lowrider interiority in the last chapter, I hold that lowrider embodiment, as a distinctive version of automobility, refracts the historical position of Mexican Americans in particular ways. Importantly, it is not a universal body that is involved in lowrider embodiment, but particularly sexed and gendered bodies, as well as raced ones. As I will elaborate below, my consideration of lowrider embodiment here is substantially incomplete because of my own gendering in field encounters, and my focus on a space of practice—that of the everyday activities of car customizers on public streets—that is historically geared toward particular constructions and territorial configurations of gender (D. Massey 2005). A more comprehensive study of the genders of lowriding remains to be done. Nevertheless, this text can contribute toward that project by advancing my argument that spatiality, and hence materiality, is crucial to lowrider significance. In this chapter, I demonstrate this by contrasting lowrider practice with depictions in lowrider media: however much everyday practice may construct restrictive or oppressive scripts of male and female gender roles, I propose that material in motion remains decidedly open to revision and does not simply reproduce ideological content found in recorded or printed mediatizations.

A central question in the burgeoning field of automobility studies is whether distinctive "car cultures" (Miller 2001) like lowriding represent relatively minor "inflections" of automobility as a social system that proceeds otherwise unswervingly in line with ideological formations such as the nation (Edensor 2004; Seiler 2008, 9). Lowriding is undoubtedly part of a larger context of automobility and the automobile nation. Commercial media culture has already effected a "representative" integration of lowriding into the great myth of American automobility through the use of lowrider style in advertising and in such events as the presence of a lowrider character, Ramón, in the Disney/Pixar film *Cars*. These incorporations present automobility as coterminous with U.S. society, a field of representation able to cover all corners of the social map. But such depictions of lowriding do not equate with its practice. While any event being represented in this way certainly gets lowriders' attention, I found that a concern with inclusion in the mediascape did not compare with their desire to participate, actively and bodily, in lowriding. Seeing a lowrider on film may be an entertaining curiosity, but it in no way takes the place of actual lowriding. In other words, it remained important for particular lowriders to "represent" on the street, even if lowriders in general were represented in media culture. To present embodied lowriding as being principally determined by an already-existing automobility, offering and incorporating already-existing identities, would be to ignore or discount the ongoing cultural production through which participants keep lowriding alive as a practice.

Lowriders' own insistence on participation and the ongoing production of lowrider style provides a basis for characterizing lowriding as a performance. I do not mean this only as a metaphor linking cars to other domains of life that may be considered more properly or specifically dramaturgical (Edensor 2004, 111). Instead, performance names a poetic function common to lowriding, the theater, and verbal art alike (Bauman 1984; Conquergood 2002; Turner 1986), a dynamic engagement of time, space, and memory. I call this function poetic in the literal sense of *poesis* as "making," and use performance likewise to describe "giving-form-to." These senses rely on the notion that expressive or signifying action is productive (Joseph 1999). An emphasis on productive practice suggests that accomplished representations in the media culture, which combine into larger-scale imaginaries, do not capture the fullness of what lowriding is, what it does, and what it is for, all of which are at stake in any particular performance. Indeed, so long as lowriding continues as a field of popular performance, such questions remain open (Butler 1993a). The broader implication is that the place of Mexican Americans within the ideological and material constructs of American automobility is not a predefined arrangement to be reflected in everyday practice as a kind of pageant, nor does it become a static relationship once textualized in media. Rather, Mexican American automobility, including but not limited to lowrider style, remains a permanently undecided and emergent relation, one that takes form only through enactments in specific, literal places.

In what follows, I unpack some of the relations and differences between lowrider embodiment as evident in everyday lowrider practice, and its mediatized representation. I first detail some examples of everyday lowrider embodiment, and then outline the gaps between distinct fields of interpretation and evaluation that feed back into cultural production. One of these fields is constituted by the community of participants and close-in observers to whom lowriders in any particular place are answerable in practice, and the other by more general social systems of media and automobility. Both of these general systems overlap in particular ways with lowriding in the construction of particularly gendered and sexed bodies. First, the lowrider media culture that has developed over the past several decades joins a media-culture industry with very specifically gendered precedents and visual codes. Second, automobility itself has a contested history of being gendered as masculine. Yet I maintain that lowrider practice is not ultimately or necessarily constrained by these points of contact. I follow these themes through several discursive and material contexts, including the problematic gender politics of erotic representation within the lowrider media, feminist critiques of automobility in general, and lowrider space. With these diverse sources, I mean to show how close contact with lowrider embodiment can yield a different view from that provided in lowrider and general automobile media. Specifically, lowrider embodiment as a materialist practice and version of automobility lends itself to manifesting an ambivalent social position, at various times indeed reproducing, but also reacting to the inherited cultural-political world.

Lowrider Embodiment

At about 11:30 at night, we were standing in a group of nine or ten in the parking lot of an Albertson's grocery store. People leaned against cars and made conversation, keeping an eye on the traffic that cruised down Pleasant Valley Road or, slightly farther away, on Riverside. The flash of a pair of rims or a metal-flake paint job rolling by caught the glance of one or two people at a time. Then a low, pulsing rumble approached from the car wash across the parking lot, and all heads turned as one. A gleaming silver Cadillac rolled slowly our way on twenty-inch alloy rims, the bass hitting on its system. The finish had the deep shine of many painstaking wax jobs. Drops of water remained on the window from the car wash. The car pulled to a stop across three marked parking spaces, and a large Latino man got out wearing an oversized, designer football jersey, enormous baggy jeans ironed to a crisp crease, a small goatee, and a gold chain draped around his neck, supporting an intricate metal charm. A thin braid descended from his hairline down the center of his back. The crowd shouted a greeting together: "Lito!"

"Damn," said Lito, showing a spattering of water spots on his jeans. A thinner young man climbed out of the passenger seat, and Lito gestured toward his passenger. "He said, 'You washing yourself or the car?' So I was like, 'Hmmm, that's starting to feel good.'" He rubbed his arms as if he were showering. "Fuck the lotion, dog, spray some of that wax on my arms." Everybody laughed.

Ismaelito ("Lito"), who routinely referred to himself in the third person as "Big Daddy," was a big guy who rolled in big cars. He was known for his show-quality customized lowrider and another late-model Cadillac daily driver. That night in the parking lot was not his only grand entrance I witnessed. One Sunday evening at the cruising in Chicano Park, a nondescript Japanese compact pulled up beside the group of people I was standing with. No one recognized the ride: it was not customized as a "Euro," no rims, no audible system. When the door opened and Lito stepped out, the surprise at seeing him in an unfamiliar car, not to mention the unfolding of his considerable girth from such a small space, made us all laugh. A cast on one hand extended over his wrist. "Hey," shouted Lito, "I'm fuckin' in-cog-nito! I'm like, damn! Roll down the other window, dog, I'll hang my arms out both sides!" He proceeded to announce that he had wrecked the 'lac, and since the show car had a knock in the motor, he was hitting the cruising spots in a car borrowed from a relative. Someone asked whether he had insurance for the wreck. "Oh yeah, Progressive hears the phone ring, they just start writing me another check." Lito portrayed himself as the veteran of many accidents, apparently indestructible. He scratched at the skin on his arm just above that cast, describing how the air bag in the 'lac had broken his wrist. "I got to get this thing off, though, dog. Let's go, I got a grinder at home. Wheeeew!" He mimed cutting the cast with the power tool.

Lito's comic performances in this anecdote exemplify how lowriding involves a close relationship between cars and bodies. It is no simple matter of fact that lowriding requires and affects human bodies—in some ways, a lowrider becomes an extension of the human body. The particular emphasis on embodiment that I found to be enacted by lowriders was both an expressed and an enacted priority: that lowriding was and should be a practice in which to participate, not an abstract aesthetic best appreciated from a distance. Lito's comparison of an unfamiliar Toyota to a disguise spoke to one of the implications of this: as I have noted already, it was fairly common on the boulevard to identify people with the cars: "Hey, I saw Martin—with that red Lincoln?"

These and other more extensive anthropomorphizations of automobiles recur throughout lowriding and related cultural productions. In an interview conversation that drifted to the subject of music, the lowrider I call Smiley referred me to the song "Rimz & Tirez" by West Coast rapper Xzibit. Released well before

Xzibit became more widely known as the host of the car-customizing reality TV show *Pimp my Ride* and a regular on *Extreme Makeover: Home Edition*, the track offers a narrative from the anthropomorphized perspective of a Chevy Impala that makes its way from the junkyard to the cruising strip, customized and revitalized as a lowrider. This figure of the automobile as a form of embodiment is thematized in literature as well as in songs like "Rimz & Tires." In Helena Viramontes's story "Neighbors" (1995), a custom car is part of the ominously embodied presence of the neighborhood clique called the Bixby Boys, which registers as an implied threat to the narrator and creates a rift between her and the boys within their common spatialized community. In Sandra Cisneros's story "Hips" from *The House on Mango Street* (1994), the narrator likens her maturing body to a new Buick, something that is at once an object of desire, a means of mobility, and an unanswered question about destination.

Conceiving of cars as bodies resembles the bodily identification with rides in the lowrider scene, but unlike Cisneros's character, lowriders whom I knew tend to talk more about what cars were—a material presence to be reckoned with—than what they represented. This is why the preparation of a lowrider is the production of a public self as much as it is the crafting of a cultural text out of an industrial product. One night when Raymond was out on Riverside Drive, watching the rides in traffic while standing beside the parked Ford Taurus he had borrowed from his mother, he anticipated a future moment when, having finished his Monte Carlo sufficiently to cruise it, he would achieve a different level of participation. "Man," he said ruefully, watching one custom car after another roll by. "Just wait until *I come out* next spring." To "come out" in this sense meant to achieve lowrider subjectivity by participating and by being seen doing so. It would mean that Raymond had invested his car with identity to a satisfactory degree and that this relationship had been concretized as he took his place among the cruisers on the boulevard. Raymond anticipated cruising as the realization of a particular, custom version of himself.

Bodily identification with the car is not only affirmative, though. As a surrogate for the owner's body, a car body can also serve as the target for violence. In the 1979 cruising/gang-exploitation film *Boulevard Nights*, which was a central event in the mediation of lowrider style around the country, gang members execute a vendetta against one of the protagonists by trashing his Impala while it is parked in front of his house. Similar traumas were related to me in stories about the Austin cruising scene. For instance, a club member who was restoring his truck told me several times about how its custom paint job had been destroyed when a jealous member of a rival club threw acid on it in the street.

Investing a car with a degree of subjectivity exposes one to the pain of loss. Anthony, whom I met at a Holy Week church breakfast on the Eastside, described the '79 Regal he had had for a while. He had put rims on it and done the paint, and was starting to put in hydraulics, when his daughter was born, so he decided that he needed to give up the car and devote resources to buying a house (he did not mention the mother's role, if any, in this decision). Once an avid reader of *Lowrider Magazine*, Anthony told me that after giving up the Regal, he didn't even want to see the magazine anymore because "it hurts too bad" to look at lowriders and not be able to participate.[1] I thought I recognized similar emotion on the face of Roman after his gold '64 Impala was mangled in a wreck. Previously, Roman had spoken with me at length about his experience in lowriding, but after the crash, he did not have an answer when I asked whether he would repair the '64. It seemed too overwhelming to consider starting over on the car that he had built over years and that, as soon as it rolled out of his garage, would be subject again to collisions and damage. The materialized self of a customized lowrider therefore accrues a capacity to affect and to be affected (Massumi 2002)—it displays to the world, stands as the object of desire, and carries the vulnerability of a physical body.

Yet such identifications are never only individual—they are freighted with the legacies of prior acts and patterns of identification: lowrider embodiment forms a point of contact between self and society at which participants both are hailed by power-infused categories of identity and "act back" against such interpellations. In the police traffic stops related in Chapter One, a stigma identity was at work that equated a certain kind of "Mexican" body (not only Chicano or Chicana, but urban, working class, and driving a lowrider) with the demonology of "gangs." This was racial profiling, to be sure, but more specifically, it was "lifestyle profiling."[2] Traffic stops provided an opportunity for Foucault's political gesture of refusal, to "refuse what we are" in the hegemonic racial formation (1982, 216), but this was as much a matter of bodily gesture as of spoken discourse.[3] Gloria, Big Beto's partner, told me a story about this kind of moment of refusal.

> They pulled [Albert] over one night . . . [Albert] had his friend [Rudy] with him, and . . . [Rudy] doesn't—his friend [Rudy] has a bad habit of not wearing a T-shirt. And, 'cause he likes to show off his body. And the cop told him to get out, and [Rudy] got out and he didn't say nothing to the cop, and . . . I don't know, they have the habit of wearing the pants half off the butt or something, and so his—he was wearing low pants with no

T-shirt and he has tattoos. So—and he doesn't have any gang tattoos, he just has one that has his name [Valdez], and one on his back that has, um, his son's name. And I guess 'cause it was in Old English, the cop asked him, "Who do you claim?" And he's like, "What are you talking about?" He's all, "Who do you claim? What gang are you with?" And he kept trying to tell the cop, "I'm not with a gang." And he finally got so mad, he ended up smarting off to the cop and telling him, "I claim zero on my W-2 forms for income tax!" And that really made the cop mad, and that's when he told him, "I'm going to take you in," and he's like, "No, but I don't know what else to tell you." And so they finally let 'em go. They kept them there for almost an hour, just drilling them, and they gave them a ticket for, um—they said he wasn't wearing his seat belt, he said he was, but—so, I don't know. And they said it was a routine stop, so . . . He let it go, but it's happened a couple of times, I mean, they see rims on a car and they're the target, you know. "Oh they're going to do bad, so I better follow them."

The condensed materiality and extended mobility of the human-car hybrid body pushes against an established order of things premised on official knowledge of human beings and their social place. Though not always driven by conscious, intentional agency, the move to materiality that lowriders make by investing identity in an object resists the fixing of social relations even as it draws on them. Thus, lowrider materialism does not exclude media culture—indeed, sites of embodiment such as local cruising scenes remain in a symbiotic relation with translocal mass media. Lowrider media outlets like magazines, mass-produced video recordings, and websites report on local scenes and offer an avenue to fame for participants. Mediated representations feed back to local scenes as lowriders consume them, both scanning for the appearance of people they know firsthand and studying what "they've got" in other locales. Part of the bargain in this relationship is that maintaining such a presence in the mediascape requires confronting and negotiating the mass media in general.

Lowrider Media

By *Lowrider Magazine*'s own authorized account, lowrider media was born in Northern California in the late 1960s as part of growing identity consciousness and activism on the part of Chicano/as.[4] Lowriders had appeared in barrio-based publications like *Con Safos*, but a magazine dedicated principally to low-riding and published on a more ambitious scale was the project of a handful of students at San Jose State University who called themselves the Low Rider Associates. The group, which included "El Larry" Gonzalez, David Nuñez, and Sonny Madrid, among others, used campus resources to organize cultural projects, including concerts and magazines aimed at students and the off-campus community alike. The associates worked with political organizations such as the United Farm Workers and the Movimiento Estudiantil Chicano de Aztlán (MECHA), garnering enough credibility for Gonzalez and some like-minded friends to ride an endorsement from César Chávez to election to the student council, which in turn allowed them to divert more funds to their efforts.[5] After a string of other magazines such as *Trucha*, *Lowrider Magazine* was born. A Chicano bicentennial dance on July 3, 1976, raised seed money, and the Gilroy Low Rider Happening, organized collaboratively by the Low Rider Associates along with car clubs and farmworkers' groups, provided material for the magazine's photographers to cover in the first run of 1,000 copies in 1977.

This maneuvering to secure the use of student-government and university money resembled the tactics of cultural-political activism.[6] Despite this and other countercultural connections, members of the San Jose group were not necessarily revolutionaries—*Lowrider Magazine*'s own history suggests that they were interested in profits as much as politics, and joining the media "spectacle" was always part of the plan. Early critics of the claim that lowriding expressed Chicano/a culture saw right through this as a culture-industry colonization of barrio style in the interest of corporate access to a growing market (Plascencia 1983). But the nature of the relationship of *Lowrider Magazine* to the communities it marketed to was and continues to be more complex than an Adornian "mass deception."

Even while *Lowrider Magazine* produced the very events it then covered as journalism, the magazine also served and continues to serve as an inroad for hundreds of local communities into the translocal media culture. With its coverage of shows, features on readers' cars, and a vibrant tradition of reader content in letters to the editor and similar sections, it is difficult to view *Lowrider Magazine* as an imposition of aesthetic norms from above rather than as a conduit of representation flowing from one street scene to others. Moreover, from its first issue, *Lowrider Magazine* assumed a critical position toward mainstream media and society, suggesting with pieces like the first editorial, "Low-Riders vs. Chico and the Man," about the controversial Chicano-themed TV series, that credible representations of Mexican Americans were absent from the media culture. Targeting a largely bilingual or code-switching barrio-based audience, *Lowrider Magazine* tapped a market most publishers and distributers did not know existed, taking a place on newsstand shelves, as *Lowrider Magazine* writer Paige Penland put it "between *Alarma* and *Hot Rod*" (1997).

It is difficult to imagine a translocal lowrider scene (what *Lowrider Magazine* has often called the "lowrider movement") existing without an organ like *Lowrider Magazine*, particularly in far-flung areas that do not see car shows on the monumental scale of those in Los Angeles or the trappings of a lowrider "tradition" associated with a place like Chimayó, New Mexico. In Roberto Rodríguez's memoir of working for the early *Lowrider Magazine*, he describes the marketing of the magazine in barrios beyond Northern California as a way of linking various local scenes into a new relation as a kind of imagined community (Rodríguez 1997; see also Anderson 1991). During my research, lowriders often made reference to "the magazine," and it was assumed that everyone would have read or seen the latest issue. Several lowriders kept extensive collections of back issues. Issues were often arranged around a car on display at a car show, indicating an ongoing commitment to lowriding and situating the car within the broader community and history of lowriding. Yet *Lowrider Magazine* is, of course, not a transparent reflection of the constituency it serves. Like *National Geographic* in its own way (Lutz and Collins 1993), *Lowrider Magazine* presents a certain view of the world and of lowriding, a visual rhetoric that underscores very specific messages.[7] Alongside a generally affirmative tone, celebratory of lowriding and everyone who finds a place under its big tent, *Lowrider Magazine* expresses concern for social justice for lowriders and Mexican Americans in general regarding the police and other authorities. It claims a relationship to the Chicano/a movement and to Mexican American history, supports Chicana/o education through essay and scholarship contests, and takes responsibility for representing Latino/as in the media culture.

To the extent that lowrider media represent an incursion into the media culture by a minoritized population—an account that *Lowrider Magazine* has often been eager to endorse—this relationship implies a negotiation with the norms and requirements of the media culture. In 1996, *Lowrider Magazine* was acquired by an automotive publishing group and was thereby formalized as a niche market within a larger media corporation (Penland 2003). This move, along with a series of changes in editorship, clarified the tensions in the already vexed relationship of *Lowrider Magazine* to local scenes. The use of female models in its imagery is an aspect of *Lowrider Magazine*'s position in the middle ground between "the media" and "the community," and one that has perhaps sparked some of the most enduring controversy.

Lowrider Model Photography and Gendered Media

The sexualized depiction of female bodies as adornments to cars conforms to mainstream norms of gendered and sexed visual representation that have proved in recent years to be relatively unimpeded (even if not unaffected) by the accomplishments of feminist theory and activism since the second wave. Sarah S. Lochlann Jain, a prominent critic of automobility, notes that the draping of cars with eroticized female bodies in the context of car shows, calendars, and so on amounts to a "performative hypermasculinity that verges on over-compensation" (2005, 196). Jain draws on Eve Sedgwick's notion of an erotic triangle to explain this: the use of women as ornamental figures of erotic desire is actually recruited to the task of nurturing relationships between men (197). Even to the extent that sexualized print and video images allude to actual courting practices undertaken in the car, the point is to "get the girl to impress the guys" (197). Thus, as Sedgwick concludes about comparable triangulations, the use of women as nonagentive bodies is geared toward cementing homosocial relations between men, and even toward constructing spaces where women are excluded.

This is more than plausible in lowriding, and many readers will recognize masculinity as a principal stake in the descriptions of lowrider style and lowrider space throughout this text. In fact, my own positionality in the field was shaped and enabled by this immanent homosocial project, even though lowriders were not intrinsically motivated to bond with me as an individual, and even though I viewed my own sociocultural position as being that of an Anglo male seeking to practice a critique of my own privilege. Yet in retrospect, I was able to form relationships with lowriders across both prominent and subtle differences of race, class, and culture at least partly because of presumed gender solidarities that I did not recognize consciously enough to question.

This problematic situation was compounded by the fact that my access to the experiences of female lowriders was restricted by the particular way I was gendered in the scene, which structured my relationships with women involved in lowriding as well as with men. At times, this relationship was one of reticence. When I met the officer of the "ladies' chapter" of an Austin club at a car show,

Figure 3.1. Cover of the inaugural issue of *Lowrider Magazine*, January 1977.

she assured me she had "a lot of words" to say about lowriding, but would not return my calls later for an interview. "Anna," who was married to the lowrider called Mario, was equally reticent when I visited their home. As we talked in the living room with a recorder running, Mario told me, "You should talk to [Anna]. She's been lowriding longer than I have. She got her first trophy like a year before I did." But Anna assured me she had nothing to say. I do not intend to dismiss these problematic characteristics of my project or of lowriding; indeed, I would add patriarchy to any list of "negative" aspects of lowriding that should not be ignored. But it is important for outside observers to understand that however oriented toward constructing and reproducing masculinity lowriding may be, this does not go uncontested by those who identify with the lowrider community. Nor is the body politics of lowriding exactly congruent with the general fields of media and automobile culture that it touches.

Lowrider model photography was part of lowrider media from the beginning (Figure 3.1). The first issue of *Lowrider Magazine* featured a woman on the cover, wearing an overcoat with a Soledad car club's name on the back: New Image. Her back is to the camera so we can read the club name, and she is looking half over her shoulder in the direction of the camera. There is a glamour element to the pose, though the clothing is not "revealing." With her back to the camera, she is presented somewhat as the passive object of a consuming gaze, but in a relatively modest form as compared to the modeling to come. Like a beauty pageant or local fair "queen," she is used to represent the "best" of a community, the idealized qualities that "our women" share or aspire to (Cohen, Wilk, and Stoeltje 1996). In other words, from the beginning of the lowrider model genre of image, objectification was at stake, even when the model was fully clothed. In November 1979, the *Lowrider Magazine* cover first featured a model wearing a bikini swimsuit (Penland 1997, 76). The result was both instant controversy and increased sales (for further discussion of this history, see Chappell 2000 and 2008). More than twenty years later, as I reviewed archived issues of *Lowrider Magazine* in advance of my fieldwork, the debate on lowrider models continued in its pages, but *Lowrider Magazine* never stopped featuring female models prominently.[8] That this has played a part in the magazine's claim to be the "most successful Chicano publication ever" (Penland 1997) cannot easily be denied.

Lowrider Magazine models are often in swimsuits or other revealing clothing that might fall in the category of "club wear" or stripper outfits. The poses proffer the woman's body to be consumed as the object of heterosexual male desire. For a time in *Lowrider Magazine*, the centerfold picture that graced every issue and presented the month's feature car included a female model in a bathing suit with the Budweiser beer logo on it. This collapsing of editorial material and advertising continues to be borne out in the other pages, where advertisements for custom wheels, paint, hydraulic components, and other products are adorned with scantily dressed women.[9] Besides resting so comfortably within the mainstream of visual advertising, this imagery trades in well-established stereotypes of the Latina "hot tamale" (Limón 1999; Nericcio 2007; Yarbro-Bejarano 1999), which does not prevent many lowriders from investing the display of Latina models with the cultural significance of patrimony. In ongoing debates about lowrider model photography, in such forums as the letters to the editor, readers often speak of the Latina models with a tone of collective ownership, constructing the magazine as a storehouse of images of "our" beautiful women as much as it is of "our" custom cars. The occasional inclusion of non-Latina models has sparked its own controversy, as have other readers' complaints about, for instance, an absence of African American models.

Despite its grassroots origins and claims to a continued connection to the street, a great deal of what *Lowrider Magazine* offers readers is access to a space of fantasy, a flight from the real. The lowrider cars that are most prominently featured in the pages are on the scale of dreams for many readers. While "daily drivers" and "stock" restorations occasionally make it into the magazine, a more typical feature presents a highly modified ride, approaching the class of national "best of show" or "lowrider of the year" winners. These cars have often been built with professional help and show the effects of months of full-time labor and tens or even hundreds of thousands of dollars of investment. Readers may aspire to build a car that is customized as much as the featured cars in the magazine, but that may also never happen. In the magazine and at shows, they consume such cars as "celebrities" in a lowrider star system. Model photography is also integral to this fantasy world.

The visual narratives of desire and its satisfaction objectified in women's bodies obliquely refers to the "real world" of lowriding by situating them near featured cars, but everyday cruising on boulevards like Riverside at the time of my fieldwork was not where you would expect to encounter the surgically sculpted and airbrushed bodies of glamour models. The bodies of those out cruising on the boulevard were also under construction, through various means such as tattooing, diet, and fashion—but this yielded results easily distinguishable from the cosmetic work of models. The visual fantasy of lowrider model photography does allude to and visually elaborate the erotic excitement associated with courting that actually goes on in everyday cruising. The fundamental difference, however, is that cruising-scene courting is a dialogical interaction, with much of the excitement coming from efforts to "talk to" or "holla at" a potential partner, while lowrider model photography offers stimulation only in one direction. The models' carefully composed postures of docile sexual availability package such ordinary desire in a consumable form requiring no

Figure 3.2. Modeling and shooting at an indoor car show in San Antonio.

negotiation other than its purchase, a commodified scopophilia (Mulvey 1975). The ubiquity of such images in lowrider media repetitively articulates a script of women as willing and available sexual partners, made all the more desirable by their contrast with the "real world" and contingencies of everyday life, including the possibility of rejection.

If no one was out cruising on Riverside dressed like a stripper, at least when I was there, the visual erotics of lowrider model photography does get reproduced locally at car shows, not only by visiting professional models, but amateurs whom I came to think of as "volunteers" seeking to launch their own modeling careers. In this way, and due to coverage of shows by the magazine, car shows represented a kind of middle ground or threshold between lowrider media and the cruising street. A local show I attended in a San Antonio park was typical, as would-be models joined the flow of spectators and participants moving around the display cars. In the parking lot designated as a display area, women posed in front of the cars, drawing small crowds of onlookers. One of the models wore a retro pachuca outfit, with pinstriped pants, suspenders, and a fedora hat. Though her top was pretty tight, she wore considerably more clothes than the typical model in the magazine. The photographer, a grey-haired man in a black muscle shirt, black jeans, and boots, was directing her to assume various poses and shooting while the crowd looked on. His camera bag, left on the ground next to the car, had a couple of old laminated passes dangling from it, including "Selena Forever—All Access," apparently a souvenir from a production of the stage musical about the slain Tejana star. Meanwhile, in front of another car, two women with bleached hair and tiny bikinis were being shot in a variety of glamour poses by a younger man (in his twenties, maybe) who was decked out in a baggy black suit—not the zoot suit that regularly shows up at lowrider car shows, but a slick, modern design. Unlike the first photographer, who presented a kind of implied professional celebrity by casually displaying his credentials from past jobs, this one projected professionalism as an aspiration.

Other photographers also appeared to be amateurs on the make, like an even younger-looking guy I saw toting a 35 mm camera while a buddy followed, hauling the camera bag and tripod. As they hustled toward the cars, the one with the camera was giving instructions: "Now, you don't take pictures of anyone in front of the cars without asking permission." These impromptu photo shoots were observed by an audience that was itself partially in costume, since a fair number of attendees had turned out in zoot suits or cholo gear for the occasion. The would-be models were hanging out all day, and when they weren't posing in front of cars, people would approach to ask whether they could take a picture, for example, sitting on the lap of a *veterano* while he made a barrio sign with his fingers, thus embodying a role that was not devoid of fantasy itself. One of the women I took to be an amateur model asked a man in a charcoal pinstripe zoot suit for his coat because she was freezing (not surprisingly), and they seemed to know each other. They strolled off, talking: "Remember that car show one time . . .?"

A general tendency during my fieldwork was that the more local the focus of a car show, the less likely it was that professional models would be there posing for photographs. It was at the bigger shows, in particular the touring *Lowrider Magazine* shows, that professional or aspiring models and photographers could be expected to make a real-life appearance. A standard feature of *Lowrider Magazine*–sponsored shows is to have certain professional models who have forged a career out of posing for *Lowrider Magazine* on hand to sign autographs and pose for Polaroids with customers for a fee. These "appearances" offered readers of the magazine a chance to temporarily enter the fantasy world it constructed and to bring back a souvenir in the form of a small color photo of themselves with a famous model on their lap or arm. Perhaps the best known of these *Lowrider Magazine* models is Dazza, who is a one-person lowrider model photography industry in her own right. Dazza garnered her own corner of the lowrider exhibition at the Petersen Automotive Museum in Los Angeles in 1999–2000 (Sandoval and Polk 2000), maintains a website, and does a brisk business selling autographed pictures, posters, and calendars at major lowrider car shows. Dazza also represents another way that the model's profession can be distinguished from ordinary life: she apparently owes her longevity in the scene at least in part to extensive surgical and cosmetic customization of her own body.

A career like Dazza's is what amateur or volunteer models with little experience might hope for after getting a break in the industry. A show being covered by a *Lowrider Magazine* reporter offered the chance to appear in the pages of the magazine, which could, as the logic goes, lead to other things. When I asked the publisher of a Texas lowriding magazine at a car show about the role of model photography, he emphasized these career opportunities in order to construct his position as being that of a benefactor, rather than exploiter, of the young women he photographed. Assuming that women dressing and posing like models at a car show harbor certain career objectives, he claimed that he was doing them a favor by providing breaks that they might not get from mainstream publications as Latinas. Not surprisingly, his narrative left out any consideration of how, for these career opportunities to be effective, they would have to align with heteromale desire—that assumption was just built into the modeling genre.

The proliferation of digital cameras and image-sharing media since the early 2000s has no doubt altered this relationship and perhaps diminished the difference between shows covered by national media and those that are not. It is an open question whether such changes amount to democratization, in the sense of women seizing more control of the production of images, or whether they reproduce a top-down, exploitative relationship between media culture outlets and the women who model for them. The decentralization of visual media does seem to have diversified the aesthetics represented in glamour photography to an extent, hinting at the possibility that through more grassroots, alternative, or underground modeling and photography scenes, women may find a measure of autonomy in their own representation. Returning to Sedgwick's point, however, this would not put glamour photography any less at the service of men.

At car shows during my fieldwork, the visual gender and sex constructions of lowrider model photography were definitely geared toward a normative heteromale audience. Beyond the professional and amateur-volunteer photo shoots, this found a counterpart on the entertainment stage in bikini contests or otherwise named events, in which women danced to compete for the strongest audience reaction to their enactment of a provocative model persona. This, too, related to widely mainstream practices. In Austin, it was not unheard-of for certain bars to feature amateur stripping nights or various modeling contests oriented toward a body part (e.g., "Best Buns"). Likewise, the Texas Heat Wave, a massive custom car and truck show held annually in Austin that drew participants from across the country, always featured a wet T-shirt contest as part of the entertainment until the venue was changed to Dell Diamond, the minor-league baseball stadium in the suburb of Round Rock. The contest was banished from the program at the Heat Wave for being incompatible with the stadium's family-friendly image, a decision roundly mocked by John Kelso, the humor columnist for the *Austin American-Statesman*:

> Reid Ryan, president of the Round Rock Express, the minor-league baseball team that plays at Dell Diamond, said the wet T-shirt contest wasn't permitted because it doesn't promote the ballpark's family-values theme. "They called it a wet T-shirt and hot body contest, and that just didn't jibe with what we wanted to do," Ryan said. "Without us being car show people, we had a real big learning curve on what a car show is." Somebody needs to send Ryan the Snap-On Tools calendar. How can you have a car show without a bikini contest? That's like a circus without the elephants. (2001)

The Heat Wave served as an indication that the objectification of women in lowrider modeling was by no means unique to lowrider style—while lowriders attended the Heat Wave, they were far outnumbered by other kinds of customizers, who brought minitrucks, hot rods, and other classes of vehicle. Like the Heat Wave's "contest" entertainment, lowrider model photography, by ascribing women to a secondary and objectified role as ornaments to cars rather than as participants in lowriding, reproduces general and patriarchal (not only Mexican American) assumptions that automobility, property ownership, and mechanical labor are all the domain of heteromales. Despite the fact that this is not unique to lowriding, the gender and sexual politics of such glamour images can cause well-meaning liberals or middle-class academics to recoil from lowriding as a whole, since it is nearly impossible to engage with lowrider media culture without encountering swimsuit-model photography. My effort to theorize lowriding as an embodied practice with the potential for social intervention, rather than as essential misogyny, is a possible alternative to this recoil, but presents its own risks. One of these is that I reproduce a romanticizing mistake all too familiar in the study of popular culture: the fallacy of locating heroic resistance to domination in strictly male activities that, in turn, are reliant upon the internal, collective oppression of women, a theoretical move that would effect a "construction of social harmlessness" (Cummings 1991).

The question at the center of this interpretive dilemma, what other scholars have suggested to me is the central "contradiction" of lowriding, is whether objectification of women is intrinsic to lowrider expression and is thus bound up in any claim to lowrider authenticity. If an "authentic" performance can be understood as one that is convincing to a constituent audience, delivering a belonging effect to the viewers, then it must be recognized that the models featured in *Lowrider Magazine* are an authentic part of the genre and that hetero-masculinity is among its chief priorities. As Kelso argued about car shows in general, modeling can be expected in any car show or magazine that conforms to precedent. Thus, the question would be settled if it were the lowrider media—more specifically, the organizers of car shows and editors of magazines—that define what lowrider style is all about. But this role of media and the notion of authenticity itself are, in fact, contested and exist in tension with the aesthetic values and enacted choices that emerge in popular lowrider practice, "below," as it were, the media stratosphere. If lowrider identity is, as lowriders themselves often insist, most authentically embodied in the process of making lowriders, not only in consuming their visual representation, then the use of women's bodies as ornaments or tokens is not a necessary part of lowrider practice, any more than last year's outdated customization trend is. This notion of lowriding not as a set iconography but as a "complex site of cultural production" (Rosaldo 1993, 217) suggests how it is that people might identify with lowriding as a general cultural field without necessarily buying into the specific matrix of gender and sexuality implied and indeed required by the genre of lowrider model photography. The consistent controversy in response to lowrider model photography from within the lowrider community is a testament to this.

When *Lowrider Magazine* first featured a woman in a swimsuit and high heels on its cover, in November 1979, the move was soundly criticized by men and women from within the readership. Some of the opposition appealed to propriety, protesting a "trashy" representation of a "nice homegirl." In fact, the model, identified as "Mona," was recognized within her own community and expelled from her Catholic high school following the publication of the cover (Penland 1997). The editors attributed a 15–20 percent leap in circulation to the model images, however, and on this basis have rationalized making similar images a defining feature ever since. This has in large part defined the visual repertoire of lowrider media since other publications, such as *Orlie's Lowriding*, *Street Customs*, and San Antonio's *Vajito*, also feature glamour images of women prominently, as do a growing number of lowrider-themed websites. One notable exception within lowrider media is *Lowrider Bicycle*, which generally has not used glamour photography, presumably also according to a logic of propriety, since it is aimed at a younger audience.

Despite this near ubiquity, lowrider model photography has been a point of contention in the letters section of every issue of *Lowrider Magazine* that I have perused:

"You make the Chicanas look trashy."
"I love the beautiful ladies."
"You can't see the cars with those girls in front of them."
"My mom won't let me read your magazine."
"When will you put some *machos* on the cover?"
"How about some African American women getting a chance?"
"The world should know that we have so many fine Latinas in *la raza*."
"Don't hate on them just because they're beautiful."

The reception of lowrider model photography thus reflects a wide diversity of positions and views on the politics of gender, representation, and identity, from feminist critique to conservative prudishness, with a great deal of affirmative sexism in between. It also is part of larger rifts within Chicana/o identity politics regarding patriarchy and gender. According to an activist e-mail listserv at the time, in 1996 the Xicana Caucus of MEChA introduced a resolution calling for the organization to boycott *Lowrider Magazine* in protest of the objectification of women on its cover. The resolution did not pass a general vote, but it prompted *Lowrider Magazine* to respond. In a letter to MEChA, female employees of *Lowrider Magazine* rejected what they interpreted as a puritanical attempt to censor women who were happy for the opportunity to autonomously display their "beautiful bodies" without shame.[10] The caucus's feminist critique stood on the shoulders of historical challenges mounted by Chicanas to male-dominated corners of the Chicano movement as well as academic Chicana/o Studies.[11] Like other backlashes to Chicana feminism that have invoked the figure of Malintzin, or La Malinche, *Lowrider Magazine*'s response to MEChA painted feminist critics as traitors: it accused the Xicana Caucus of being divisive and betraying *Lowrider Magazine* after the magazine had supported MEChA and other movement causes in print.[12]

It is a testament to the heterogeneity of responses to patriarchy, and to the history of feminism, that both MEChA activists and glamour models may consider themselves "gender radicals," on one hand by challenging the objectifying practices of patriarchy from a feminist point of view, and in the models' case, by launching professional, financially rewarding careers as media personalities uninhibited by conventional strictures of modesty (see Del Castillo 1996; Yarbro-Bejarano 1999). It is important to note that the kind of criticism represented by the Xicana Caucus does not deny the Chicano/a identification with lowriders in general, though it may take issue with a particular aspect of how lowrider culture presents itself. The idea, implicit in a proposed boycott of *Lowrider Magazine*, that lowriding and even *Lowrider Magazine* could be reformed and salvaged from patriarchal practices of representation underlines the depth of the identifying links between lowriding and Mexican Americans, demonstrating why controversies around gender and representation do not go away.

Despite entanglements with the media culture industry, the lowrider niche remains a "minor" medium (Schulman 1994).[13] As much as lowrider media reflect a desire by producers and participants to join the culture industry, lowriding writ large remains answerable to the community, a public primarily comprising the Latino/a residents of urban neighborhoods where lowriding is popular. This accountability, or at least this expressed desire to be answerable, along with self-constructions of lowrider media and personalities of some renown as "positive," have directed responses to the questions raised about lowrider models.

One such response has been a kind of liberal equal-time approach to objectification, evident in some of the larger car shows. As Bright noted, the "bad girl" modeling contests that were a part of lowrider car shows in Houston in the mid- and late 1980s had their counterpart in the zoot suit contests in which men modeled costumes celebrating the cultural pride and "¿y que?" attitude nostalgically associated with the pachuco era of the 1940s. As Bright observes, the female modeling contests revealed double standards with regard to gender and the value of being "bad":

> Men and children of either sex are able to evoke a reading that they are
> cool and disinterested. They are judged on these standards alone. Women

are usually not able to evoke this image. They have the problem of trans-
mitting contradictory messages that lie uncomfortably close to the truth.
The idea of being a zoot suiter is to be good at being "bad." While men
and children can achieve this, it is difficult for women. Men, boys and
girls can all appear in a non-sexual image that is disjointed from their
personality. Women cannot. If they appear "bad," they can be interpreted as being promiscuous. This creates difficulties for a contest that is
intended to show a positive ethnic image. For this reason, the "bad girl"
contest has been dropped in some car shows and replaced with a "most
beautiful" contest. (1986, 70)

I would quibble with the idea that modeling performances that show less
skin, such as a zoot suit performance, are nonsexual, but Bright's point is well
taken that the stakes in performing sexuality and presenting the body for visual consumption are different for men than for women. Most directly, this is
because modeling at car shows occurs within a larger visual-cultural context
in which the sexualized representation of women is the norm. Bright reports
that in the 1980s, another alternative was sometimes posed by "Madonna look-
alike" contests in which models mimicked the singer in parodying an up-front,
"bombshell" sexuality. The ironic agency that has been ascribed to Madonna's
performing persona of that time may have been present in such reproductions,
but in the context of my research, car show modeling appeared to wholly embrace the objectification of female bodies for visual commodification and
consumption.

More recently, however, car shows have begun to include "hard body" contests in which men display their bodies on the stage. In keeping with Bright's
observation of the unequal consequences of "bad girl" contests, such displays
occur in a field of gender politics and visual practice that is already so tilted as
to make any claim to "equality" illusory. A far cry from the zoot suit contests of
earlier lowrider shows, which displayed both purchasing power and cultural
competence, including evidence of knowledge from history or collective memory (Bright 1986, 66, 70), macho man or hard body contests have become more
about body building and the display of a sculpted, heavily muscled body. Just
as bikini contests have intensified to resemble the displays of professional or
aspiring strippers (who, by going public in this role, have already left behind
the possibility of maintaining certain conservative notions of "decency" in the
community), these performances accentuate the distinction between the car

show stage and ordinary life. Indeed, while the bikini contests bring to the fore the inequalities in male and female relationships to the power of the gaze and the imbalanced distribution of ascribed subjectivity and objectivity, hard body contests mime this structured difference in a carnivalesque inversion. Women in the audience of a hard body contest are invited to objectify and consume male bodies in the way that men habitually do to female ones, and thereby to briefly occupy the social role ascribed to men, but not in a way that offers any real threat to the mundane order of bodies and genders.[14]

A second response to gender-themed critiques, one akin to the equal-time objectification offered in hard body contests, is the uneven and inconsistent but clearly noticeable opening of lowrider media to women's mechanical work. Contrary to stereotype, there are women who build their own lowriders, organize clubs, and even command professional fees for displaying them as featured cars at shows. For *Lowrider Magazine* to pay attention to women as lowriders themselves is an important step beyond noting the support role women play for male lowriders, which lowrider researcher Denise Sandoval found to be a common refrain in her interviews with lowriders. In the narrative of "support," women in lowriding play a background role, providing the invisible domestic labor that keeps men alive, fed, clothed, and free to pursue their interests (D. Sandoval 2003b, 183). Yet women have participated in lowriding in all capacities, as mechanics, car owners, car show competitors, car club officers, and so on. Part of the gender politics of lowrider media is how *Lowrider Magazine* and other outlets respond when women who have long participated in lowriding make a claim to their share of fame that being featured in lowrider media represents. With *Lowrider Magazine* functioning as a point of access to the media culture industry, the question of which cars, built and owned by whom, will be featured in the magazine, and how, is a matter of great import. Given the constructions of gender and sexuality that are conventional within lowrider model photography, a significant issue this question raises is what a photo feature of a woman's lowrider should look like.

At various stages in its history, *Lowrider Magazine* has suggested numerous responses to these questions, which remain unsettled. Some women have posed in front of their own cars in modeling outfits for *Lowrider Magazine* photo sessions. Others eliminate the ornamental model role altogether and pose in street clothes: the mechanic-owner and her car. The November 2004 issue used a narrative of increased female participation within lowriding as a marketing angle, presenting a special feature on the "ladies of lowriding."

Figure 3.3. Cover of *Lowrider Magazine*, November 2004.

This approach adhered to the noncritical, equal-time solution: while the women who had built the featured cars posed beside their rides as men often do, some of the photographs included female lowrider models as well. The cover exemplified this, resulting in a visual depiction of a specific, delimited range of role possibilities: a model stands on one side of the featured car, and the owner on the other (Figure 3.3). Even in presenting their work as mechanics, engineers, or painters, however, the magazine subjected women lowriders to conventions of female beauty and presentability, posing them in high heels, short skirts, and the like. Indeed, in the November 2004 cover, the model holds a wrench and the owner the keys. Thus, agency is presented as equally available and divided between the two, and their division of labor in the erotic presentation is "just different." In effect, the magazine's attempt at inclusion negates the differences between being a woman lowrider and a lowrider model—both are "ladies of lowriding." The implication is that building a lowrider competently does not deliver women from strictures of gendered behavior and appearance, a theme that also appeared occasionally in earlier features, in which the female owner appeared as both mechanic and model, albeit wearing more clothes than a professional model typically does.

These issues have been taken up by Liz Cohen, a Colombian American artist who grew up in Arizona and who places the continuum of gendered lowrider embodiment at the center of her work by building and customizing cars herself and then posing in a bikini for photo shoots. According to a newspaper article covering one of her projects, which involved an East German Trabant that could expand into a Chevy El Camino with a chromed-out V-8 engine, Cohen attempts to play three roles simultaneously in her foray into car customizing: "The people who build them, the people who own them, and the people who represent them—the models. I'm hopefully going to be all three" (Irwin 2006).

Cohen works closely with customizers who vouch for her legitimacy in the shop as a mechanic, thereby endorsing the meritocratic line. But the idea of giving equal time to female models and mechanics (itself never even close to being accomplished) does not extend to broadening the category of "lowrider model" itself. *Lowrider Magazine* has never featured an obviously male model on the cover, hard bodied or otherwise, which suggests that while projecting an inclusive attitude, *Lowrider Magazine* remains strongly invested in maintaining a heteromale address in the magazine, one that imposes limits on the degree to which women lowriders, male models, or certainly any as yet unrecognized lesbian, gay, bisexual, or transgendered lowriders could be accommodated. Larry Gonzalez, quoted in a *Los Angeles Times* piece about the magazine, takes a "strictly business" position on the issue: "'We get criticism every issue for the girls,' Gonzalez acknowledges. 'But, hey, we're a business. We're aimed squarely at 18- to 25-year-old males, and they're interested primarily in two things. Cars are one of them. And until our audience revolts, we'll keep using the girls'" (O'Dell 2000).[15]

Lowrider Magazine's jovial affirmation of "the ladies of lowriding" is a slick sugarcoating of a much more conflicted relationship of lowriding to gender and sexuality. What Gonzalez does not acknowledge is that the group he identifies as the target market for *Lowrider Magazine* is not the entirety of the population interested in lowriding. Indeed, his comment completely discredits the wide readership of *Lowrider Magazine* by women, which is at least suggestively indicated by the number of letters to the editor whose authors identify as female (D. Sandoval 2003b, chap. 5). If women are not entirely absent or unwelcome in lowrider space, they are obviously not encouraged by Gonzalez's marketing attitude and others like it to take part in lowriding actively. Particularly in mediations of lowrider style, they are aggressively relegated to an objectified role even when being paid lip service for their participation otherwise. This relationship demonstrates how the specific forms that lowrider embodiment takes and the relative values ascribed to them in different contexts represent a point of contact, under negotiation, with the media culture industry as a larger cultural-political formation.

As Sandoval succinctly notes, in the pages of *Lowrider Magazine*, "The representations of Chicanas ultimately serve market interests" (D. Sandoval 2003b, 207), even as the magazine serves as a tangent point between commercial and community spheres whose interests are considerably diverse. Within this contact zone, lowrider models fall within a mainstream genre of representation commonplace in advertising and entertainment: so-called glamour photography or the almost ironically termed "non-nude modeling." They also reproduce a mainstream association of women-objects with cars and, especially, custom cars, a visual coupling that is as easy to find in the pages of *Hot Rod*, or in the print ads and calendars of auto-parts and tool companies, as in lowrider media. The persistence of such habits of representation in lowrider model imagery is evidence that the agency and dynamics of customization do not in any obvious or automatic way subvert or interrupt conventional ascriptions of automobility and mechanical labor as men's concerns and men's work. Beyond visual representations of the body, these fields of automotive practice form another point of contact between lowriding and larger social histories.

Automobile Genders

Recent critical work implicates lowriders in the "consequences"—cultural, political, geographic, and otherwise—toward which automobility as an ideological formation has historically tended (Seiler 2008, 3). Yet the materiality of automobility, in particular as it is privileged in lowrider embodiment, suggests that however likely these consequences may be, they do not necessarily always appear in local manifestations of automobility. Thus, it is essential for critics to avoid too easily pasting arguments about automobility in general onto all specific instances of its practice. Jain, in a trenchant critique, finds violence to be characteristic of automobility in "the gendered and classed spaces of the auto itself" (205, 188). The question that lowriding necessitates is "which auto itself?" I will take a moment to engage a piece of Jain's work, not to disagree that automobility produces gendered and classed spaces, but to assert that "the auto itself" cannot be used to describe a universal one of these; the phrase does not describe a context, but a category of contexts, all of which are gendered and classed in specific ways, and which require iterative reproduction to conform to ideological mandates (Butler 2004, 134).

In her article "Violent Submission: Gendered Automobility" (2005), Jain analyzes Guy Ritchie's short film *Star*, which was part of a high-art advertising campaign for BMW.[16] Jain shows how, in the film, an expensive, high-performance European sports car is a particularly legible sign of masculine power, and beyond that, a brutally effective blunt instrument used by the male driver in Ritchie's film to beat down an uppity woman, played by Ritchie's then-spouse Madonna. Jain's incisive critique of the film's portrayal of gendered violence by automobility is clear and accurate; in fact, the film's gender politics may be worse than Jain lets on, since I wonder whether she overestimates Madonna's agency by raising the possibility that her performance is a parody of masochism. There is little room to doubt that the auto in Ritchie's film is a tool of patriarchal violence. But this analysis of a media text about automobility in order to access cars as cultural objects "in the fullness of their materiality and semiotics" (Jain 2005, 186) also demonstrates why it is crucial to engage automobilities in everyday practice.

Jain's decoding of Ritchie's BMW film is a work of semiotic analysis of a mediation that gestures toward materiality as a referent; it is not a material engagement.[17] Jain's argument that "automotive technology, engineering studies, and cultural notions of masculinity carry notions of gendered violence" (2005, 188) is ultimately an ideological diagnosis, ascribing content—"notions"—to automobility that can then be assumed to carry over to all contexts in which cars appear. Yet if cars are indeed encountered and engaged for analysis in the "fullness of their materiality," that fullness complicates ideological content.

While the appeal that cars hold for lowriders can by no means be understood as devoid of the notions or meanings of gender and class privilege that Jain is talking about, just as certainly the gendered and classed space of automobility depicted in Ritchie's film is not one that the lowriders I interacted with in my fieldwork would ever expect to have access to, apart from in a kind of fantastical relationship as spectators.

Jain's discussion of the gendering of automobility as a form of masculinity is premised on her observations of the roadway-vehicle system, which prioritizes and indeed mandates aggressive sociality on the part of the driver-subject, and submission from the public. Yet this "space-taking" (Jain 2004, 195), ingrained as it may be in the cultural habitus of automobility, must be read differently against the historical backdrop of the erasure of Mexican Americans from the public. To use a car to take space in this context is as much a refusal of submission as it is enforcement of it (and men and women alike took space on Riverside). Furthermore, the particular rhythms and forms of lowrider automobility enhance rather than overwhelm dialogical sociality, re-creating the "vibrant street space" that automobiles historically displaced (196). For these and other reasons, including the gap between the agency implicated in purchasing or driving a luxury vehicle and that involved in deploying working-class skills to build one, the cool, entitled, ruthless masculinity portrayed by Clive Owen's character as the driver, embodied in his mastery of a machine that is a supreme product of European engineering and manufacture, could represent nothing for lowriders so much as a gap between the "textual and social subject," a contrast somewhat similar to that which films aimed at a specifically patriarchal-bourgeois audience pose for women viewers (Gledhill 1999, 68).

It is easy to imagine possible contradictions posed for Mexican American lowriders viewing a media text like *Star*, and the industrial-commercial normativity that it presents: for instance, male lowriders might at once identify with its patriarchal subjectivity, but not with its bourgeois character, which expects and claims total control of its immediate environment and trajectory.[18] If such a class identity were not a priori exotic to working-class Mexican American viewers, it still suggests a gap in that the media culture industry always represents this class culturally as Anglo, and most often (still) as racially white despite occasional attempts to inoculate the mediascape against charges of racism by portraying wealthy characters of color.

Jain (2005, 195) grants that the gender politics of automobility is historical (race and class are somewhat less her concern), and in doing so notes that the

masculinization of cars was an ideological move to counter the broadened possibilities offered by their materiality, including the expansion of women's mobility, and with it employment options, and so forth (see also Seiler 2008, 85).
Early automobility, in fact, occasioned a crisis of gender, as technology and activities requiring mechanical skill presented a sphere of instrumental meritoc-
racy where women could prove themselves the equal of men (Parchesky 2006,
174). If a woman fixed a car, there was no disputing it, and machines either
ran or did not, without prejudice. Joan Cuneo is the iconic figure of this conjuncture: among the most successful auto racers of the early twentieth century,
she embodied a threat to male dominance that was met with social regulation
when women were banned from the sport (Jain 2005, 195). Thus, ideological
controls imposed from outside the realm of mechanics and motoring contributed to the shoring up of automobility as a masculine sphere.

Lowriding is by no means immune from this gender regulation, and indeed it could be said that most lowriders use customizing as a means of masculinity. A lowrider club that was the subject of a feature story on a major TV
network in 2009 made no bones about their policy of not accepting women
members, which the female reporter answered with only playful indignation.
Such a gender-restrictive rule was not something I ever heard articulated by
an Austin car club, though women members were by all accounts more the exception than the rule. Lowrider space was saturated with implicit rather than
clearly stated gender politics, evident in discourse and in the spatial arrangement of cruising sites. It was relatively common in my fieldwork to hear a car
referred to as "bitch," posing the conundrum of using a dehumanizing term
to refer to a machine that had been to some degree humanized by customization—perhaps it amounted to a form of humanization as subordination. This
was not considered derogatory, however, and would most often be used as affirmation of an aesthetically satisfying ride: "Man, that bitch was *clean*." Used in
this way, the term carried connotations of both beauty and a measure of mean-
ness, in contrast with other usage of the word as an insult or mock insult. In
tune with street culture recognizable from mediations as well as everyday discourse, when men called each other "bitch" out of mock-aggressive gender play
in the friendly spaces of everyday lowriding, it would typically be only an ironic
quotation or hyperbolic parody of aggression, a kind of billingsgate between
equals (Bakhtin 1984; Limón 1994). The stakes would have been considerably
higher if a woman were to be called the same, which I rarely, if ever, heard.
Likewise, homophobia was the norm in ordinary talk on the street, with male

friends routinely affirming their friendship and heteromasculinity by gay bait-
ing each other.

What I heard of this common trafficking in sexism and heterosexism occurred mostly in casual times before and after car club meetings, at shows, or
between meetings and late-night cruising. These spaces often drifted into a
loosely homosocial configuration, with the men talking together in one area,
and women and children mainly in another group. This arrangement reflected
the club-meeting structure, since no women were official members of the Custom Kings while I spent time with them, meaning that no woman showed or
cruised a car identified with the club. This had not always been the case, but
more to the point, many women were de facto members of the community surrounding the club. The absence of women on the club roll was never, in my
experience, an exclusion of women from lowrider space.

The boundaries of the gendered microspatial arrangement of a meeting
were also highly fluid and porous. People moved between circles of talk, men
played with kids, women joined conversations among male members, and
so on. Smiley, for instance, maintained platonic friendships with several of
the female regulars at these gatherings, chatting with them and playing with
their kids. Vero, the Latina wife of one of the club's Anglo members, favored
the mechanic's aesthetic of wearing a Dickies jacket and was likely to be found
in otherwise male conversations, where she could hold her own in aggressive
verbal play and automotive shop talk alike. Therefore, while separate spheres
seemed to manifest at times in the microspace of informal lowrider gatherings,
they were by no means absolutely separate. Women often proved themselves
perfectly capable of joining in tough talk and verbal play with the men. Therefore, while sexist billingsgate certainly operated within a linguistic context of
normative patriarchy, it was not effective in the exclusion of women from lowrider space—sexist talk was recognizable by all who were there as a norm of
discourse on the street and theoretically open to cooption and resistance by
women who were tough in their own right. The same cannot be said of heterosexism, and lowrider space would not have been considered gay or lesbian
friendly.[19]

In all these ways, lowriding reproduces wider prejudices and patterns of
automobility and the street as "masculine" spaces, requiring that embodiments
involve performances of masculinity. This resonates with Sandoval's point that
"lowrider culture is anchored within a patriarchal and sexist framework where
a woman's role is highly visible, yet problematic to say the least" (D. Sandoval

2003b, 207). But deviations within that reproduction prevent such a gendering from being seamless or taken as permanent (Del Castillo 1996). Beyond patterns of mundane discourse and practice, by privileging the materiality of lowriding as an embodied practice, some lowriders denied its absolute masculinity as an ideological position. The type of positive club that the Custom Kings represented adopted a mainstream liberal posture of nondiscrimination in general, with membership based primarily on the state of one's ride (in practice, interpersonal relationships also played a large role). The all-male membership, not to mention the masculine club name, was thus implied to be a result of historical patterns of automotive work being undertaken more by men, not an intentionally or explicitly exclusionary strategy.[20] The distinction may not be convincing, but it does reflect a wider move to deny or question lowriding as a male-only activity. Penland offers a similar narrative in her history en route to a "you've come a long way, baby!" account of progressive gains of women lowriders:

> Of course, female automotive enthusiasts have always faced special challenges, and the quest to roll low was no different. Like early hot rodders and kar kustomizers, lowriding's pioneers bought their first cars with the G.I. Bill, a government subsidy that most women didn't have access to. Moreover, until the late '60s, women weren't expected, or in some cases allowed, to work. Chicanas, born into the lowriding cultura, faced even higher hurdles. Most young Mexican-American women celebrate their quinceañera (15th birthday) with a lavish party, rather than with the car that their brothers traditionally received. Thus, throughout early lowriding history, women with their eyes on the prize had to defy tradition and get a job to earn their own ride. They would make only a fraction of what a man did for the same work, but these few, persistent lowriders eventually rolled onto the boulevard alongside the best of them. Despite their efforts, however, the majority of Chicanas in the '50s and '60s still had to settle for the shotgun seat. (Penland 2003, 44)

What Penland terms the "tradition" of giving a boy a car on his fifteenth birthday was not something any lowrider ever described to me, and is probably more an ideal than a financial feasibility for most. I did hear numerous parents refer to the *quinceañera*, or "sweet," that they planned or wanted to throw for their daughters. This did not necessarily go along with a fully elaborated system of "traditional" expectations. José, the model-car customizer and single father I got to know, both discussed plans for his daughter Maria's sweet and proudly let me know about her participation in a precollege enrichment program at the University of Texas.[21] She had had some trouble at school "just because of who she was, how she dressed," and, he said, because of his time limitations as a working single parent. But despite academic struggles, she and her friends "want to go to college, [and don't] want to get pregnant." Among other things, this desire to avoid teenaged parenthood represented an attempt to dodge the statistically disproportionate dropout rate of Latino/a youth in Austin. José also talked about it in the context of other moves to challenge tradition, though. Maria had participated in recreational wrestling and boxing clubs, and when she asked her father whether she could try out for football, he said yes, to her surprise. She eventually let on that she didn't actually want to play, but had wanted to see what the answer would be, and was impressed that he would have allowed it. With José's encouragement, Maria took some graffiti classes offered in a community art program. In keeping with a general discourse of "positivity" in urban expressive arts, he figured that if kept busy with such creative outlets, she wouldn't "go out at night" and get involved in illegal activities. He told me he thought that "delinquency" happens when you forbid your children from doing things. He wants to keep them busy because "there's a lot of stuff out there to take them from you."

While José's account may not conform to how Maria experienced gender regulation in her activities, the way he characterized his daughter valorized a streak of rebelliousness against limitations imposed on her by both mainstream or official and specific "cultural" expectations. He said, "Latino men are so macho against Latina women. I'm just like no, you've got to come up," that is, accept the challenge of going to school. He didn't care where she went or what she did as long as she wouldn't stay at home "cooking, getting pregnant, that's it." She had expressed interest in a couple of area universities and the air force.

José's parental encouragement of his daughter had counterparts in lowriding: younger girls frequently won trophies for lowrider bikes at neighborhood shows. Some of these rides had obviously been done for the girls by their parents, and by the time young women were old enough that working on their own cars might be possible, other constraints would have presented themselves, such as the unequal earning potential of jobs ascribed as normative for men and women.

Gloria was one of those women enthusiasts who did talk to me. An aspiring lowrider, Gloria was saving her paychecks as an auto-parts store clerk to move toward her dream of customizing a new Volkswagen Beetle as a "strictly show car," as well as setting up another car as a "full-body hopper." She told me:

> I started learning how to work on cars from my grandfather growing up. He's like, no granddaughter of mine is going to have to depend on a man with a flat tire. He showed me how to change out the belts . . . how to tear apart an engine and name all the parts on it . . . Now I work on cars at the Auto Zone. Lots of people say girls don't like it—oo, don't get me dirty!

She said that people get the wrong impression by assuming that lowriding is a "guy thing," a stereotype that she attributed to the lowrider model imagery in *Lowrider Magazine* and elsewhere. But she rejected the underlying implication:

> Same issue's been going on forever and a day that females are inferior to the men. Men can do a lot of great things, but so can females, whether we know it or not . . . I just want to trip everybody out so they say, "That's a girl! That's [Gloria's] car!"

Ambivalent Embodiments

When Adrienne Rich calls the body the "geography closest in," she names an analytical method that radically specifies the position of subjectivity vis-à-vis social formations:

> I need to understand how a place on the map is also a place in history within which as a woman, a Jew, a lesbian, a feminist I am created and trying to create. . . . Here at least I know I exist, that living human individual whom the young Marx called "the first premise of all human history." (2001, 64)

Critical attention to the body and to embodied social practice underscores this observation that materialism not only calls for large-scale analysis such as political economy, but also ought to direct attention close-in, taking practice to be a necessary form of materiality (Bourdieu 1977). Thus, materialist research cannot begin and end with big-picture narratives of classes and modes of production, but must also attend to the physical details of bodies in motion and in relationship to one another. Both "the social" and "space," can thus be located at the scale of the body (Harvey 1998a; Lefebvre 1991, 40; Soja 1996, 113).[22] This is not to claim access to some prestructural or natural experience that renders identity categories that resonate at larger scales irrelevant; indeed, a theoretical turn to embodied materiality has enabled work on the specificities of race and gender—for example, a major contribution of Gloria Anzaldúa's celebrated work lies in her rendering of intimate spaces, rather than the grand-historical ones favored by nationalist politics, as sites of struggle and knowledge (1987; see also Rosaldo 1993, 216–217).

Lowriding engages this cultural politics of historical particularity as an embodied practice. As in my treatment of interior aesthetics, a principal finding of these efforts to draw close to lowrider embodiment is the awareness that lowriding as a general field of practice is ambivalent: it is both overdetermined by its relation to heavily ideological historical constructions such as the gendering of automobility, and invested with lowriders' desire and hope to be "positive" and to find "pride," "culture," and all manner of good things in their practice. Ultimately, the performativity of lowriding, which is to say, its manifestation in embodied acts and their perpetual reiteration, is what maintains this ambivalence as a state of multiple potentialities brought together in a material conjuncture. This is why I view lowrider significance to be grounded like Anzaldúa's "new *mestiza* consciousness" and Chela Sandoval's "oppositional consciousness" (2000) in historical circumstances and experiences of dislocation that are themselves located and manifested materially. Yet unlike the scholars who have developed theories of multiple or mobile subjectivity, lowriders do not necessarily do their work through textual practices that culminate in the formation of a consciousness. Instead, the politics of presence is a matter of material practices that generate particular affects, which can register as feelings, and produce space.

None of this negates what is undeniably a problematic gender politics that infuses lowrider media. Indeed, my project raises its own problematic by drawing connections between the theoretical insights of Chicanas and Chicana feminist thought—which have made some of the most far-reaching and influential contributions to Chicana/o Studies as a theoretical field—and a material cultural practice that is dominated by men and that often bears strong threads of sexism, heteronormativity, and hegemonic masculinity. The crucial point, however, is that such negatives do not constitute an unchangeable core of lowriding. In addition, when my representation of lowriding becomes vindicationist, it should not be read as a rebuttal of feminist critiques of lowriding, which

I would argue must continue. If anything, my position is that such critiques should be nondismissive of lowriding as a whole (a redemptive position evident in work such as Denise Sandoval's). For its part, lowriding can take it.

Lowriding as a detour from the ideological trajectory of industrial-commercial car culture shows that automobility is not a static system so much as an emergent and proliferating web of relations built on and with material remnants of the historical past. Attention to lowrider embodiment reveals an important but otherwise easily missed aspect of this emergent character, which is relevant to many other popular practices: that it is precisely the material emphasis within lowriding that creates its open-endedness. This contrasts with a certain philosophical perspective that takes an interest in materiality and things as being driven by a desire to secure meaning and nail things down (B. Brown 2001). In contrast, I argue that lowriders prioritize embodied materiality precisely because it is on this scale that social structure is dynamic and malleable.

This is an implication of the notion of culture as a generative process distinguished as a particular way of making that does not foreclose on what will be made. Lowriding is a culture that you do, more than culture that you have or carry. Such a notion emphasizes the centrality of a tension between history and innovation, finding identity not in absolute conformity, but in the grounded creativity of a version. Taking full advantage of the concreteness of cars, the undeniable presence and substance of things, lowrider materiality nonetheless displays a sophisticated familiarity with their contingency. It is thus on a bodily scale that affective politics offer the chance to diverge from entrenched ideological precedent. Such changes, if seized to show that masculinist or misogynistic aspects of lowriding are not essential, gesture toward the hope for a politics of presence not dependent on the privileging of certain bodies and the oppressing of others.

work
The Producer as Author

I arrive at a garage on the outskirts of East Austin in the hours between close of business and dusk. Smiley passes me on the way to the sink. "Hey Ben! I'd shake your hand, but . . ." He holds up both palms, which are black with grease. I notice he is wearing a T-shirt from a lowrider car show a couple of years back, but not the gold chain he usually has on while out cruising.

About seven or eight men are gathered around a clean El Camino painted green with gold-plated trim and gold rims. A skinny Anglo guy, I guess in his early twenties, is holding a compressed-air tool and trying to chisel out a notch in the bed of the truck. He is Frankie, and this is his shop, he will tell me later. He wipes his upper lip and studies the bed. "This ain't going to do it." The hard metal of the bed will not give way.

Beside the El Camino on the floor of the shop is a frame of welded angle iron, some four feet across. This is what will hold down the bank of six to eight batteries, the "juice" behind the car's future hydraulic setup. The frame is from another car and does not fit the El Camino exactly. Notches in the bed will allow it to be secured. But first the notches have to be cut.

Locomoco is leaning on the El Camino. His head is shaved, apparently a few days ago, and under the stubble I can make out an Aztec calendar tattoo spanning the globe of his skull. He straightens up, a huge man well over six feet tall, and remarks in a deep baritone, "I'd take the torch to it."

Tony, the owner of the car, is smaller and energetic. "I don't know, man. That gas tank is right there."

"It wouldn't heat it up that bad."

"Nah, but one spark. Damn."

Frankie does not seem concerned that the possibility of using an acetylene torch in the immediate vicinity of a gas tank is being discussed in his shop. He puts away the air tool. Others weigh in.

"Use a grinder, then."

"Nah, dog, that would be even hotter."

Tony is stewing. He has paid nobody to be here tonight, calling in a favor owed to his brother as a way to get Frankie to open his shop to them. But Frankie, like everyone else there, is probably mostly motivated by his own interest in the project. Everybody, whether watching or working, wants to see this car get lifted.

Tony turns to his brother. "How much would [Ralph] charge me to install a rack?" Ralph owns a shop just down the road. He is known for his work on hydraulic systems and reinforcing frames, including the setup he did for Tony's brother. The cars with the most respected hydraulics on the street are Ralph's work. He is also known for being rather temperamental in conducting his business.

"Install it? I don't know. Probably seventy-five. But that's building a new rack, too. You know [Ralph]. He's got to do it his way."

"How long would he take?"

"Depends on if you're on his good side."

Tony weighs his options. The sun is setting, and they have been working on the car since getting off work. The current approach seems unlikely to yield much progress, but still, seventy-five dollars is seventy-five dollars.

Locomoco takes a torch and almost meditatively starts cutting a length of pipe on the shop floor. He leans close to the small geyser of sparks, no goggles or mask over his face.

Tony abruptly turns away from the El Camino and starts packing a toolbox. "Fuck it, I'll call [Ralph]." He climbs into the car, fires it up, and pulls out of the shop. Before Frankie closes the doors, four men push a dead jeep into the place vacated by the El Camino—tomorrow's business. There is some joking around as most people stroll to their cars to drive home. Tony looks around at the few who are left. "Whattya say, fellas? Get a six-pack and go back to the house?" This is the first form of compensation I have heard offered or discussed tonight.

《 》

The previous chapters have in various ways suggested that the preferences and aesthetic criteria of lowrider style refer to a particular social position, that is, they resonate with a particular object by virtue of its embeddedness in historical social relations. Among these are relations to education, property, and authority. Elaborating on the last chapter's discussion of embodiment, I return here to my project of drawing close to this social position and its embodied spatiality by considering one of the most prioritized modes of the politics of presence: work.

One Sunday evening, I showed up a little early at the park where cruising usually went on, and passed the time in conversation with the one other person who had arrived, Thomas of the Kings. I mentioned that I had been offered a chance to teach a course on lowriders in Mexican American studies at the University of Texas, and he was incredulous. Apparently, this was not his idea of what people studied at UT. "What are you going to teach them," he asked, "how to wrap a frame?" I tried to explain how my research emphasized "the cultural part" of lowriding, rather than technical concerns like how to reinforce, or "wrap," the frame of a car with steel in order to gird it against the shock of hydraulic hopping. At the time, this exchange seemed to illustrate a gap between Thomas's and my own understanding about what education was for, a gap between vocational training and nonapplied humanistic inquiry, a decidedly classed distinction.

But our conversation was not only about distinct concepts of education— part of the contrast was also in what we each assumed a course about lowriders would entail; that is, what was important about lowriding. My assumption that the importance lay in the cultural part reflected my training and the genesis of the project within ethnographic and cultural-studies traditions. Yet the notion of material embodiment advanced in the last chapter suggests that the value that lowriders find and cultivate in their rides is not reducible to what they represent, which is to say, something other than material concerns like "how to wrap a frame" (Keane 2005). This may have been one of the most direct instances of a lowrider calling into question both the textualist convention established by most scholarship on popular culture (Grossberg 2006, 9) and the relevance of seeking out cultural texts legible and indeed amenable to academic "reading."

Those scholars who try to deviate from the habit of accessing culture through texts note the importance of the "poetic wisdom" embedded in culturally specific processes of making and occupying a particular social space (Fernandez and Herzfeld 1998, 101). Opening scholarship to this practical knowledge is the motivation for the participant side of ethnographic participant-observation. The idea of poetic wisdom shares some resonance with recent interest by certain authors in productive labor or craft as a form of knowledge (Crawford 2009; Sennett 2009). But long before these publications, lowriders were suggesting, even in the textual mediations of our conversations, that the line between cultural concerns about meaning and mechanical things was a blur. In a space close to the everyday practice of lowriding, rather than in more formal conversations or written works about it, it becomes difficult to divorce *poesis* from the practices of *tekhne*, creation from technical production (see Cintron 1997, xii). Attempting to move into this proximate space, I decided to build a car. This chapter reflects on the materiality of working-class experiences in Austin at the time of my fieldwork, which I attempted to glimpse through not only dialogue with lowriders, but also my efforts (ultimately incomplete) to earn the necessary funds for a car as well as to navigate the lowrider economy and find a ride.

As is the case for all inquiries into "the ordinary," this chapter includes observations that some readers may find unremarkable—hardly discoveries at all. I recognize that much of this text is implicitly addressed to a middle-class audience, and in this way it relies on a certain stereotype of those who will take an interest in an academic book. While the class background and location of academics cannot be generalized altogether, I would argue that moving from a university campus into the spaces described in this chapter meant leaving a site structured by one set of class norms and entering another. As much as my Anglo background and phenotype, class marked the line of difference that I crossed in research, and my relation to the university and education in general was a principal indicator of this. One lowrider affiliated with the Kings was a student at the local community college, and I had a passing acquaintance with another who, raised in East Austin, was completing his undergraduate studies in mechanical engineering at UT. No doubt there were others pursuing higher education whose paths crossed mine in the field, but it seemed that most low-riders I met were through with formal education and, in any case, worked in jobs that did not require a degree.

My point is that in the process of trying to get into car customizing myself via wage labor, I gained insight into the contrast between the economic position afforded by a college education, let alone graduate school, and that provided by a working-class job. The seasonal cycles of tuition payments and loan disbursements prepare students to function according to the calendars of salary and mortgage. The constantly rising costs associated with higher education are justified with reference to "investment" and deferred gratification in the interest of a later reward. These are just small examples of how academia remains a gateway into bourgeois class culture (Lubrano 2004). The spatial displacement of going to the field in the same town where I studied was in part a matter of switching between places engendered by very different sets of assumptions.

Lesson one: a lowrider can get expensive. This begins to explain why it is highly desirable to start out with as cheap a car as possible—all the more so if you are going to customize the paint or body, since then the car doesn't have to be in pristine shape to begin with. Austin lowriders talked about potential rides according to what they needed mechanically to be functional, but beyond that, primarily whether the chassis was "straight." Within and around the lowrider scene, there was also an active market in barter and trade—Locomoco, for instance, once ran down his personal history of lowriding for me, which started with the purchase of one car for less than $1,000 and ran through a series of trades with friends and relatives. He had had a string of three or four cars, but had paid money only for one. After a car has been secured, adding hydraulic systems, seriously modifying the metal car body, applying polychromatic paint jobs involving many layers of lacquer, and installing multimedia entertainment systems would all incur substantial costs. At first, this would seem to offer support to two stereotypes that I encountered during my fieldwork, but the struggles lowriders go through to finance their rides reveals them to be misconceptions.

One was that, given the association between lowriders and minoritized barrios that had a reputation as being crime ridden, as well as the place of lowriding within a broader urban street culture, some outsiders could make sense of extravagantly adorned and modified automobiles only by imagining them to have been purchased with money from an illicit source such as the drug trade. Occasionally, I heard rumors of illicit funding for one car or another, but many lowriders I met disparaged such rides—like any car already customized when purchased, these lacked the prestige granted to one known to be the product of legitimate hard work. It was certainly not a given that the only source for financing a lowrider was the illegal economy.

On the other hand, it was also off base to deduce, as a local reporter once asserted in a feature article for the *Austin American-Statesman*, that lowriders are now mostly middle class. This was partly a problem of attention and partly one of definition. The reporter seemed to be responding to articles and rumors about the multiple thousands of dollars, even hundreds of thousands for the upper echelon of show cars, that a fully customized car would require. While it is true that the most elaborate lowriders that dominate the competitive show circuit require sums of money well above the figure that represents the "middle" of U.S. annual incomes, these professional lowriders represent a small elite and not the everyday lowrider community that is my focus. It remains true that a thoroughgoing, "frame off" customization, the kind likely to produce a professional-level, national-show-winning car, requires funds and control of one's time beyond what is typically available to the working class. The most elite show cars also frequently involve radical modifications, the timely completion of which requires hiring specialists, so that the owner of the car becomes less its builder than the director of a customization executed by an ad hoc team of professionals. This status was not enjoyed by anyone I met in the Austin lowrider scene, and indeed would have implied a distance from the particular sociality of what I am describing as everyday lowrider space. Less descriptive of most lowriders, the journalist's remark was more a reiteration of the commonsense ideology that "ordinary" Americans are all middle class.

In contrast with both of these stereotypes, most lowriders I met could be considered working class because of their overlapping relations to education and wages. As I have noted, they typically worked without the credential of higher education at jobs for an hourly wage in an at-will service sector of what was still considered at the time the "new economy." Many worked in a sector often inaccurately called "unskilled," a term that referred to a kind of work requiring skills that were not valorized by the public culture. Not surprisingly for car enthusiasts, many lowriders sought work in automotive jobs as mechanics, parts clerks, or drivers. Lowriding thus represented an aestheticization of skills and activities that, outside the leisure time devoted to lowriding, also earned lowriders their livelihood.

Lowriders often represented themselves to me with the same kind of appeal to respectability that the reporter may have been trying to indicate with "middle class," but lowriders' own appeal was more often based on the integrity of one's work rather than a particular level of income. For instance, in several interview situations in which Eddie presented the public face of the positive car club of which he was president, he sought to counter stereotypes of lowriders as gang members by claiming a mainstream status as "blue collar." Similarly, when I first met a lowrider named Victor, he made sure to remark that lowriders were not "all pachucos" and that he held a decent job in the warehouse of the main production facility of Dell Computer, operating equipment that lifted pallets of goods worth many thousands of dollars. Not every lowrider shared Victor's disdain for "pachucos," but the claim to respectability that hinged on legitimate work was common.

These protestations of respectability push against a long history of public discourse stigmatizing Mexican Americans as a likely criminal underclass, as well as the enduring association of the term "Mexican" with "cheap labor" (Garza-Falcón 1998; Vélez-Ibañez 1996). People commenting on the history of lowriding have often identified financial stability as one subtext of a clean custom ride. At the same time, one characteristic of the barrio spaces where Austin lowriders lived and cruised was an attenuated ability to escape the presence of illicit work such as drug dealing, which is what compels those presenting a positive narrative of lowriding to specifically distance it from ill-gotten gains, even if it is widely known that certain custom cars have been financed by the odd drug deal.

Beyond these contested relations to the legitimate and the unrespectable, the status of lowriders' work took on specific resonance in the setting of my field research. In the early 2000s, Austin was a high-tech boomtown, one of a number of metropolitan areas that represented either the epitome of an information economy already in full swing or a bellwether for where the U.S. was headed soon (English-Lueck 2002). Like many cities around the United States, Austin scrambled to style itself as the "Silicon Hills" counterpart to California's Silicon Valley and New York's Silicon Alley. By 2011, parts of the boom had proved to be temporary fads, rather than heralds of Austin's future—the city remains a hub of information and creative work, but the manufacturing sector associated with companies such as Motorola and Samsung has declined considerably (Ladendorf 2009). This has likely exacerbated a situation that was already emerging during my fieldwork: blue-collar labor was indispensable to the local economy, but largely invisible in public constructions of Austin as a place. The embodied space of this particular relation to political economy is thus a part of the elusive "experience" of lowriding that may not be easily conveyed but is known intimately to participants. Just as important as the mechanics of car customization, the poetic wisdom of lowriding is also gleaned from participation in two related but distinct economic spheres: labor at the hourly wage level in an information- and service-based economy, and experience with the relatively informal market in used cars and replacement or custom parts through barter and trade that makes lowriding possible on a restricted budget.

《 》

When I first met Roman at a car show, some younger friends and admirers of his were gathered around his 1964 gold Impala Supersport, almost like disciples. They pointed out the features that they would imitate in their own rides as they built them from the frame up with their own hands, which, as they told me, was as a lowrider should. One of the acolytes disparaged some of the cars on display at this local-scale show, saying, "Here, they think if you put rims on a car, that's a lowrider. Like that blue car over there. That ain't a lowrider. A lowrider is your heart and soul." I asked whether they had ever heard of people buying a lowrider ready-built. They had, but as another one said, "It's not your car. A lowrider, you have to build from the ground up."

Later, in an interview, Roman gave me an idea of what this took. Roman's dad had first bought the Impala from a friend. He offered to sell it to his son for $1,750. Roman helped his grandmother clean offices, making $3 a day; on break from school, he cut yards; on weekends, he collected cans from under the bleachers at stock-car races, picking up around $15 or more for three trash bags full of cans. He bought the car from his father in the eighth grade, when he was fifteen years old. He started by sanding down rust spots and polishing the old hubcaps. Eventually, he paid a painter to give the car a primer job, which restored its uniform surface and made it look "even better." He knew something about cleaning up cars from doing some detailing work with a friend. The car took another "big step up" when he bought fiberglass wheel skirts at a car show, had the engine rebuilt, and got a friend to do the upholstery. He went for the original look in the interior. The car was his transportation to school and work, and he continued making gradual improvements until it got "too good to drive to school," at which point he left it in the garage and started taking the bus.

Most of the club members I met in my fieldwork were older than fifteen, working grown-up jobs for regular wages, but it was still a struggle to keep up their commitment to lowriding. Richard, the longest-standing member of the

Custom Kings club, was at nearly every meeting, but I never saw him join the cruising afterward. This had to do with the fact that his '68 Impala was in the body shop, gradually getting a "makeover," in his words, but it also had to do with the weight of Richard's other responsibilities as a homeowner, husband, and father. Richard worked two jobs to pay the bills. At the club meeting the week he was hired for his second job, I heard him discussing it with another member.

"So after the shop closes, you go over to Wal-Mart?"

"Just three, four hours a night."

"What are they going to pay you?"

"Ten."

José also struggled to stay in the lowrider scene and support his family, two teenage children he was raising alone. Although he hadn't had a custom car for years, he drove a respectable, serviceable "family ride," a Chevy Lumina. As an office clerk for a county agency, he had a stable, decent situation, but with a son and daughter in high school, the pay was not quite enough. The summer after I had gone over to José's apartment to work on lowrider model cars, he told me he was going to have to quit the hobby for a while to start working nights, cleaning an office building after his own closed for the day. His brother-in-law, who was also visiting that evening, asked for details.

"You're going to go over there?"

"Yeah, it's just a couple of hours."

"I can't believe you're going to do that. And they're paying you what?"

"Six an hour."

Awhile later, José chatted about his second job while hanging out at the car wash after a club meeting. He said, "I had to go get my fingerprints [. . .] Shit, it's just janitorial, but I had to do a drug test."

Eddie teased him: "Watch out, the FBI's coming in right now. And you're doing that for how much money?"

"Six-fifty."

"Man, you're taking those hours?"

"It's just a few hours every day."

Low Finance

How long must it take to scrape together the surplus cash to be a lowrider? How many extra jobs, overtime hours, and off-the-book hustles? I had not written a car into my research grant proposal, and I suspect it would have been less likely to be funded if I had. The stipend I had coming in, and the assistantships and loans to which I had access as a student, marked out my "difference" from the community I was working in, which, not coincidentally, also authorized me as a researcher in the eyes of the larger academy. I decided that the experience of working for a car would be most valuable if I attempted to breach this gap and work not only at an earning level similar to that of my lowrider friends, but also in a job like what I heard them describe when they chatted about their everyday lives. I inquired at a car-stereo shop and an auto parts store, but they had no openings. The local grocery chain was always hiring, including the store that was one of the only supermarkets on the Eastside. As part of the interview process, the manager asked me whether I had looked for a job at the University of Texas. I said that I had been a teaching assistant on campus but that I was involved in a research project based in the Eastside community and now wanted to get to know the area and my neighbors better. He assured me that I would. A high percentage of the clientele at the Eastside store came on foot, indicating that they lived in the immediate area. The manager glanced at my application form.

"It's just that, someone with your level of education . . . I would worry that you would get bored with the work." I told him that I had worked at routine jobs before and that I was willing to start at entry level. He then asked some questions that he told me were "behavioral based." One of these was what experience I had selling. I told him I didn't have any. He said, "Let me clarify: when I say selling, it's not—when I think selling, I think, oh, a used car salesman. What selling means here is—at the checkout, we have these baskets that are impulse items, and they're around a dollar. The selling I'm talking about is suggesting, just mentioning, in your conversation with the customer, would you be interested in these? Are you open to doing that kind of suggestive selling?"

I said it sounded like part of the job, and he wrote on the form "Open to suggestive selling." I was hired, at $8.50 an hour.

《 》

The rhythm is set by the scanners. As seven of us in the row of checkout lanes drag packages across the glowing lasers, the computer beeps its confirmation, as if to say, "Check." The beeps set a cadence, offering a framework for comparison between us: How many beeps in a minute? Am I ahead or behind? What does this do to my average? Beep.

As I reach for products and try to speed up my beeps, the conveyor belt jerks toward me. An electric eye is supposed to stop the belt when items get close to the scanner, but somehow it misses them, looks right through them, and they start to pile up. A box of crackers, flimsy yogurt cartons joined in a six-pack, a Styrofoam plate of meat wrapped in a transparent "cello-pack." The plastic wrap does not slide well across the stainless steel surface at the end of the belt. Can of coffee, frozen juice, bag of pork rinds. Unaware of the pile-up, the belt advances. The package of meat, gripping the steel counter, is upended by the progress of the belt and is now flipped over. I grab at it to keep the clear wrap from tearing, and one of my fingers pierces the plastic barrier. Beep. I toss the meat to the bagging station and enter a code for the produce that is next. Glancing down, I see blood on the keypad of my cash register. Beep. Another package of meat, this one with a bone protruding through the wrapping. I should offer the customer another one, but I am more focused on the possibility of *E. coli* on my hands and now on my pants leg.

The groceries are piling up downstream of me. I look around for a bagger, and see one of the high-school kids sauntering in from the parking lot after a carryout, taking his time. I feel fury rising in my belly. If I have to bag the load myself, the clock doesn't stop, which wrecks my items-per-minute average. Beep. I reach back without looking for the next item, and when it comes into view, I am gripping the snout of a frozen hog head. Beep. My customer asks, "How much is that? I only have eighty-five. I'm going to have to take some things off." I have a new target for my anger.

"Ben when you go on your break, come and do your Shrinktrax, okay?" There is no sign that I am in trouble with my shift manager, Lila, but Shrinktrax is never a good thing. The checkout system at this major grocery chain was designed to be as automated and efficient as possible. Still, a human checker is indispensable for navigating the diverse kinds of pricing—by number, weight, or barcode—coupons, and other intricacies of checking out. And humans are necessary to guide our species-mates efficiently through the work of buying. Thus, a human body is a necessary evil in a much larger, integrated retail machine (each cash register was part of a computer network that, we were informed, could be monitored from corporate headquarters at any time).[1] Yet in the view of the corporation, the human checker stands in the way of the ideal profits that would be attainable if the machines could run at capacity. This human factor in reducing profits is known as "shrink."

Once a week, the three checkers who are seen as producing the most shrink are identified by the computer and pulled aside by the manager. You go

ABOVE: 1964 Impala in Chicano Park.

ABOVE: *Día de la Raza* celebration on the Eastside.
BELOW: Cruising Chicano Park.

ABOVE: Cadillac street ride with custom paint. Photo by Adrian Romero.
BELOW: Monte Carlo in Chicano Park.

ABOVE: Car show hopping competition. Photo by Adrian Romero.
BELOW: Modeling and shooting at an indoor car show in San Antonio.

ABOVE: Wire spoke rim and show cars on display. Photo by Adrian Romero.

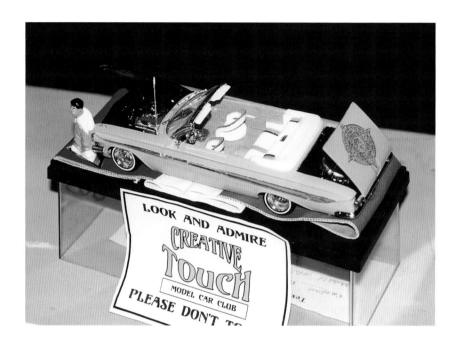

ABOVE: Model lowrider with a Homies figure, on display at a car show.
BELOW: 1964 Impala model lowrider painted in blue metal flake by the author.

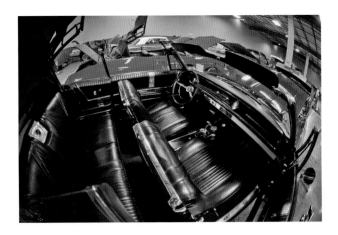

ABOVE: Tucked velvet upholstery and bar accessories on a show car.
BELOW: Restored stock interior on a show car. Photo by Adrian Romero.

ABOVE: "Bombs" in Chicano Park.

over the numbers that mark you and sign a paper showing that you understand what you have been told. This amounts to a tacit contract: "I won't do it again," but you often do.

"So, um, you can see that your percentage of produce is at 11 percent and the target level is 16." Lila is just being realistic about Shrinktrax, which means that she realizes that we checkers control some of the variables Shrinktrax measures, and not others. "I don't know how you're supposed to raise the amount of produce a customer buys, but . . . Your IPMs are at 22 and they should be at 25."

IPMs are items per minute, the quantitative measure of your effectiveness as a checker. There is no financial incentive to improve your IPMs, but some competitive streak and some ingrained desire to please make me want to score higher, and to my own surprise, make my anger flare at anyone who stands in the way of my IPMs. Fundamentally, IPMs are about "through-put": success lies in moving product, because profit is measured against time—that is, against the cost of labor. The more products you can get through your line, the more money you can make for the company in the time you are on the clock, getting paid. This is the opposite of shrink. Paradoxically, it means shrinking the degree of resistance that your body offers to the onward march of the conveyor belt. At some stores, checkers are encouraged to move products across the scanner with both hands independently, "in a swimming motion." Thus the line of checkers fell into a pattern, almost coordinated like a Busby Berkeley water ballet with a one-note score (see Kracauer 1995). Beep.

《 》

The concept of shrink dramatizes one aspect of labor in a retail context, in which workers sell their bodies in units of time. In exchange, we are contracted to get out of the way of the accumulation of profit, to make our intrusion in the functioning of a hyper-Fordist machine of distribution as minimal as possible. The space of retail labor, it would seem, is not big enough for both of us—thus, to curb the company's "shrink," we must diminish our own impact on the system. My efforts to avoid shrink as a grocery checker resonated in some ways with Barbara Ehrenreich's widely read account of low-wage work. In a series of articles for *Harper's Magazine*, later published together as *Nickel and Dimed: On (Not) Getting By in America* (2001), Ehrenreich went undercover in several low-wage jobs, trying to live on only what she could earn. The project was one of several similar attempts to encounter the Other of the much-lauded new prosperity at the turn of the millennium.[2] Although she limited her field-work to a month in each setting and had no illusions about other limitations to her research, Ehrenreich nonetheless took the crucial ethnographic step of attempting to occupy bodily the social space she was trying to understand.[3] One of her experiences was a kind of rage that resembles what I felt in the grocery checkout line. Even when her shift at Wal-Mart, replacing tried-on clothes on the appropriate racks, is going well,

> somewhere around 6:00 or 7:00, when the desire to sit down becomes a serious craving, a Dr. Jekyll/Mr. Hyde transformation sets in. I cannot ignore the fact that it's the customers' sloppiness and idle whims that make me bend and crouch and run. They are the shoppers, I am the antishopper, whose goal is to make it look as if they've never been in the store. At this point, "aggressive hospitality" gives way to aggressive hostility. (2001, 165)

Not only the worker's body, but also the physical presence of customers, which renders the inventory disorderly, threatens the efficient operation of the retail machine.

At the grocery story, my fellow employees and I had to regulate customers' flow through the checkout lanes in order to keep the whole system running. One coworker, Lizette, was particularly a stickler. I found this out when a non-English speaker entered my line, which was designated as "express"—ten items or fewer—by a lit-up sign. The customer unloaded a huge basket of groceries onto the belt. Lizette, who happened to be looking over, said "No, don't let her do it, Ben. That's why people get mad." I tried to explain to the woman that she could check only ten items, but either she found my Spanish incomprehensible or she simply ignored me. Lizette came over and started unloading groceries from the belt back into the basket, saying, "No, ma'am, you'll have to go to another line." Customers lined up at Lizette's register waited while she unloaded my belt. Just then, two things happened at the same time. My phone rang. I picked it up, and it was Lila, saying, "Ben, turn off your 'express.'" I hesitated, not wanting to undercut Lizette after she had completely reloaded the customer's groceries into the basket. Meanwhile, a woman from Lizette's line was going around to everyone in a uniform and saying, "Miss, would you tell that lady to come back to our line? We're waiting here." The system was fouled up, and you could almost hear the IPM figures dwindling toward zero. Looking around,

I discreetly switched off my express light in obedience to Lila, though the customer had moved on.

Later, I found myself trying to avoid a repeat of that situation when it occurred to me about midway through a transaction involving Spanish and a complex coupon situation that once again my customer was way over the ten-item limit though the "express" was on. Not wanting to provoke a confrontation between Lizette and anyone, least of all me, I switched off my sign unilaterally. The next couple of customers had small loads, so I went back to express. As far as I was concerned, the idea was to make the terms of my check stand match, as nearly as possible, the reality that was unfolding. Unlike Lizette, I hesitated to make this happen by altering the reality and sending customers with too many items away—I preferred to alter the terms. Behind me, I could hear her arguing with a customer: "No, that's ninety-nine cents. You have to buy five for the discount. You have to have an in-store coupon." But I was not alone in my conciliatory approach. The same day, there was a little bag of crackers that didn't scan, and the customer couldn't say what they were supposed to cost. Jared, the manager, was right there, so I asked him. He didn't know, but said, "Maybe thirty-five cents or something?" I asked the guy, "How does thirty-five cents sound?" He was agreeable, so I entered it. In training, I had learned that such fudging of price and cash flow is actually worth it for generating satisfaction in a customer, since the average buyer at this grocery chain spent around $16,000 annually at the store. In a training session, which was in a centralized facility that served all Austin locations, my instructor owned up to hating IPMs, since he thought they were counterproductive for customer service. On the checkout line, however, they reigned supreme.

The combined mandates for workers to discipline themselves and their customers to the flow of the retail machine are perhaps best endured when a worker reaches a semiconscious state of muscle memory and ingrained habits in which the body seems to take over and work to do itself, a degree of incorporation that Ehrenreich and I both experienced, and which has its pleasures. This must be something like what performers or athletes call being "in the zone." Ehrenreich describes it thus:

> The breakthrough comes on a Saturday, one of your heavier shopping
> days. There are two carts waiting for me when I arrive at two, and tossed
> items inches deep on major patches of the floor. The place hasn't been
> shopped, it's been looted. In this situation, all I can do is everything at

once—stoop, reach, bend, lift, run from rack to rack with my cart. And then it happens—a magical flow state in which the clothes start putting *themselves* away. Oh, I play a part in this, but not in any conscious way. (2001, 176)

This experience, almost rapturous, of being in the zone of the service industry, is short-lived, but it is no joke. There is a very real pleasure in incorporation. Walter Benjamin noted the tendency of human beings to mimic and repeat actions that were initially learned as forced adaptations to technological and social conditions. For instance, the human eye had to adjust historically to seeing the kinds of moving crowds that appear only in a city, but "the assumption is not impossible that, having mastered this task, the eye welcomed opportunities to confirm its possession of its new ability"; hence, the fragmented flecks of paint in impressionism, which force the eye to dart around the canvas, ultimately were embraced by viewers (cited in Buck-Morss 1989, 269). In an experience that is somehow related, the anthropologist Donald Brenneis found, to his none-too-pleasant surprise, a certain rush at being incorporated into a data-processing machine as part of his experience on the review committee of a major fellowship competition (1994). In retail work, the principal pleasure offered by incorporation may be the rapid passage of time, the shortening of drudgery. Ehrenreich reminds us that this comes at the cost of losing agentive control of one's body and becoming at once bigger (more active) and smaller (less consequential) than oneself: "What you don't necessarily realize when you start selling your time by the hour is that what you're actually selling is your *life*" (2001, 187).

A tiny archive of such lives sold was in the grocery store's request book, a three-ring binder that sat near the clock-in computer terminal in the break room. Rather than being hired for a certain schedule, I had been asked about how many hours I wanted, and had to return to find out whether and when I had been granted them. The request book was where you would ask for changes to the hours you were scheduled for. Written on the inside cover in permanent marker was the admonition: "Requests are just that—they are not guarantees." I noticed that some people had signed their names and written "Honeymoon" or "Family need." One person wrote, "Please, I really need off this day." If requests were not granted, you had to be prepared to trade shifts with someone.

Retail labor trades on time and bodies. Yet what capital can be gleaned by a worker from the transaction can also be turned to carving out instances of the "illusion of escape"—times and spaces that appear to transgress the limits of the everyday. The cars that lowriders produce as extended bodies and fantastic interiors also seem to place them out of reach, temporarily, of management measures like the surveilling Shrinktrax. In contrast with the "zone" of incorporation at work, moments of pleasure derived from lowriding are the products of bitter struggle to wrest a delimited domain of freedom temporarily out of an everyday life saturated with necessity (see Lefebvre 1992:40).

Finding a Ride

More than money is required to get into lowriding at or below a living wage. Shopping for bargains in the used-car market requires the knowledge necessary to estimate the potential value of a car against the costs of restoring or customizing it. In the market for project cars meeting the specialized price criteria of potential lowriders—less than $1,000 was a good benchmark—time was a critical resource. Decisive action was required to land a bargain, and if you didn't know everything that a particular ride would need, you had to know someone who did. Thus, lowriders were purchased not only with money, but resources such as experience, intuition, and social networks that would not typically be counted by the outside world as capital.

When I first met José, we immediately started talking about his car situation. He had recently bought a Chevy Lumina that he had not customized, though he was hoping to get some rims for it. His daughter called it a "family car," apparently disparagingly. Before that, he had had a truck that he was not proud of. He would not take it cruising, because of its state of disrepair, and was not sure it was mechanically sound enough to make it around the state to car shows. But immediately after he borrowed money from his parents to buy the Lumina, he found an '80s Cutlass that needed some work but was pretty sound, for $600. He kicked himself because he could have cut into the down payment on the Lumina to get the Cutlass, "put it up somewhere," and started to work gradually on another lowrider. As he put it: "So now I've got my daily driver . . . but I could've had a *car*!"

José's aesthetic distinction made more and more sense to me in the course of my fieldwork as I became closely attuned to the cars I passed in traffic. Seeing a clean Impala rolling by delivered an aesthetic effect, enough to evoke an involuntary "Yeah!" from me, as if I were a bebop fan in a club listening to a cat blow. I could not see a junked GM car standing in a driveway or a vacant lot without wondering whether the owner would sell, and for how much. One evening I came back late from cruising and clicked on the television while I wound down. A rerun of a sketch-comedy show was playing: the skit was a parodic combination of a game show and a Jerry Springer–style trash-TV chat show. The contestants were stereotypes of working-class folks, white trailer-park residents, and a black "ghetto" couple. The characters' dialogue satirically outlined a context of social pathology: violent relationships, substance abuse, and especially poor taste. In a finale that underscored the low-rent style of the game show, the host revealed the prize they were all vying for: a 1984 Chevy Caprice Classic. I had to laugh, not at the buffoonery of the show's depiction of poor people, but at my own reaction—"Yes!" It was just the kind of car I was looking for.

After weeks of poring over classified ads, I found a winner: "1980 Cutlass Supreme. Runs great. $700." The address was in a relatively affluent, far-north suburb. It took me nearly an hour to drive there from the Eastside. I wondered whether the owner realized what he had—that the old beater car he was ready to unload was in fact a highly desirable potential cruiser, easy to work on, requiring only cheap and available parts, and with a solid frame that was good for hydraulics. The owner had said on the phone that he hadn't "buffed it out" in a while, but it looked to me more as if the paint were corroding away. The vinyl top was scratched and torn, as was the interior. The seat belts were frayed. I met the owner, and he gave me the keys. The car started easily and ran smoothly as I pulled out onto the street for a test drive. I cornered, and the turn signal lever came off in my hand.

I had no idea how much it would cost to fix up the car. I returned it and thanked the owner, saying I needed time to think about it, then drove to a strip mall nearby. I asked at the first store (a video shop) whether there was a phone I could use. My plan was to call Smiley's cell to ask him for Big Beto's number, since he did interior work, and then get an estimate from Beto for what an entire interior overhaul might cost. The number Smiley gave me was busy. In any case, I didn't have the money with me. It was Sunday, so I drove to a bank with an ATM. I punched in the numbers to withdraw $600, more cash than I had ever requested before. Denied—apparently it was over my limit, but the ATM did not say so in so many words. I tried $500, then $400, then $300 before I saw any cash. Holding the stack of twenty-dollar bills in my hand, I was emboldened to go ask the owner whether he would accept a down payment and the balance the next day. I drove back to the house, but as I pulled up, two women and a man were walking away from the house—he got into the Cutlass while the women went to another car. It had been sold.

Next ad: $700 for a 1979 Monte Carlo. When I drove to another suburb to look at it, the owner assured me that 1979 was the last good year before MCs went "soft." I knew this car was also lowrider material—I even had a miniature model '78 MC lowrider with functional hydraulics that was nearly indistinguishable from the '79. This car was customized for racing, though, which hindered my ability to gauge its potential—I had trouble envisioning it lowered, rather than raked, and with small wheels, not big slicks. The owner had half-finished a project to install power windows in the place of the stock manual ones, and a jumble of wires and dismantled door panels filled the front seats. Most importantly, was this the body style I wanted? Unable to commit, I put it on the back burner to see whether something better would come along.

Nothing did for a couple of weeks. Steve told me at a club meeting that he had a friend who was "getting ready to go back to jail," and who had a Regal for $200 and a '65 Impala for $500. Somehow neither one ever came through. There was a Regal parked in a yard on Holly Street with "$500 needs motor" written on the windshield. I walked by to look at it and saw some serious rust on the roof. I drove out to the suburb of Pflugerville to a car lot to look at a '79 Regal that was advertised in the paper for $975. It looked very good from a distance, but as I got close, I saw "skin cancer" rust on its roof so advanced that some of the metal was flaking away. When I started it up, the dealer said he didn't know why, but you had to start driving in the automatic transmission's low gear and then shift your way up to drive. I left it there. Later, Eddie confirmed my suspicions about the rust on the Regal by saying that you could replace metal in the fenders or quarter panels, but not so easily the roof. On the other hand, Steve suggested that I cut off the roof and make a convertible. There was an ad for a 1980 Regal in the auto parts column of the paper for $300 (I assumed no motor). They never answered the phone.

All of these near misses were for project cars that were GM models from the late 1970s or early '80s. Such "G-body" styles were popular as lowriders, but they couldn't compete with an Impala from the 1960s. For that reason, it caught my eye when, riding my bike to work at the grocery store, I saw a primered 1965 Impala parked with a sign on its window: $2,000. This was not a lot for a car, but represented a different level of the market I had been frequenting. I was going to work only to check the schedule, so I circled back to take a closer look at the car and recognized two brothers, John and Jesse, whom I had met at the park the last week. They were both working on cars in the carport and were glad to see me stop by. John took me to look at the '65. It needed a lot of work inside—John told me that a dog had gotten into it and torn up the seats. The body was also visibly not straight in several places. Scanning the car and noting other holes and imperfections in the sheet metal, I pretty much ruled it out for $2,000.

The brothers had two other Impalas in progress in their carport. One, a '63, was jacked up off the frame. They were meticulously sanding the frame "down to bare metal" in order to "shoot it" with an epoxy primer, then paint it the same color as the car. They showed me the rear quarter panel that had to be replaced because someone had done some clumsy patchwork there and the metal was a mess. Jesse showed me the engine that had been in the car when he got it—a straight-6 that was sitting on the ground near the driveway. He had a replacement engine already, a 350-cubic-inch V-8 that was all chromed out but not installed yet. When I told him I was thinking about an MC I had seen advertised in Round Rock that might have engine problems, he said, "You might want to just get a motor, drop it in. Three-fifties are a dime a dozen right now."

We talked for a while about the car I wanted to find, and I gratefully noticed that they didn't try to push the '65 on me. I told them about my experience with the Cutlass, how I hadn't moved fast enough to get it. The interior problems with the Cutlass had been all up front, unlike any potential motor problems with the MC. Had I been more prepared and fully integrated into the network of people with specialized repair skills, I might have moved faster and landed it. The MC was a different story. Without much knowledge of engines, I had a hard time judging what exactly it needed. Jesse showed me how to take off a radiator cap and check for a milky, creamy substance "like chocolate," which would indicate that water had been circulating in the engine. Also, he said I should check the crankcase fill cap. He said that if fluid around the dipstick is foamy, then "that engine ain't no good." When I said that I didn't know about working on cars, but that I would like to get a cruiser up and running, Jesse offered to help me out. Both brothers worked at car dealerships in the service departments, and Jesse said he could do "side work" at his shop, making use of the space and tools after regular business hours. Jesse proposed that if I got a car, he would do an inspection and tell me what it needed, and then if I came back the next week with the parts, he would do the work that day.

John told me they go to a lot of swap meets to get parts. He said the quarter panels he needs for his Impala were usually $400, but he found one at a swap meet for $125. They said that going to a swap meet like that is like "going to the mall": "You keep looking in your pocket, and it's, like, damn! I ran out of money already." You have to buy things quickly, though, or somebody else gets them. Eventually, I left, shaking their hands and making plans to talk at an upcoming car show. I said, "Sometime, I'll probably pull up with a car and ask you what's wrong with it." Jesse promised to help me out.

After a couple of weeks of chasing leads, an opportunity finally arose only two blocks from my rental house on the Eastside. Passing a residential double lot with several cars parked in the yard, I noticed a Cutlass with a "FOR SALE" sign. The body seemed to be in much better shape than anything I had looked at so far, and the sign said $1,500. I went to the house next to the lot and waited at the gate, where two small yapping dogs announced my presence. A woman came out the front door, apparently Latina and maybe in her forties. A little boy, barefoot in shorts and carrying a soccer ball, was underfoot. I asked her whether she was selling the Cutlass, and she said yes, it was an '84. I asked how much, and she shook her head as if in resignation and said, "A thousand dollars."

After the heaps I had seen, I was subject to being dazzled by the mostly clean vinyl roof and chrome trim. The paint was well past its prime, but I expected that, at a minimum, a simple paint job would be part of making the car my own. We looked at the motor, and I felt the crankcase oil (a little grit) and looked at the coolant in the radiator (full, no foam). She said that the engine had been replaced two years before. She pointed out some problems with the doors—both the inside handles had broken off—and the power windows weren't working. She had new switches in the back, and just hadn't had time to install them. There was a CD player and a subspeaker box with a "power booster," as she put it.

Dumb but eager to get going, and probably half blinded by the moderate bling of the intact chrome, I decided to take it without even starting it up. I told her I had only $700 and asked whether I could put some money down. She was agreeable, so we went in to write up a receipt on notebook paper. She said, "I just figured some punk would turn it into a lowrider or something. I've had a few kids from the neighborhood look at it and tell me they wanted it, but then it's 'Oh, I've got to go ask my parents for the money,' and they never come back." I smiled and said, "Well, I do want something to work on, fix up," but left it at that.

Barbara, whose name I learned from the receipt she wrote out, said that she worked as a truck driver with her husband and was not home enough to make use of the car. She had bought it from her friend for $1,500 and had only taken it to the store occasionally. I noticed a small sticker on the rear bumper that read "Bitch Goddess." I agreed to bring by the rest of the money the next day, sometime after noon.

I went back around five with the $300. I counted out the money and she got out the title. It was still in the name of the prior owner, who had signed the transfer without dating it or noting the mileage or sales price. Barbara had not paid sales tax on it, and she left the sales price empty so that I could decide how much tax to pay. The Cutlass started right away. As I pulled out of the yard and into the street, it stalled. I restarted and revved the motor. I tested the power-window switch. The passenger window lowered, stopped about halfway down, and would move no further in either direction. I reached down to try the power seat and found the switch by moving the seat forward uncomfortably close to the steering wheel. I reversed the switch to move it back, and the seat didn't move. From this cramped position, I managed to pull the car into the dirt driveway behind our rental house and then pry the door open with the stump of a door handle. An old shower curtain thrown over the open window would keep it something like dry.

Despite its shortcomings, my purchase was met with approval in the lowrider scene. Clearly, this was a car worth working on, plenty of potential. At a Sunday-evening cruise at the park, I mentioned it to Jimmy, a veterano of the local scene. "A Cutlass?" he said, "Oh, that's good. I was afraid you might go Euro. You know what you bought—you bought a *frame*." On a different night, at the weekly Custom Kings club meeting, I asked Eddie where there was a good junkyard to get a new seat motor for the Cutlass. Overhearing us, Richard suggested that I just get regular seat tracks and bolt the seat down, unless I was wedded to the idea of power seats. I was not. He also told me that any GM car from the early 1980s would provide compatible interior parts. He directed me to a salvage yard in South Austin.

I drove down on a weekday morning, and it was already hot when I got there. I walked up to the desk and asked where the GM wrecks were. The clerk pointed me in the right direction, and as I walked out to the junkyard, I passed a sign near the front door to the garage. It read: "One night a week I sleep here with my shotgun and my rottweiler. Burglers are welcome to guess which night." Rusting, stripped, with shattered windshields and torn upholstery, the car corpses sat baking in the sun. After having seen so many cars in need of parts that might not be available, I saw the wrecks as a gold mine. I didn't know how the yard priced parts, but I had the idea they were practically free. I picked my way around, finding a power-lock switch here and a door handle there, prying parts off and trying not to scratch the chrome finish, sweating at the effort. I gravitated toward cars that were stacked on others that had been crushed, which placed the work area at chest level, meaning I would not have to bend down. One car had a few large scraps of Styrofoam packing material lying in its backseat, one of which I took and used as a box to hold the small parts I was collecting. Eventually, I found the right kind of seat and, with no small effort, removed the bolts holding it down. The less-accessible bolts posed particular problems: I had to bend over the seat and peering underneath with my head upside down, my glasses sliding down my sweaty nose and rendering everything invisible. Finally, my shirt was soaked through with sweat, my hands were coated with a layer of grit, and my socks were collecting burrs from the weeds that pushed up around each wreck, but I had the seat tracks I needed. I marched proudly to the cashier and plopped my Styrofoam basket of parts on the counter. He glanced at it. "Cash or charge?"

I felt a couple of bills in my pocket. "Cash."

"That's forty dollars."

"Oh. I guess charge." More than I had expected, but still not bad compared to what the parts would have cost me at NAPA or AutoZone.

《 》

The Custom Kings were gathered in a parking lot on Riverside after a Saturday-evening meeting, discussing where to go eat. It was still too early for cruising, but late for some fast-food dining rooms, and Smiley was making some calls to ask how late places were open. Raymond had his 1970 MC out—it was in primer, prepared for an anticipated paint job, but the hydraulic system was ready, so he was already cruising it. While playing a bit with the hydros on the way to Riverside, he felt that something was wrong with the system, so while the club was parked, he popped the hood to check. There was oil on the side of the engine well, near one of his hydraulic cylinders. He asked Smiley whether he had a Crescent wrench to tighten the valve that connected the hose to the cylinder. Smiley said, "What's that, five-eighths?" and went to the trunk of his glitter-painted compact import, where he kept a heavy toolbox. He came back with a wrench, but it was too small. Raymond said, "Nah, it's eleven-sixteenths." That wrench fit, and he tightened the nut. Looking on, Lito said, "Shit, just chain that motherfucker to [Eddie's] car and make it really tight!"

Despite the competition on cruising nights and at car shows between individual lowriders and between clubs, there was a general ethos of mutual aid in the lowrider scene. John and Jesse's offers to help me on the first day we met were not only neighborliness. Whether making impromptu adjustments like this in a parking lot, or staying late in a shop for some side work, lowriders collaborated to get work done on their rides. Often this was motivated by good will and a shared desire to see a car come out, regardless of who owned it. In other situations, the informal exchange of labor was all business. Eddie's hydraulic setup, which was the envy of everyone in the Kings and well known outside the club, would have cost upward of three thousand dollars had he contracted it out. While Eddie was a skilled mechanic, he wanted the frame wrapped by Ralph, who was known to be one of the best at reinforcing cars for hydraulic hopping. Short on cash, Eddie worked off the $1,500 bill over months by helping out in Ralph's shop.

Specialized skills or equipment became part of a person's reputation, and a resource not only for customizing one's own ride, but also for myriad cottage industries and small-scale startup enterprises. Very much like the independent musicians for whom Austin is known as the "live music capital of the world" (see Shank 1994), lowrider painters, upholsterers, metalworkers, and mechanics seek to invent careers out of the work that is their interest and passion, sometimes without the benefit of formal, structured jobs. Friends could be counted on to support such efforts by providing business and referrals, but commerce also sometimes strained relationships when agreed-upon charges went unpaid or work didn't get done.

My next glimpse of the informal economy of customizing came when I began looking for wheels for the Cutlass. Rims were the easiest, most basic modification for marking a car as a lowrider. Having a car with rims was also the basic criterion for membership in a club like the Kings, and it was generally agreed that rims with a different diameter—either larger or smaller—than stock wheels was a customization. The classic lowrider rim was the spoke style made by Dayton Wire Wheels, but also widely imitated. Molded alloy wheels, "dubs," and free-spinning rims were popular in the cruising scenes that lowriders frequented, and so the question of which kind of custom wheel was acceptable for membership was a frequent concern. There was also a politics to the formation of diverse camps in wheel aesthetics.

Albert had left me a message saying that he knew someone who was selling some knock-offs, chrome 100-spoke Players. These were classic lowrider rims, though not posing as much of an investment as the actual Daytons they were modeled on. Albert had Players and said he was happy with them. The guy had five to sell, and he was asking $500. It was not a bad price, and a rare deal in that a spare was included, which could thus be integrated into a custom design—displayed in the trunk, for example. I called Albert back on his cell phone, and Gloria answered. She said they were at Anthony's, and handed it over to Albert. He told me the deal: one of the rims was dented, but it was nothing that couldn't be hammered out by Eddie or somebody. He said we should go look at them and maybe "show him $400." He had told Albert that he wanted $500 but then asked whether he thought that was a good price, so Albert thought he might come down.

He said that he would call the guy and then call me back. A little later, he called and said the seller was going out to dinner with his family and would be back around eight. We could make arrangements to meet then. At about 7:45, I finished eating and drove to the bank to get money out. I had about $40 in cash at the house. The ATM wouldn't give me $460, so I tried $400, and it went. In the parking lot at the bank, there was a Cadillac Coupe de Ville convertible that I coveted; the rims were old-school Supremes.

Back at the house at a little after eight, I was nervously waiting for Albert to call. Eventually he did, and we arranged that he would pick me up and we would meet the seller at Rundberg Lane, far to the north, at nine fifteen. He must have been coming from a northern suburb, maybe Pflugerville. Albert showed up at about eight thirty, so I took a minute to show him the Cutlass. Albert said that he had had a Cutlass as his first car with hydraulics, before he got in the club. He told me that the full vinyl roof on mine was custom. I showed him a few cracks I had discovered in the fiberglass around the headlights and grille, and he suggested getting a "Euro style" front clip from an '87. This was a front-end unit that featured composite headlights, a popular style that had been made for only a couple of years. He said he got a Euro clip for $150, had it sanded and painted to match the car, and that was it. He asked whether I was going to paint the car. I said that that had been my intention, but that I wasn't sure. When my research funding ran out, we would be leaving town, and the emerging plan was to sell the car in whatever shape I had managed to get it, but keep the rims for a future project. He asked how much I wanted to get for it. He was looking for a car because he wanted to work on his truck and do it right—break it down to the frame and do it all. He knew his way around a Cutlass, too, from having one before. Knowing Albert's truck, which was in much better condition than the Cutlass, I suspected that he inquired mostly as a formality. But on the other hand, it is advantageous for a customizer always to know what is for sale and for how much.

We drove up I-35 to Rundberg Lane and stopped in the parking lot of a convenience store. Albert kept the motor running, the AC and radio on, while we talked and waited. Finally, a royal blue and white Cutlass pulled in front of us. Two white guys got out, looking as if they were in high school or just out. There was a sticker on the car that said "Pimpmobile," and hip-hop was playing on the system. We walked around looking at the wheels. I was distracted by the dirty tires, which did not flatter the rims. The driver had short red hair and a goatee. He showed us the spare and the place that needed to be hammered out. His friend had long dark hair and wore a cap on backward; he quietly observed the proceedings while nursing a Black and Mild cigar. Both had tall takeout cups of coffee. The car owner said he was planning to replace two tires before selling the wheels, and Albert saw an opening to bargain: "Tell you what. Leave it like it is, and we'll give you $400 cash for 'em." The guy said that he had to get his factory wheels back from Lalo (someone whom he and Albert knew in common) and that Lalo had to put a new tire on his factory wheels because of a blowout. Albert proposed that we find him some factories to roll on until he got his own fixed, and that way we could switch out the wheels in the next couple of days. I could barely follow this complex arrangement, but the seller agreed.

On the way back, I asked Albert which wheels he had in mind for the switch. He said that he had some that might work, or Eddie might have some. He very gently broached the subject of using the factory wheels off the Cutlass, if I felt all right about that. He even suggested that we could "put it in writing," though the main reason it was safe to lend my wheels to the seller was that "he's easy to find." I said that the car wasn't really ready to drive yet, and Albert offered to come over and help me take the wheels off, put them in his truck, take them to the shop where Eddie worked, put them on the seller's Cutlass, and take his wheels off. We had worked out the details. The cash was still in my pocket.

When Albert dropped me off, he took another look at the Cutlass standing in the driveway behind my house. "Are you planning on keeping it here?" I said yes. He offered me the use of a car cover he had once I got the wheels on—I think to deter theft. I looked at the Cutlass. There were small scratches on the paint and sap droppings from the trees were starting to accumulate. A few birds had left their mark on the vinyl top. The shower curtain spread over the window that was stuck open was held down with a pair of bricks on the roof. I still had the power window to fix. As it was, it didn't look like a target for a thief, regardless of the "power booster" in the trunk. I thanked Albert, and we said goodnight.

Time passed, and I kept up participant observation in the cruising scene in my Toyota "family car," but I never heard back from the rims guy. Eventually, my grant was spent and our family was preparing for the next gig: my wife, Marike Janzen, had a research fellowship that would take us to Germany for a year. It was not clear whether this marked the end of my attempt at lowriding or whether there were some way to hold my place in the scene until I could get back. Albert had not shown any further interest in using the Cutlass as a daily driver while working on his truck, but it occurred to me that this might work for someone else. José was telling me about a half-finished Monte Carlo that he now had on blocks at his parents' house, and I proposed a deal. If he wanted to sell the MC, he could buy the Cutlass from me and have a car with a reliable engine that nonetheless could look respectable with rims. He was very interested, but after a couple of weeks, he had not found a buyer for the MC, and he couldn't front me the cash.

Less than a week before we were going to leave town, I spray-painted "FOR SALE" on a piece of scrap plywood and leaned it against the rear window of the Cutlass. A couple of days later, a Latino man and his teenage son stopped by. They lived on Third Street, a couple of blocks away, in a house I had noticed because of the 1980s-model Monte Carlo in front with rims and a primered quarter panel. The father told me his son had wrecked the Monte and was looking for a car to start over on. I mentioned the stereo components that would come with the Cutlass, since Brenda had made that a selling point, and he shrugged, uninterested, telling me that he planned to "take everything off the Monte Carlo, and put it on this." I demonstrated what I had learned about the motor: it was generally sound, but needed some new vacuum hoses to make it run more smoothly in low gear. They took the car for a test drive around the block, and I was relieved to see it reach the corner without stalling. A short while later, they returned looking satisfied. "What did you want for it?" the father asked me.

"750."

"Well, I got to go to the bank, but I'll come back in a couple of hours."

So it was done. I cleaned my pawnshop tools out of the front seat, went back into the house, and waited for him to arrive with a roll of cash.

Work, My Work, Side Work

One weekend afternoon after the Kings had been invited to display outside a local restaurant as part of its anniversary celebration, a few of us decided to ride around awhile before the club meeting. Arturo said, "They still got that . . . Oak Hill?" Eddie said yeah, and we decided to go check it out. Oak Hill is a suburb near the Austin Community College's Tower Campus on the southwest side of town, and car enthusiasts gathered there on Saturdays in the parking lot of a grocery store. It was just beginning to fill up when we got there—hot rods mostly, with some minitrucks on airbags, some '70s Trans Ams, and some classic pickups. We pulled up, got out, and stood around the cars, checking out the others from a slight distance. Almost before I got out of my car, Eddie and the others were working on theirs. Eddie dug around under the dash for a loose wire because his taillights were out. Oscar was rooting in his trunk to figure out why his subs were emitting a strange noise. It turned out that a screw had worked loose, so the subs were just hanging out of their cabinets. Eddie's problem was more mysterious, and he was deep into it when an old-timer who pulled up in an old Chevy stepside truck came over and perused his car. Since Eddie was preoccupied, the guy moseyed away without starting a conversation.

Eddie told me that sometimes they get grumbles from the hot-rodders, elaborating with a little imagined dialogue with an Anglo hot-rodder over the proper diameter for a set of wheels. "Why'd you do that to your car? Why you got thirteens on it?"

"Why you got fifteens on yours?"

"'Cause fifteens is the right size."

"Thirteens is the right size."

"No, fifteens fit my car."

"Thirteens fit *my* car."

At this point, we had heard no actual grumbling from the mostly Anglo crowd we were visiting. Still, Oscar said, "I feel out of place!" and Eddie replied, "Why?" with plenty of irony to show that Oscar was stating the obvious. Then Eddie said, "It's okay, we'll just take Ben hostage."

Arturo laughed and agreed: "You go, 'help!'" As me, he waved in a half-hearted way.

Eddie said, "No. Ben, go over and talk to them. I don't speak white."

The parking lot continued to fill up, with no police in sight. When a baby blue stock '58 Impala pulled in, Oscar said, "There. That's my dream car." Eventually, an old-timer came over to talk about the '50s Chevies. As we started to move toward our cars to head to the meeting, someone made a comment about being on summer vacation. When the Anglo hot-rodders had moved on, Eddie said, "No wait, we're Mexican—we don't get vacation!" Everyone concurred, laughing. "We have to call in to get vacation!" On the way to the car wash for the meeting, Eddie played with his hydraulics in traffic, hitting three wheels with abandon at a major intersection, as if casting off the minor tensions raised by the visit.

People turn to lowrider practice as a resetting and valorization of mechanical practices that are wrongly classified as unskilled in an information-oriented economy. As an activity of leisure, lowriding represents an attempt at unalienated production: the struggle toward an appropriation of time and resources from the domain of "work" for "my work." Along the way, lowriders step out of relegated places in the economic order: they seek to make meaningful the cars that they build, within a historical context in which economic value and social status is afforded to work with information, by people who write, or "create," computer programs, for example. What was called the "new economy" at the turn of the century has appropriated "creation," colonizing the vocabulary of art, along with the antiestablishment poses of bohemia, for the domain of business and a certain sector of the privileged class (Ross 2002).

In contrast with those sectors of business now classed as "creative" (Florida 2001), what, then, is "unskilled labor"? In use, the term refers to work that is theoretically available to someone who has not finished high school or pursued further education (skill being equated with the authorization provided by formal education). Clearly, much "unskilled" work requires extensive and specialized skills (see Striffler 2002). Also, not everyone sees a stigma in such work. Smiley, who had greeted me at Frankie's shop, worked a desk job as a purchaser in the parts department of a high-tech hardware firm. This was not in a category with the glamour jobs of web designer, code warrior, or startup entrepreneur, nor did it have the wide career horizons of microchip engineering, but as a job in the high-tech industry, Smiley's would have been basically desirable. He was riding the technocultural wave. Yet in the bedroom of his parents' house where he lived and granted me an interview, Smiley told me that his dream was to open his own garage and work on cars. He was taking courses at the community college to obtain technical certifications that would move him closer to this goal—ironically, trying to study his way out of high tech.

In his work on the rhetorics of everyday public culture in the Latino population of a small midwestern city, Ralph Cintron contests the mainstream economic definition of "skilled," deploying the classical term *tekhne* in order to draw attention to the artful aspects of "mundane skill," the kinds of work, of production or poesis, that do not hold the status or the cultural capital of an art. These are the areas of everyday performance, the "surfaces of public culture," where he, as a rhetorician, looks for meaning: "Hairstyles, clothing, car decoration, musical styles, talk, the geometries of city streets and street names" (1997, x). For Cintron, *tekhne* marks a concern with habits of making that has been lost or corrupted in the modern world, since the objects and work worthy of meticulous attention are defined as rarefied, other than ordinary:

> Has this ancient concept of *tekhne* or art devolved in the modern world
> into something more debilitating, a cleavage, say, between artistic skill
> and other skills? The detritus of romanticism, particularly the idea of the
> alienated and sacred artist, survives in the modern fetishization of the
> art object. With such fetishization, art becomes aggrandized, a product
> of the mysterious, irrational, creative, and individual mind; in contrast,
> mundane skill becomes a product of generic minds. I am using the notion
> of *tekhne* here to level that fetishization and to see the art in mundane
> skill and, more significantly, in day-to-day life. (Cintron 1997, xii)[4]

Forces are arrayed against Cintron on this move. What is at stake in naming kinds of work is the matter not only of fetishization, but also of hierarchies in kinds of processes and kinds of products—the matter of who gets to fetishize what. In the discourse of computer industries, programmers involved in designing websites sometimes "build" them as "architects" (though, notably, this is not called "the Internet construction business"), but more often it seems that in the information industry, people "create" things. Often what they create are "solutions," postmodern indulgences that promise to deliver consumers from various annoyances or blockages that impede one or another kind of flow (purgatory is the place occupied by users of last week's technology). This flow is understood to be a channel from a vast, inexhaustible, and fungible resource—the imagination—to productivity. What solutions do is to allow us access to this resource in order to get our humdrum limitations out of the way, stop the shrink on creativity, and do our part for eternal economic growth.[5] There can be no top to the information economy, Bill Gates and Steve Jobs alike tell us, because its base is not material, but lies in the domain of human ideas.

To produce in this economy is to foster "ideation," as in: "I've created a solution that allows you to maximize ideation." Before the high-tech bubble burst, that kind of talk and a domain name of your own could have landed you a spot among the elect of the information technology and its promiscuous venture capitalists. In prior epochs, rising elites liberated themselves from work by seizing ownership of private property; now there is a synthesis possible between the Protestant mandate to produce and a liberation from bodily concerns—who even needs a body, after all, when production can take the form of ideation? The investment in ideation also situated an agent different from *homo faber* at the center of "no-collar" work. As Andrew Ross (2002) documents, the pendulum in a longstanding debate about whether progress should yield better compensation or a more comfortable or tolerable working experience swung toward the latter—rather than being well compensated, workers ought to be fulfilled. Rewarding work (in a psychic, not an economic sense) is not merely an amenity of late-modern life; it has become a responsibility. If you are not gratified by your job, there might be something wrong with your software, or you may just need an upgrade.

Recession brought the material base of the information economy back to light—we learned that computer wizards were not squeezing resources endlessly from a turnip; instead, they were convincing (sometimes conning) people in control of accumulated capital to release it into circulation at unprecedented levels of complexity. When the financial returns did not materialize as promised, the benefactors retreated, and now the Internet is no longer the land of the free. Millionaires on paper became stock-broke overnight. Yet social commitments to a particular class rather than to the public were rendered clear during the crisis. Being "too big to fail" became a euphemism used in bailouts to distinguish the entitled from the not, suggesting American society can get along without homeowners or debt-free students, but not without the rich.

The lowriders I met occupied a specific place within this class structure. They generally did not talk about "creating" cars—they "built" them. When the terms of art are employed to talk about lowriding, it generally signals an intentional effort to grant the status of art to car customizing, often by an outsider. I heard a community activist call lowriding "public art from the barrio." An advertisement for car wax in *Lowrider Magazine* uses "Some artists work with paint and canvas; others work with metal" as a caption to a picture of a tricked-out lowrider being contemplated by a man wearing cholo style with a goatee and a shaved head. Like "culture," the term "art" confers status to the object and the practice of lowriding, but neither of these terms occurred very often in the everyday conversations in which I participated. People were much more likely to refer to lowriding as a "sport," addressing the competitive aspect of car shows, but also invoking leisure practices that figure much more prominently in everyday life, if only vicariously through *Monday Night Football* and the college game on Saturday. Sport also invokes gendered ideas about the proper outlets for creativity and imagination. Only occasionally was there mention of "creation," but again, this was not casual diction: it carried a rhetoric of promotion, the stuff of car club or business names, such as "ATX Custom Creations."

The car is a contact point between the classes said to create and those who build and repair. One of the most visible public signs of the new-economy prosperity that graced (some say afflicted) Austin in the late 1990s was the appearance of luxury cars in traffic. Rolls-Royces, Dodge Vipers, BMW Z3s, Boxters, Ferraris, and any number of other status cars routinely turned up on the streets. Of course in Texas, there were also the mammoth trucks and SUVs that stood ready to take off over rolling prairies, if only they hadn't been made into golf courses. Luxury cars served some of the bodily needs of an industry that advertised itself as being an enterprise of the mind (carpal-tunnel injuries and the side effects of caffeine ingestion notwithstanding). After all, minds must sometimes be physically transported from subdivisions and lakeside ranch houses to office towers if their owners don't e-commute; even if they do, a vehicle is needed to visit consumption palaces such as the newly ubiquitous "stadium seating" cinemas or to take in Austin's famous music scene. Cars are necessary for taking advantage of the lifestyle options and amenities offered by a decentered information-driven city.

Luxury cars may be paid for by ideation, but someone also changes their oil. Someone rotates their tires, checks their plugs, overhauls their brakes, details them inside and out, and gives them state-mandated inspections. Thus the car is a tangential point of contact between two kinds of work. Rubbing between these domains, the car makes it clear that discerning one kind of *tekhne* from another, labor from creation, work from "my work," is not a natural science. These terms are stakes in a contestation. By building lowrider cars when members of rarefied sectors of the economy are creating ideation all around them, lowriders weigh in on the contest. They do so every bit as seriously as a startup ideator pursues his or her dream, and with none of the ironic detachment or dismissive humor of a postmodern consumer.

《 》

After being away for almost a year, one Saturday night I was back in town and went to a club meeting at the car wash. I was greeted warmly. "For those of you who don't know," said Eddie, since the club had grown considerably, "this is Ben. He's done some media stuff for us, getting us out there." The idea that I had done "media stuff" came from the fact that since Internet searches on lowriders sometimes turned up my name on a conference program or a working paper from my faculty homepage, I had been approached by a couple of reporters, whom I referred to the club for interviews. The result of my research was not always entirely clear to everyone, especially as it went on over years. At times in the dissertation phase, people asked me about the paper I was writing.

I saw others on that first Saturday back in town, however, whom I had known from the beginning of the fieldwork and who knew that I had my own project in the works, beyond a de facto role as a media liaison. One of these was Richard, whose '68 had undergone a makeover lasting more than a year.

"How's the book coming?" he asked.

"Oh, you know. Little by little. I'm going to try to get it done, graduate this year."

"You working on what, notes?"

"Yeah, a lot of notes. Trying to make sense of them."

Richard nodded. I don't think he said this out loud, but he could have meant, "It takes time." Plans fall through or change, the money runs out, the body-shop guy gets busy or the painter distracted. It is a matter of patience, connections, funding, support, luck, commitment, and, most of all, time. No one knew this better than Richard, since he paid regular visits to the shop to check on the Impala and maybe indulge in a daydream about when it would be mobile again. At that point, I wasn't sure which one of us was going to "bust out" first.

Neither Gangsters nor Santitos

The sad part is that any minor infraction was grounds for rude behavior, for "provocation," for abuse, for arrest and many times for violence. The reason it is sad is because when the pleve [folks] went out to cruise, not everyone was a santito or santita. When people go out to have a good time—often times, there is drinking involved. Even rich people and gavachos [whites] do it.

Roberto Rodríguez, *Justice: A Question of Race*

At two o'clock one July morning in 1998, the owner of a punk rock club on Sixth Street and her boyfriend were walking to her Chevy Suburban in downtown Austin. According to newspaper coverage of the trial that followed, the two saw that a window was broken and someone was in the vehicle. The boyfriend, Paul Saustrup, drew a handgun and shouted, "Freeze! Anyone else comes jumping out of there, you'll be the first to die!" The man in the car, twenty-year-old Eric Demart Smith, got out. Accounts differ about what happened next. Sasha Sessums, the club owner, said that Smith was shirtless and drunk—she could see his "gang tattoos." Later, another news report stated that Smith's shirt came off as he and Saustrup scuffled. According to Saustrup, Smith walked away, then turned toward him and reached for his waist—"going for something in his pants" was what Sessums told the 911 operator from her cell phone—and Saustrup fired. A man who lived in a nearby alley remembered thinking that Smith was trying to get away, with Saustrup chasing him. Saustrup shot Smith twice, the bullets striking him behind each shoulder blade. In the first news story on the shooting, the front page of the *Austin American-Statesman* on July 9, 1998, read in part:

> Smith, also known as "Blue Devil" and "Eloc," was convicted of posses-
> sion of a controlled substance and attempted burglary of a habitation on
> Feb. 18, 1997, according to court records. . . . Smith was also convicted of
> five misdemeanors including a conviction on Dec. 21, 1995, of burglary of
> a vehicle.[1]

Saustrup was eventually indicted for murder. When the case moved into court, the defense followed the lead of the newspaper, putting the deceased Smith on trial. Saustrup never denied the shooting, but mounted a plea of self-defense. In 2000, he was acquitted of murder on these grounds. During the trial, the defense attorney displayed life-size photographs of Smith's torso and his tat-toos. The lawyer told the jury that it is easy to tell good guys from bad guys. He pointed to Saustrup: "Here's the good guy." "And here," he continued, picking up the photo of Smith, "is the bad guy. He's dead because he's the bad guy."

The issue of good guys and bad guys—of criminality—is a key stake in popular aesthetics and the contestation of public space (see Chappell 2006b). There was no direct connection between Smith's death and the lower-intensity harassment that lowriders reported as the ubiquitous experience of being pulled over in traffic, but as the high-profile trial proceeded while I was begin-ning my research, it was a grim reminder that semiotic politics, filtered through constructions of "bad guys" and the risks they pose, carried life-and-death consequences, at least for certain people and in certain spaces. In this chapter, I attempt to address the complexity and contradictions of the criminalization of lowriders. This brings back under consideration the stereotypical associations of lowriding with gang culture, which I raised in the introduction. Lowriders, well aware of this as a meaning ascribed to their aesthetics in public culture, often protest that they are "not all" gangbangers. In the end, the question of whether lowriders are gang members is not particularly useful, not least because it reproduces the common misperception that gang membership is a black-and-white variable that tidily divides American society into two columns: legitimate and criminal. In fact, families, friends, and people connected in oth-er ways often share an appreciation of barriological aesthetics with gang mem-bers without committing crime themselves. A more illuminating approach to the issue of "gangness," criminality, and violence is to attend to how notions of "gangster" get constructed and circulated, by whom and with what effects.

As a small contribution to such an inquiry, which is crucial for understanding lowriders but which cannot by any means be subsumed under the project of this book, here I present perspectives gleaned from the vantage of lowrider space. First, I sketch some examples of how "gangster" as a fluid and contested aesthetic principle operates within barriological lowrider space. Though there are pleasures and even some power to be gained from embracing a gangster aesthetic, some lowriders also went to lengths to refuse this label, either by deflecting it onto others in contrast with themselves or by describing cliques and fighting as something in the past that they had matured out of. In any case, countering the stereotype of lowriding as a manifestation of gang culture was a priority for numerous car clubs. For all these positive efforts, however, proximity to active gangs and everyday violence can keep the issue alive, infusing the competition for space and prestige among and between lowrider groups with the possibility that it could escalate into something more, into "drama."

Returning to the question of how public space is regulated, I propose that the stigma of gangster criminality is closely bound up with the minoritization of space. This involves both the police practices of regulating space that I introduced in Chapter One as well as the chronic insecurity of a certain social position, which reinforces constructions of masculinity tied to violence. I close the chapter by relating some lost opportunities to resolve the stigmatizing cycle that criminalizes spaces and populations, anecdotes showing that police, in their efforts to innovate their work through "community policing," and lowriders, in their attempts to change their image with the police, basically talk past each other.

Gangster Aesthetics

Raymond showed up to a meeting decked out in gangsta finery. A crisply ironed bandana encircled his smooth, shaven head, tied at the top in a neat square knot. He wore an oversized baseball-style jersey, hanging down over long Dickies shorts pressed to a sharp crease. His athletic socks were spectacularly white, pulled up to his knees. A thin gold rope hung around his neck, and his watchband and a ring were also heavy and gold-colored. A Black and Mild cigar with a filter tip was stuck behind one ear.

"Looka here! It's Tube Sock!" said Eddie as Raymond strolled up to the group at the car wash. It was true that Raymond's look seemed to be heavily influenced by the late Tupac Shakur, a popular icon in the lowrider scene. Raymond was with his older brother, who was wearing a retro bowling-style shirt and a porkpie hat. "So, you going to roll around with us tonight?" Eddie asked Raymond.

"Nah, I got to go somewhere."

"Where?"

Raymond smiled. "Oh, just somewheres."

"The club?"

"Nah, just somewheres."

Eddie pressed gently for details, but none were forthcoming. Perhaps Raymond had plans that did not jibe with the Kings' requirements (drug free, gang free, no alcohol at meetings). Or perhaps he was going "somewheres" to meet someone, and it would just be inconvenient for Eddie to know. What happened outside of car club events was difficult for Eddie to comment on. He quit prying and turned back to meeting business.

no where was Ray going?

《 》

The portion of barriology that overlaps with an urban gangster aesthetic has long been a site, among others, of cultural exchange between Mexican Americans and African Americans, premised on shared experiences and social spaces.[2] One of these shared experiences is that of being the object of "gangster" interpellation, resulting in parallel relationships to law enforcement. Both black and Latino people, for instance, have been subject to profiling and the use of potentially lethal force by authorities in the context of public gang scares that have also given impetus to attempts to connect identified cultural performances with criminal behavior. An aspect of this common experience is that when law officers use aesthetics as a targeting principle in gang investigations, it can compound the problem of state repression of entire populations seen to be contaminated by the gang stigma—indeed, Mike Davis (1990) noted in his critical history of the 1980s LA gang scare and the violent response by the Los Angeles Police Department that antigang measures looked beyond the illegal acts of individuals to constitute and criminalize gang members and their families *as a class.*[3]

Because gangness references behavior—the use of identifying styles like tattoos, clothing, and language; being in a gang-identified location; taking part in gang-marked activities—gang identification short-circuits the race question in yet another version of lifestyle profiling. Police or vigilante violence against a black or Latino person is publicly and legally excused when it can be recontextualized and construed as violence against a criminal, particularly a gang member, who is by definition a threat. In this way, notions of criminality are animated by an available racial script, as Judith Butler observed in her analysis of how the jury interpreted video evidence in the Rodney King case:

> The fear is that some physical distance will be crossed, and the virgin sanctity of whiteness will be endangered by that proximity. The police are thus structurally placed to protect whiteness against the violence, where violence is the imminent action of that black male body. And because within this imaginary schema, the police protect whiteness, their own violence cannot be read as violence; because the black male body, prior to any video, is the site and source of anger, a threat, the police effort to subdue this body, even if in advance, is justified regardless of the circumstances. (1993b, 18)

Although gangness is racially marked, it is not identical with race. But while the history of the struggle to discredit both explicitly racist laws and racially selective enforcement has gained enough ground that the state is always required to offer lip service to equal protection, "culture" and behavior remain fair game for public generalizations about criminality. Behavior and outward signs thought to be gang affiliated have become the subjects of "gang science." Police, parents, teachers, and other authority figures compile concordances of data in the interest of interpreting visible signs as signals of criminal behavior. Gang experts offer to share their expertise in interpreting the dangerous signs of urban style: baggy pants, athletic jerseys, colored bandannas, tattoos, Gothic-style lettering that lowriders call "Old English," and other signs are taken to be symptomatic of gangness.[4] This becomes an intensely motivated form of police ethnography—attempts to answer questions such as who are these gangs and how will we know them—directed and backed by the full force of the state.

Significantly, according to the Austin Police Department's (APD's) Gang Suppression and Joint Juvenile Gang Unit (formed out of the Hispanic Crimes Unit and the Street Crimes Unit), the Texas Penal Code places expressive culture at the very center of the definition of a gang: "three or more persons having

a *common identifying sign or symbol* or an identifiable leadership who continu-
ously or regularly associate in the commission of criminal activities" (my emphasis).[5] The unit's website also alerts parents and teachers to warning signs of
varying levels of gang involvement. Under the heading "Factors Contributing
to Gang Affiliation" are standard sociological variables drawn from underclass
theory and psychology: ineffective parenting, low self-esteem, a family history
of gang involvement. The next set of red flags, called "Early Warning Signs of
Gang Involvement," takes social deviance or delinquency as a theme: drug use,
truancy, keeping late hours, declining grades. After "Contributing Factors" and
"Early Warnings" comes the decisive category, "Definite Signs of Gang Membership." These consist primarily of expressive practices: wearing gang clothing
or colors, graffiti, using hand signs, keeping photographs of gang images. So
while self-destructive, "deviant" behaviors serve as indicators of possible gang
affiliation, aesthetic choices of a kind that mark the subject and embrace a connection to urban, minoritized places and sociability are considered definitive—
the sine qua non of that special degree of deviance that is gangness.

The purpose of this public information is to help communities and families
intervene to prevent the undoubtedly devastating effects on young people of
participating in organized crime. But a focus on "gang signs" caters to a public that seems always hungry for spectacular symptoms of urban or racialized
depravity. This allows style to be conflated with criminality in a way that both
invites and justifies the policing of signification. It also becomes a proper obsession beyond the police force, among school authorities for example, since
banning gang signs is something that can be done in the daunting face of urban violence. Regardless of whether banning gang signs does anything to curb
violence, the legal scholar Ann Kordas points out that a symptomology of the
signs of gang-related and other types of violence has inspired wide-ranging
prohibitions on imagery, including religious symbols such as the Virgin of Guadalupe, which raise particularly problematic constitutional questions (2000,
1457). Kordas indicates the extent of these prohibitions by enumerating the
kinds of clothing and accessory styles that have been targeted by cities and
schools:

> baggy pants, pants cut off at the knee, overall straps worn off the shoul-
> der, untied shoelaces, caps worn tilted to the right, caps worn tilted to the
> left, black clothing, red clothing, maroon clothing, blue clothing, blue-
> black clothing combinations, black-gold clothing combinations, Chicago

Bulls jackets, Duke University baseball caps, black nail polish, bandannas, clothing bearing "profanity," clothing associated with "violence" (e.g. black trench coats), "morbid-themed" or "Goth" clothing or accessories (e.g. black clothes, white makeup), Marilyn Manson T-shirts, Confederate symbols, headwraps, earrings, shaved notches in eyebrows, sunglasses, and red or blue pens worn behind the right or left ear. (1455–1456)

The sense of panic associated with such signs is accentuated by the APD website's self-described purpose, to work against "the ever increasing wave of violence which had been inundating the city."[6] The flood metaphor situates the gang-suppression efforts within a conservative narrative of decline, brought on by a contamination of the normative community by essentially bad elements. Therefore, the gang scare is a classic moral panic, one in which expressive cultural practices are seen as leading youth down a slippery slope to deviance; like many other moral panics, the gang scare is implicated in and constitutive of racializing discourse—the Hispanic Crimes Unit meets the Street Crimes Unit.

Despite the fact that most lowriders I met were interested in dispelling the association of their style with gang culture, this did not necessarily mean that they tried to distance themselves from iconographies that were publicly labeled or understood as gang signs. Assuming and stubbornly preserving a certain "gangster touch" (Phillips 2000) in one's style of everyday living not only reinforced barriological authenticity, but also offered what Dick Hebdige called "the power to discomfit" (1988). Various factors imbue a custom stylistic gesture with particular affectivity, including reference to historical precedent, collective memory, and a dialogical transaction between performer and audience. This affectivity registers in a sense of close connection to place and community, the assertion of a self unapologetically marked by this propinquity, and the power to affect others noticeably with one's presence. Together, such affects give certain versions of the gangster touch a kind of beauty. In a context like lowrider space in East Austin and South Austin, this was an oblique and oppositional energy, claimed by people whose access to the power to affect their situations, including their spatial location and spatialized relations with other social actors, was often curtailed, deferred, or nonexistent. Often, cruising nights would find lowriders on the boulevard playing with gang-identified references, deploying them sometimes in jest, but never abandoning or repressing them entirely in some whitewashed claim to legitimacy. Sometimes these references were ironic allusions to gang-exploitation cinema, such as the films *American Me* or *Blood In, Blood Out*, which could be seen as perpetuating stereotypes of gangness as a cultural attribute of Mexican Americans, but which nonetheless were part of a media-cultural repertoire that lowriders shared.[7]

During one of the postmeeting meals that the Kings and their families routinely enjoyed, a nonmember in attendance made a joke at Aaron's expense. Aaron's sister Elisa, who was sitting several tables away, hadn't heard the joke, and asked what was so funny. Nobody would tell her, and she persisted because Aaron, who was relatively soft-spoken, wasn't about to repeat it. Finally, when Lito, who was sitting closer to the joker, responded, "Nothing, nothing!" Elisa turned on him with mock aggression: "Now, I don't have [Eddie's] knife, but you know I will cut you!" Everybody laughed again.

Lito leaped up and played out a prison murder scene from *American Me*. "I'm walking out and get shanked! Uh!" He mimed a low stab from behind. "Don't look at me! Don't look at me!" When Eddie came back from the bathroom, Lito complained, "Man, [Elisa] threatened my life!"

Refusing to Be Gangster

Playing with gangster themes was in part an embrace of barriological knowledge and in part an ironic critique of the stereotyping to which all lowriders were subject. To perform a gangster role among friends was one thing; to be targeted as a gangster in public, however, was quite another. Even though lowriders admitted that they were not blameless in the pattern of being stopped in traffic by police, Smiley also faulted the police for either not discriminating between those who "cause trouble" and those who do not, or willfully ignoring the difference. When I asked him why he thought he got stopped in his lowrider, Smiley said

> Stereotypes. Lowriding. "Oh, that's a lowrider." And then I had a sticker in my back windshield, [Custom Kings] sticker, you know, my logo. I know a few police officers asked me, "So, what is this [Custom Kings]? Is this a gang?"
>
> [*Sarcastically*] Yeah we're going to really let our gang out like that, you know, so, "Oh yeah, I represent that clique right there." No, you

know, I mean—but they would always question it, of course, while they were checking up, you know, seeing if I have any warrants. It's the first thing they say: "So you're [Custom Kings], huh?"

Say, "Yeah, I sure am." You know, and, um, they'll find out I don't have any—they'll come out empty-handed, you know. No warrants. Nothing. I mean, they can search my car if they want. I'm not going to have anything. [. . .] but at the same time, it's good to show what car club you're in, 'cause they know who's—they know which car clubs out there that are causing trouble and which ones are not. 'Cause, yeah, there are some out there that do cause a lot of trouble in the community. But, um, I mean they pretty much—they know, actually, which ones out there are bad and which ones are not.

Members of the Custom Kings repeatedly described themselves, to me and to others, as a positive lowrider club that maintained a strictly antigang posture. Along with the prestige of its cars, whether a club was "positive" was a matter of debate, and such reputations carried potentially significant consequences. Once I got to hear Albert pitching the Kings to an unaffiliated lowrider when their conversation turned into a recruiting opportunity. The guy had been approached by another club called Lyfestylz. He took a purple card out of his wallet and showed Albert, who examined it and handed it back, advising that it would be wise to check out any club to find out what he was getting into. The other guy mentioned that he liked the fact that Lifestylz claimed to be "Drug and Gangsta free" on its card.

"Thing is," Albert said, "somebody can front that on a card, or they can front that in conversation, but how do they act? Some people are drug free and alcohol free during the week, but then on the weekend, they get drugged up, they drive like that, and they get popped." Beyond getting "popped" by an accident or a police stop, what was at stake more generally was reputation and standing in the barrio community. Albert said that the Kings had a good relationship with most other clubs in town and that this spirit of coexistence insured them against petty crime, implying that being victimized by criminal acts would indicate an envious or otherwise problematic relationship with particular community members. The guy asked whether there was a monthly membership fee, and Albert said, "It's ten bucks," adding, "Thing is, you factor in getting your window broken, your stereo stolen, are you paying more for that or more for the ten bucks a month?" The guy asked about another club that was nationwide but was starting an Austin chapter. Albert shook his head gravely and said, "I'm not going to even give a response to that. There's good and bad everywhere. To each his own. The club I knew out in Las Vegas wasn't good."

Smiley offered further perspective on how the reputation of a club situated it in specific relation to other organizations, including not only gangs but also community groups.

> We've got a strict rule: no gang members, no drugs. There are car clubs that don't look into that. I know there have been car clubs that have gang members in the club. I've seen a club go down because they had two members in the club from rival gangs. The presidents can say when you come into the car club, you leave that behind, but . . . Deep inside they still supposedly represent that. They can be cool with the person from the other clique until some little thing—it starts up. We had one member that used to be involved in a gang. He thought that getting in the car club would stop it, but the gang wouldn't let it go. They taunted him, they messed with him. The president went to talk to the main guy in the gang: he wanted to get out of it. He let them know that they needed to back off. The club had already been out for a while, had already done the second annual car show at Travis High School. We really made it known to the community that we were a gang-free, drug-free car club. The radio mentioned our name and what we were about. LULAC [the League of United Latin American Citizens] also sponsored the show. The gang had that in mind, and after that, he didn't have trouble with them any more. He left on good terms. He looked to car club as an escape route. Nowadays, you can't get out of gangs. He had a life planned for him, and he needed to move on. He thought the only way to do that was joining us, 'cause he saw how we were. Back then, we were strong. The gang would leave him alone because they were big. We had other car clubs that had our backs at that time. We helped them out, so they will help us out.

Smiley's narrative raises the point that lowriders are up against not only unfounded stereotypes by the police, but also problems associated with actual social and geographical proximity to established gangs. The antigang stance is not only an attempt at good public relations, but also an effort to prevent gangs from confirming stereotypes about lowriders and the lowrider scene. The car club is an alternate group in which to find protection and support. Thus, as a type of mutual-aid and self-defense association, the car club assumes one of the roles that a gang does for members (see Vigil 1988, 90–91).[8] Along these lines, Chris told me:

> It's like so close akin to a gang—I mean, it is almost parallel. Not necessarily from the finer clubs, the [Custom Kings] are positive, but [Just Cruzin]? You get just a couple of people with attitude, and having a sticker becomes a hazard because you're associated [. . .] It's normally the older folks who have a little bit more respect. They're in it for the style, for the art. [. . .] I'm in it purely for the art.

If a commitment to mutual defense was an aspect of lowrider car clubs that made them "so close akin to a gang," this was tempered by a notion of responsibility, namely, that adults should avoid conflict. Hence, gang activity was something that the Kings spoke about growing out of, and those who were unwilling or unable to leave it behind were considered troublemakers. Before cruising one night, there was a joint meeting between several car clubs that were planning a benefit event. As the meeting broke up, some of the Kings discussed who had shown up. One of the Stylistic Syndicate members was there in a newly painted Suburban, and Eddie pointed it out to me—"He just put airbags on that thing last week," he said. There were also a couple of people Eddie knew from high school—one guy, Jesse, "used to tag 'Jesus'" as a graffiti writer. Eddie also recognized somebody who had been really quiet in high school, and he recalled, "Man, we used to *beat his ass*. Every day. He couldn't get to school, man."

Smiley said, "Man, [Eddie] you were mean!"

Eddie: "Well, he was the only one dumb enough to join a rival gang! He came to the high school and was the only one representing the other set."

Smiley: "What clique was that?"

Eddie said some name that sounded like "Mental."

"You going to talk to him?" asked Smiley.

"Nah," said Eddie, "I'm older now. That shit's over."

When Eddie mentioned gang activity as a kind of youthful indiscretion, it underscored how gangs were part of the social landscape of the city: along with sharing certain mutual-defense functions and stylistic iconographies, lowriders and barrio gangs shared a certain space. Like Eddie, other lowriders spoke of gang affiliation or just fighting as being associated with a particular life stage, something that they had grown out of. They were careful to contrast those practices with lowriding, calling the latter a "lifestyle," implying a permanent commitment to a more mature and sustainable activity. Still, the best intentions were not always enough to motivate former gang members to leave street violence behind.

Killers

Regardless of personal decisions and commitments regarding gang identity and behavior, lowriders were close enough geographically and aesthetically to gang members that contact between the two was inevitable, which, along with permanent tensions with the police, affected how people responded to gangs as a threat. José told a story that illustrated this, recalling the details from memories more than a decade old:

> **JOSÉ:** My car, when I had my Cutlass, I had found out there was a guy in the [Familia] that had a car the same color as mine. But he had some cheesy rims on it, you know, his was, you know, the back was dropped, the front was jacked up, he didn't have no hydros. I didn't have hydros, but mine was leveled out. And I had my car shot at twice. And I was never in it—good thing I was never in it. Once I was at a dance, and someone, they did a drive-by. But they did it with a shotgun. They missed my car—well, they missed the car, the windows, but they hit my hood. So I had all these—you know, they scraped my paint job on the hood. You see all the pellet marks—I mean, just scattered across my hood. And the other time, I was at my mother's house, [and] they shot out my back window at my mother's house. Someone had shot my—because I had it parked in the—I usually parked it in the backyard. But that time I had gone home late, so I parked it in the driveway. Someone had shot my back window out. You know, and that, it was just because—I found out it was because they thought I was that other guy, and I wasn't. But I was lucky. I had a friend of mine, well, all her cousins were in that gang, and, you know, I went with her. She took me, and I went to the guys, and I told them what was going on. And they said, "Aw, well, you know, we're sorry, we're sorry." And they—after that, you know, it never happened, you know the str—I got it straightened out. But it was just because, you know, my car looked like his car.
> **BEN:** What was that like?
> **JOSÉ:** Man. [*laughs*]
> **BEN:** I mean, going, "Look, you got the wrong guy . . ."

JOSÉ: And it was crazy, too, because I had kids! And I was lucky I was never in the car. I mean, if I would have been in the car, I mean—who knows what would have happened? Or they would have, you know . . . And I had seen instances, you know, where guys were getting dragged out of their cars, you know, for stuff. So I was like, "Aw, man. You know, I got kids." You know, I went with them, and I had my son—no, I didn't have my son with me. You know, I was like, "Aw, look, man, you know, I got kids, and I'm not this guy y'all are after, you know. Look, you know, my car's way different than his, you know. I'm coming to you straight up, you know." He's like, "All right, all right." They—he was cool, you know. It tripped me out. I would think, like, "Nah, you know what." But, I mean, he understood, and after that, you know, they straightened it out, so I was like, [laughs] "All right." But, I mean, I was sc—I didn't even want to go out, 'cause, like I said, I just didn't want to run into the wrong person and just—they think I'm someone else and just take it out on me. But it was a trip, you know, that was—that all that happened.

《 》

"They ain't got shit," one of the new members told me as we watched a Just Cruzin car roll by in traffic. "It's all nothing but factory." "Factory" meant that the cars were not customized. Worse than factory was a car that had been customized clumsily or with poor aesthetic effect, like another Cruzer's beat-up Olds Omega, which had decorative, nonfunctional exhaust pipes on the sides. While the Kings whom I was hanging around with at the park spoke disparagingly of the Cruzers' vehicles, they did so as if noting a character flaw. This ran parallel to subdivisions of class and the relative expense of modifications. The Cruzers "flew" their club logo on a window sticker, while the Kings flew metal plaques that had been dipped in chrome or gold.

The tension between the two clubs, which festered throughout my research period, also intensified around a Romeo-and-Juliet-style romance between a young man affiliated with the Kings and a woman whose brother was in the Cruzers. Several club officers among the Kings spoke often about the need to "squash that shit." The Cruzers were not exclusively culpable for the bad blood, however. One week when they kept rolling by where the Kings were posted up, Raymond bounced up and down like a boxer in his corner, saying, "I'm ready, I'm ready." He and Smiley then grabbed plaques and stood on the curb, holding them above their heads while the Cruzers did their signature honking routine. As the night went on, the clubs kept a wary eye on each other. Later I walked up to a conversation as Raymond was relating the drama he had had with them the week before. He and his brother had run into Cruzers who made some comments about the King who was dating the Cruzer's sister. I didn't catch all the details, but apparently at some point, they "stepped to" Raymond's brother or Raymond, who started to "talk noise" as well, with Raymond's brother eventually saying, "Fuck you, motherfucker," to a Cruzer. The Cruzer started to talk a lot about how hard he was, how he had been shot and stabbed. The situation escalated until some cars from a club friendly with the Kings showed up and evened the sides enough to deter a fight through mutually assured destruction. Raymond said then they were all shouting, "[Just Cruzin] sucks!" as the Cruzers drove away.

Such drama gave expression to an existing rivalry between the clubs, but it hardly rose to the blood-feud level implied in the notion of a gang conflict. Paradoxically, lowriders seemed bound by an ethos to stand up for themselves and yet not to let things get out of hand, so as to avoid being branded as troublemakers. The intensely competitive lowrider scene could be a catalyst or instigator of drama. Jimmy, the veterano I chatted with once in a while in the park, pointed out a young black man in a '63 Impala one evening and said, "That's a troublemaker right there. He got in a hell of a fight last night." I asked what the issue was, and Jimmy said, "Somebody thought their car was better than his." Competition formed tensions between individuals as well as clubs. Thus, contestation over criminality is a matter not only of lowriders relations with the police but also of relations between and among lowriders themselves.

《 》

It was the first time I was ever scared at the park. We were standing in our usual place, and the two women who had been riding around with Aaron were crossing the parking lot. They were in front of a stopped truck, so it was hard to see them from the other way, and a nondescript white car came peeling out to pass the truck from maybe thirty yards off. When the two stepped out from in front of the truck, the white car hit the brakes, squealing to a stop. The driver let them pass and then floored it again and raced to the edge of the lot. The driver had a shaved head and no shirt, and was slumped forward, leaning on his seat belt.

The car was some early-1990s compact. One of the taillights had been patched together with transparent red tape in order to pass inspection. He paused at the edge of the lot and peeled out again out of there.

Everyone around me got quiet when this car came racing through. Eddie soon started complaining, though. "Where are the laws now? They come through telling everyone to park straight, and then when this happens, where the laws now? Sonofabitches!" The curse could have been directed at the police—"the laws"—or at the driver. Eddie's anger underscored the threat that had been posed by a stranger acting unpredictably—a loose cannon.

A little later, I was talking to a rapper named Chaz, who was walking through the park to sell his CDs, when the white car came back through, again peeling out and racing through the tight space of the lot. The driver was leaning over even more and mad-dogging like crazy. He stared intently at people around him, but since no one would maintain eye contact, he kept looking around for somebody else to stare at. As he came by, I also lowered my eyes and didn't look at him. He pulled up behind a truck that was stopped on the way out of the lot, with a booming system and two people riding in the bed. The guy in the white car stared at the people in the back, dancing to the music with exaggerated motions as if mocking it, but without laughing, just staring like an insane person. The truck pulled out, and the white car peeled out again.

Chaz said gravely, "That's a killer right there. That fool's just looking for something to start. A lot of people's killers out here, but most of them, you have to mess with them for them to mess with you. He's just ready for any little thing. I don't even talk to people like that to sell them a CD. Or I talk to them just real quick, and then cut out across the park. Turn around, they're like, 'Where's that nigga go?' Like this—" he did a quick sidestep around the corner of a car, like a running back evading a tackle. "That's how you got to move out here sometimes."

《 》

At a meeting, Eddie had made a speech about how he wanted the club to have nothing to do with Just Cruzin. "If you're at Pizza Hut and they show up," he said, "I don't care if you've been there two hours: leave." In fact, there had been some talk about moving the cruising back to South Congress, which had been the cruising spot some years before, because Riverside was getting too "hot" with police and the Cruzers. Several people were talking about a rumor that somebody from the Cruzers ("And this is a *car club*," Eddie interrupted to emphasize) had shot a member of Clique 182 in the head the night before. Clique 182 was the name of one of the long-established gangs in town, many members of which had been locked up in a recent police sting. If the rumor of a killing was true, it seemed that the Cruzers were trying to gain recognition as a gang in their own right, or at least as something more aggressive than a car club. Smiley pointed out that Clique 182 members might be out to retaliate, another indication that anyone cruising should take care.

Another week, I headed out to Riverside from home. I caught a glimpse of Raymond's car at Pizza Hut and made my way back. Only Raymond and Steve were there, with a guy from the Stylistic Syndicate. Steve's little boy Andre, about four years old, was there in the Blazer. I greeted them, shook hands with Steve and Raymond, and noticed that Raymond's girlfriend, Ceci, was sitting in the passenger seat of his car with the windows rolled up, playing the stereo. Bass hummed out of the trunk. We stood around watching traffic and talking. The lot was pretty empty other than us. A little crowd of four or five people was up at the back of the lot around a Euro compact.

Steve had been on his cell phone when I arrived. "What's up . . . This is [Steve] . . . no, [Steve] . . . White Boy." Steve finally identified himself with the nickname by which he was commonly but not rudely known. "Where you at?" he spoke into the phone. "Yeah, for real? Who's all out there?" Steve turned to Raymond. "They're at the Pinky's up there at Congress. Everybody's there; he's naming a whole list right now." Then back to the phone: "Yeah? Well we're waiting to meet Eddie [. . .] I guess we'll head over there when they get here."

It was past midnight. A Buick Regal pulled slowly into the lot. I could see the sticker on the rear window: LowTimez. Eddie's brother was in that club—it was on good terms with the Kings. The car was not radically customized, but impeccably clean. Raymond called over to his car: "[Ceci]!" He nodded, and she hit one of the hydraulics switches. The front of the MC leaped once, as if taking note of the Regal. Those of us standing outside laughed; Ceci looked bored. The driver of the Buick slowed to a creeping roll and answered the MC's hop by hitting his pop trunk. The lid slowly rose to reveal glowing blue neon tubes running down each side of the trunk. The large mirror lining the lid presented a view of the spare wheel, a chrome, thirteen–inch, bolt-on spoke, like the other wheels on the car. The car stopped, and a short, solid man with a shaved head stepped out. He greeted everyone and shook hands.

"See those laws up there?" Steve pointed up the hill toward the parking lot of another business. "When you came in popping the trunk, they got out of their cars." The two police cars were parked on the side of the street, partially concealed in a shadow. Raymond turned back to his car, signaled to Ceci to lower the window, and stuck his head in to speak to her. She touched a button on the dash, and the bass emanating from the trunk ceased. The song continued without the lowest-end frequencies. We waited for the police to approach, but they never came.

A Euro went screaming down Riverside. "Oh, they don't go after *him*," said Steve. But one of the officers made his way to the car and started it up. He pulled up to Riverside, paused at the stop, and headed out almost casually after the Euro. I wondered whether the cops opt not to chase street racers sometimes because they know they can't catch them and don't want to look foolish.

The other officer had moved on by the time Just Cruzin showed up. One of their Euros pulled into the Pizza Hut, and Steve said, "Here they are." The sticker logo covered most of the rear window: "Just Cruzin."

Raymond turned to look and swore: "Shit." He reached for the front pocket in his baggy jeans and pulled out a utility knife, the folding lock-blade kind that many lowriders carried routinely and that I had seen used to cut coolant hoses and birthday cake. He emphatically flicked it open and crossed his arms, tucking the blade away under his armpit so it was hidden. The first Cruzer car parked across the lot where the Euro had been waiting. The new car opened, and a woman and young boy got out and leaned against the fender. Next came a couple of more Euros and the Olds Omega. Steve tried to keep the mood light, speaking through a nervous smile as if half joking: "Shit, man, we better go, or we'll get in trouble with [Eddie]." Andre was asleep in the Blazer.

Raymond said, "Man, fuck [Eddie]." He stuck the knife back in his pocket and started to pace, taking another look at the Cruzers, and then took off his navy blue, embroidered Custom Kings T-shirt. Underneath he was wearing a white tank undershirt. He carefully rolled up the club T-shirt and held it in a small bundle in his hand. He shifted his weight from one foot to the other, glancing up at the gathering crowd of Cruzers, then put the shirt in the car. Ceci didn't say a word or move from the passenger seat.

More and more Cruzers were arriving, and Steve got Eddie on the phone: "Where you at?" Eddie and Albert were washing their rides at a car wash on Oltorf, some distance from Riverside. We decided to go join them. Leaving the situation with a sense of purpose besides retreat seemed to relax Raymond a little, and he asked me almost cheerfully, "Ben, you going to follow us?" I said yeah, and we went.

The tension of that standoff gradually dissipated in the course of the night. Later, after the club regrouped and was cruising around in various combinations, Raymond and I ended up riding in Aaron's car—Ceci had gone home. Aaron put in a CD that I would later learn was by the Memphis rapper Project Pat, and tapped the volume button until his speakers were hitting hard with a slow, dirty southern jam: the beat was composed of low, syncopated bass hits and sixteenth-note subdivisions on the high hat. The bass rang like a fat, heavy bell, spreading a layer of sound outward and setting off a sympathetic vibration in one of the windows. Project Pat rapped, "Y'all niggas ain't no killas, / Y'all niggas some hos." Raymond draped one arm on the open window and bobbed his head to the music.

Both the assertion of killing as a manifestation of agency and the emasculation of one's foes as "hos," or whores, conform closely to what Pancho McFarland describes as a violent form of patriarchal masculinity that pervades the street culture he identifies with Chicano rap music (McFarland 2008, 15; see also hooks 2003). There can be little doubt that in "feeling" the music, Raymond was embracing and taking some pleasure or reassurance in a construction of violent masculinity that McFarland ties also to the rejection of femininity as a sign of weakness. Chicano nationalism, among other theories of liberatory politics, has at times fallen into a similar kind of dichotomy by gendering resistance as a form of masculinity, a move justified by some as countering the emasculation of Chicanos through their colonization by Anglos. Subsequent critical work by Chicana and queer scholars has taken this stance of resistant masculinity apart and imagined more thoroughly liberating futures through the refusal of received or essentialized gender roles. These crucial theoretical moves were not in wide circulation in lowrider space, but that is not to suggest that the destabilization of gender represents an elite exercise inevitably distanced from popular everyday experience. On the contrary, there is evidence that gender categories can become malleable on the street as well.

A small but significant example of this is documented in Norma Mendoza-Denton's work with Latina gang members in Los Angeles, who appropriated the concept of "macho" to describe themselves, albeit with the feminine ending—hence, "*macha*." As one of the young women told her, "When I wear my eyeliner *me siento más macha* [I feel more macha], I'm ready to fight!" (2008, 154).

Decoupled from a body sexed in a particular way, "macha" for these young women stands for characteristics of defending territory and "taking care of business," both aspects of the "traditional" notion of "macho" as a specific construction of masculinity. Mendoza-Denton argues that the appropriation of attitudes or behaviors hitherto considered masculine actually works to defend the young women against the long-term "social injury" associated with sociological correlates of gang involvement (154).

While this does not disprove McFarland's suggestion that violent masculinity is claimed in the rejection of weak femininity (for this may be precisely what macha women are doing), it does open the possibility that some of the appeal of a macho/a pose lies in an experience common to the men and women who adopt it, rather than in an interest in proclaiming, accentuating, and maintaining their differences. Indeed, I propose that in both examples, Raymond and the female gang members depicted by Mendoza-Denton, Latinos/as embraced what resembles a particular version of masculinity out of an engagement with their setting, as much as anything. That version, expressed as "taking care of business," is performed in an assertive stance of survival in a hostile context. The tragedy this poses for urban people of color occurs when such a stance manifests as belligerence toward others in a similar situation, who, apart from also adopting their own "macho/a" postures, have no direct culpability in what makes their circumstances hostile. Moreover, this articulation of violence and gender is compounded by a more general cultural context in which patriarchal masculinity is viewed as a source of power even as everyday experience informs people of color that the state cannot be depended on to "serve and protect" them and, hence, is vacant as a source of personal security.

A capacity for violence, as well as the ruthless will to exercise it, as performed by the "killer" who was mad-dogging in the park, is a script that forms part of the cultural repertoire that both gang members and their nongang neighbors share as part of a certain local barriological imaginary. But that is not to say that anyone involved in street culture on any level is therefore necessarily bound by the script. Indeed, Austin lowriders' ascription of fighting to an immature stage of personal development suggested the possibility of change.

Moreover, if machismo is in part a principle of self-defense in response to hostile circumstances, it is not the only imaginable response. A macho/a stance presents an individual ethos for survival in urban street culture, but a collective alternative lies in solidarity, the pact of mutual support and defense among fellow club members. Expressed as "having one another's backs," solidarity

natural
for group

is another overlap between gang members and lowriders. The bonds between gang members are the source of both their strength and their threat to a society steeped in ideologies of individualism and self-reliance. A passionate and even self-destructive devotion to the larger whole of the clique or barrio is a stereo-typed characteristic of a gang member. Perhaps to hold this specific character-istic or its criminal consequences at a distance, lowriders most often cast the value of solidarity in terms of familialism. Gloria told me, as others had, that lowriding was a "family thing," but then she reconsidered, saying that, in fact, the car club was more devoted than a family. As an example, she told of a time that Beto's vehicle had broken down some distance from home. Club members came to pick him up and, at the same time, spotted him the money to buy a replacement part. She said, "I know my family wouldn't do that."

Criminal Spaces

Performances of gender and criminality were tied to space in the sense that they dealt in and engaged barriology, but that is not to say that they reproduced entrenched scripts inevitably. By drawing a connection to context, I mean to complicate the notion of criminal behavior, showing such practices to be en-tangled in the production and reproduction of their contexts. In the question of who was to be categorized as criminal and whose claim to being "positive" would be recognized, behavior mattered only to a degree. For all the effort that Austin lowriders put into disclaiming gang affiliation, individual behavior and commitments were in some ways less relevant to police than location. This re-lated to an emerging cartographic approach to policing in which certain areas were identified as sites of potentially criminal activity, what the APD termed "hot spots" (see Chappell 2010). In turn, this spatial identity mapped a prob-able criminality onto its occupants. The "algebra of probability" (Nichols 1994, 35) of an emergent actuarial approach to policing, conjoined with the infamous "driving while Mexican" kind of racial profiling, resulted in a science of crimi-nal places within which people were presumed to be likely offenders.

Such "hot spots" of crime were defined in public discourse about policing partly by arrest statistics for different crimes, but were also identified by patrol officers and citizens, including the city manager. Hot spots could be identified as much by areas where crime was expected to occur as by actual incidents. Lowriders also used the term "hot spot," without referring to the police usage of the term. For instance, Mario employed a discourse similar to that of the Austin Police Department in an interview to explain the common knowledge that lowriders get pulled over by the police disproportionately. Unlike most lowriders I spoke with, Mario was not ready to say that they were targeted only because of their cars, but instead pointed out: "Where we cruise at's a hot spot anyway. It's nothing but nightclubs. Going cruising you should expect to be pulled over. They're looking for drunk people."

This profiling was part of a wider history of attempts to regulate lowrider cruising and other forms of social automobility elsewhere. The 1979 release of the film *Boulevard Nights*, a fictional film that centers on the lowrider cruising scene of Whittier Boulevard in Los Angeles, caused some concern about the glorification of gang culture in East LA. In the same kind of preemptive moral panic about urban youth crime that later greeted the release of the film *Boyz n the Hood* (1991), police shut down cruising on Whittier the weekend before *Boulevard Nights* was released. Roberto Rodríguez, a photographer for *Lowrider Magazine*, witnessed police attacks on someone he took to be an innocent bystander. Rodríguez took pictures of the violent arrests, and was attacked and arrested in his turn, charged with assaulting an officer with a deadly weapon—his 35 mm camera.[9]

In his memoir *Assault with a Deadly Weapon*, reprinted in his book *Race: A Question of Justice*, Rodríguez details the criminalization of a population defined by its participation in the cruising on Whittier, which was taken to be coterminous with the racio-cultural-spatial complex of an East LA identity. When the boulevard was closed to cruising, anyone caught driving in the area was considered suspect, a "potential violator." Rodríguez claims that the perceived gang threat, rather than acting as a motivation in its own right, was a rationale for police intervention in the spatial organization of the city, displacing but not eliminating the actual threat: "Many were saying they wanted to close the Boulevard down because of the violence, but the truth is, those that wanted the Boulevard closed were not interested in curbing the violence—all they were really interested in was moving the violence away from the Boulevard" (1997, 28). The use of a cruising scene as the focus for displacing a population and remapping space resembles a form of spatial governmentality (Chappell 2006b, 2010; Merry 2001) that was emergent during my fieldwork. Under this form of governmentality, the charge that "deviant" bodies be disciplined into orderly behavior was replaced by measures that both defined the boundaries of public spaces to which self-governing citizens would have access and designated which populations, deemed undesirable, were exceptions to "the public" and so were to be "moved on" or excluded.

José recalled cruising Chicano Park "back in the day," the 1980s, when there was something of a "peace structure" between lowriders and the police, an understanding that Chicano Park was a place for lowriding.[10] Police controlled the situation, but also afforded lowriders a chance to use the space, even if not everyone conformed to the squeaky-clean standard of a "positive' car club.

ha!

> Like I said, back then, you know, the cops were there. But it was just, you
> know, no one did nothing. That's all it was about, just cruising, checking
> everybody out. And then in Chicano Park, you know, we used to go park,
> and, you know, we were drinking. And then, it was nothing, you know,
> the cops just drive by. And if they did stop us, it was just, I mean, if they
> did come up to us, it was just to check our, you know, checking out IDs,
> but hey, we're all—you know, we're all over the age, so they didn't do
> nothing to us. You know, I mean, that's how, you know—they had their
> spot, they stayed there, ten o'clock, they started, you know, they turned
> on their lights, but everyone knew, oh, hey, it's time to go. You know, we
> all left, and that was it.

This arrangement was shattered by a rise in visible gang activity in the mid-1980s, represented by an event that José described to me as the "Easter Day shootout," in which lowriders found themselves caught in the crossfire between rival gangs.

> Yeah, it was like '86 I think? [. . .] 'Cause I know now with the Internet, I
> was trying to find out—if I could find out, like, in the archives and stuff
> in the newspaper? And it was on a Easter, that's how I remember, it was
> on a Easter over there at Chicano Park. Fiesta Gardens? And then that's
> when the [Familia] and [Clique 182] had that big shootout. I mean, it,
> you know, it was on the news, they, you know, tore up people's cars, and
> . . . 'cause my daughter—I trip out on [the fact that] my daughter remem-
> bers that. And she was little—she was like five, six years old, and she
> remembers, um, 'cause I used to take them with me. You know, Friday,
> Saturday nights we'd meet down on Sixth Street, you know, with all my
> friends in the car club. Sundays I took them with me, we went to the park,
> 'cause, you know, it was a park. Go park, you know, my kids play with my
> friends' kids, you know. And that day, I mean, you know, my kids were
> with me that day, and, uh, these two friends of mine, both of them took

off, when they saw this was going on, you know, her car was parked at
the front, you know, we're all lined up. You know, they grabbed my kids,
took 'em in her car, and she just took off, you know. And we were stuck
there behind our cars, you know, guys just going back and forth, man,
just capping at each other.

José related this traumatic event in the history of the Eastside to more stringent
regulation of the use of the park by the city and the police:

They started putting up the, you know, the NO PARKING signs, they
started putting up the—the . . . open container . . . signs . . . you know,
cops started showing up on horses, you know, that way they look into
your car and see what you're doing, and . . . and after that is when it just,
you know? [. . .] That's when they started blocking the street off. We used
to park behind the Texaco, you know, we—both sides. You know, that's
where people used to go against each oth—you know, start hopping on
each other, but, you know, they started putting up the NO PARKING signs
all along there, and . . . I mean, that's—you know, they just started cutting
down on everything. And that's when I stopped.

As a result of heightened surveillance and spatial controls, the cruising scene
was curtailed by intimidation and dislocation. José went on to describe lowriders' attempts to rekindle the cruising scene since the 1980s, without reaching
the scale of participation that had gone on before:

They started up again, but, you know, the cops are out there like that. So
it lasts, like, maybe an hour, two hours. But, you know, back then, I tell
them, you know, six to ten? Psh. Four-five blocks, you know, *lined*. Just
people just trying to go through the park. You know, check each other
out—that's all it was. [. . .] Sixth Street, too. I mean . . . we used to cruise
down Sixth Street, and we used to be all the way up to, like, that Texaco
on the other side of IH-35, where the line would start of people going
down through Sixth Street.

If the newer cruising did not live up to the nostalgia of veterans of "back in the
day" like José, this was a matter not only of reduced numbers, but also of a new
mobility necessitated by the police running off crowds of lowriders that got too
big or stayed too long in a place.

I went Sunday 'cause I didn't have my kids with me. And I went to Fiesta
Gardens 'cause my friend had told me, "Yeah, man, they're going out
there." So we went Sun—I went Sunday. But it wasn't Fiesta Gardens, it
was the—there's a small parking lot on the side of a football field. And
that's where the—I mean, it was packed, and the line started up way back
here. I was like, "All right, all right." But then I looked, and there you go,
the cops started going through the grass, started blocking off, like, where
people are driving around in circles. And so, you know, they started
rerouting traffic, and I saw, like, four cars in front of me, and I'm like,
"I wonder where these guys are going." So I followed them. Everybody
headed down to Pleasant Valley, right near the baseball fields, to the
parking lot.

The vibrant cruising scene José remembered from earlier times was only just
beginning to be reproduced in new locations before the police moved in to
disperse the crowd and cut off the circuit, the "driving around in circles." The
cruising scene thus shifted from site to site according to the dynamic with the
police.

Yeah, everybody I saw over there ended up over here. And again, I think
all it was, was they were trying to stay, like, one step ahead of the cops.
'Cause I was there like a good hour before the cops started showing
up over here. But within that hour, man, you know, when I drove in, I
parked. I mean, I just started seeing guys you know *going*. There was a
Cadillac doing 360s while doing three-wheel. You know, there was two—a
Monte Carlo and a four-door Buick Regal started hopping on each other,
and I was like, yeah, this is what I remember, you know from back—you
know, we could do all that. With no problems, no hassles. So, you know,
everybody just started parking, just started showing up, and I know some
guys started turning up their systems, you know, like, going against each
other. It's like, "Yeah." But then, you know, again, here come the cops.

Community Policing and Taco Plates

In the spring of 2000, the Austin Police Department held a series of public
townhall meetings to present the public with the new "community policing"
model that had been official policy for almost a year, and to hear feedback
from constituents as part of that program. The meetings were held in a highly

charged political context stemming from a series of controversies involving the police department over the last five years. The trial of LaCresha Murray, an eleven-year-old African American girl who was charged in 1996 with the murder of a two-year-old toddler, brought countercharges that Murray's confession had been coerced by police officers when she was isolated and intimidated in their custody, an issue that mobilized a high-profile, statewide protest movement and led to the case being dismissed in court. Meanwhile, funds were being distributed from the settlement of the so-called Cedar Avenue case (1995), in which police forcibly broke up a party attended by black teenagers in East Austin, leading to a lawsuit for police brutality. Also, prosecution in the so-called Yogurt Shop murders, a 1991 case in which four teenage girls were murdered, was being hampered by allegations that a police officer had held a gun to the head of a suspect during questioning. A police officer named Samuel Ramírez was charged with soliciting oral sex from a civilian in 1999 while on duty and wearing his gun. Although he was later convicted, the case sparked protest, since the charge was not rape but "official oppression." Nationally publicized cases of police violence, such as the slaying of Amadou Diallo in New York City in 1999, brought added attention to deaths and injuries of suspects in APD custody.[11] All these controversies were in the public view during the renegotiation of the police officers' union contract, a process that led to a movement for a civilian oversight commission.[12]

While not a direct response to these events, the public meetings in spring of 2000 were part of a hegemonic process to win political support for the police department and foster solidarity between officers and civilians. Community policing itself was much more than a public-relations effort, and with its new policies, the department joined a trend that had been applied widely elsewhere for more than ten years. Nevertheless, public relations were necessary to the extent that the new policy depended on a degree of trust between officers and civilians, and there was reason to believe that establishing such a relationship might pose a challenge, especially in East Austin.

The public introduction of community policing included, besides town-hall meetings, publications and even trading cards aimed at children. To get a sense for how this was being received, I attended several of the meetings in different neighborhoods, including a relatively affluent middle-class area in northwest Austin with a population that included a lot of Asian immigrants and Asian Americans (though the meeting was attended almost exclusively by whites); the working-class, predominately black northeast Austin; and the mainly working-class, Mexican American Eastside.[13]

The meetings varied markedly in tone at the different locations, and this coincided with a shifting definition of "community." When the dialogue was fairly consensual in tone, such as at the northwest Austin meeting, the definition of community was unproblematically identified with the civilians in attendance. Where this consensus was not assumed to exist, such as at the northeast Austin meeting, it highlighted how certain issues were excluded from a citywide category of public concerns and treated as merely private, local, or neighborhood matters; although these were precisely the issues of concern to those in attendance, they were not necessarily central to the APD's agenda for the meeting. Furthermore, even when there was a sense of shared identification with a notion of community, which there was at the Eastside meeting, the discourse was haunted by references to persons not present, who were being tacitly defined out of "the community" yet who inhabited and claimed as home the spaces under discussion.

The meetings were ostensibly intended to bring the police and civilians together, but the two constituencies sometimes worked at cross-purposes as officers tried to explain the new community-policing program, and civilians tried to air grievances or otherwise be heard. The balance between these competing interests was structured very differently in different places. In northwest Austin, for example, questions from the public tended to be about details of police programs and how those programs responded specifically to the interests of the local community, as represented by those residents who had shown up. In contrast, the dialogue was much more charged in the northeast Austin and Eastside meetings, the most general subtext being the question "why are we not being served?" In the Eastside barrio, a time limit of three minutes a question was announced; in the predominately black Northeast side, there was both a time limit and a limit of two questions a person. I recall no such limits being enforced in the northwest Austin meeting.

Although the three meetings had very different atmospheres, several common themes emerged. First was an emphasis on the notion that community policing depended on partnerships with the community. Underlying this discussion was the recurring theme of surveillance as a spatial tactic of citizen participation in the community-policing program. For example, at the northwest meeting, when an officer spoke of the need for civilian-police partnerships, he mentioned corporations like the local cable TV and telephone companies as partners. At first I understood this as a reference to corporate sponsorship, but then he mentioned that "they're our eyes and ears." This implied that the need for civilian involvement in community policing was, at least in part, related to constitutional limits on official and electronic forms of surveillance.[14] Surveillance by both police and civilians was presented as a means of evaluating crime levels in a particular area—or more generally, with respect to a category of quality-of-life issues that I will discuss below—a place's overall health or quality. Officers invited civilians to join in this specular evaluation. When someone asked how the police know whether they are doing a good job, an officer said that they could know that by noticing "who's out walking on the street": "Is it the drug dealers? Or is it people sending their kids across the street for milk?"

The northeast neighborhood and Eastside meetings seemed to represent the opposite of the consensual feel of the northwest Austin meeting as an evaluation of a public institution by its loyal constituency. East of the highway, there was less talk by the police of trying to recruit "partners." On the contrary, the civilians in attendance, who seemed to be already quite practiced in surveillance (whether as agents or objects thereof), often angrily confronted the police about criminal activity that they had witnessed but that had not been, they thought, suitably addressed by the police. At the same time, African Americans and Mexican Americans spoke of the experience of being objects of surveillance as the victims of profiling.

Eastsiders demonstrated that they were very much aware of their area's reputation as a hot spot of crime, and at times did so with humor. An apparently Latina woman from a homeowner's association said she was from New Mexico, but that Austin was the first place she had lived without being arrested. She said that the meeting was not the night for problems, but for thanks. She specifically wanted to thank Jovita Lopez, a local sergeant. She also gestured toward the crowd and said, "It's good to see some white folks in East Austin . . . We haven't killed anyone in twenty-four hours!" Many of those attending the meetings were apparently prepared to join the panoptic apparatus of community policing. Yet what often went unsaid was what, exactly, the partners were supposed to look for when serving as the "eyes and ears" of the police. Another theme addressed this obliquely by enumerating the quality-of-life issues with which the community was supposed to be concerned.

As I walked into the town-hall meeting at the North Austin Christian Church, a discussion was already underway. A middle-aged white man asked about the junk vehicle "problem," stating that there was a "backlog" of vehicles to be confiscated—some 2,500—and that this was a "huge problem citywide, especially east of I-35." His concern was for the "quality of communities," and he wanted to get volunteers involved in the seizure of the cars. The police said no: all that citizens could do on that matter was to volunteer information.

After the meeting, I approached the man who was concerned about abandoned vehicles. I asked him about "the problem." He said that he lived in central East Austin, where he had some investment property, and that the problem of broken-down cars was really getting bad: "There will be some lots with twenty cars on them." I asked him whether those were residences, and he said yes: "The way it works is when your car breaks down, park it and leave it. It's really affecting the quality of life." He said that the junked vehicles attract rats and give them "channels," and that the old trunks latch easily without an inside catch to release them, so "it's really getting dangerous for the kids, it's really a health hazard." But then he came to the crux of the matter: "The main thing is, it makes property values go down." I asked him about his investment, and he said he owned a duplex just south of the golf course in the Martin Luther King neighborhood.[15]

At the Eastside meeting, a new officer stepped up to talk about the state of the neighborhood. "Claims" had dropped in drive-by shootings, and the new issue was "boom boxes." Right when he said that, a car rolled past the rec center with a stereo thumping. Everyone laughed about that one. Also of concern were, again, "junk vehicles" and prostitution: "That's what the community is concerned about." It was a peculiar moment: at a meeting for the airing of community concerns about police matters, a police officer was reporting to civilians what the concerns of the community were.

The "junk cars" and "boom boxes" named as threats to the quality of life and as possible markers of a crime-ridden "hot spot" might be exactly the "parts cars" and "systems" that, for lowriders, were part of a positive quality of life. More importantly, lowriders were implicitly excluded from the community because of the way that police pullovers interpellate lowriders as members of a criminal—or at least suspect—group.

This continuing stigma of criminality clashed with personal relationships between lowriders and police that might have provided the social material for a "partnership," as José narrated while talking about cruising in the park.

> **JOSÉ:** But, it's—and it's funny, too, 'cause we know cops now, too, you know, have some friends, that are, are officers. And again, they would tell—'cause we went to Chicano Park one time in my mother's car. And they, a cop came up behind us, but it was somebody we knew. He knew my son. And he saw

my son, he—but he put the lights on, he pulled—right in front—right in the
middle of Fiesta Gardens, you know, pulled us over. And then, you know
how two-three cops show up? Well, he was talking to me like he was thinking
about throwing a [custom car] show. So he was calling his buddies, it was, you
know, three police cars pull up, all these guys get out, and we're in the car. But
they're just talking to us about, "Yeah, man, we're thinking about doing this,"
and my daughter's like [*stage whisper*], "Dad! Tell these guys to take us somewhere!" You know, like, everybody's just like, "Man, what's going on? They got
this dude surrounded!" But, I mean, people just automatically thought, you
know, there's something going on. My friends come up, "Hey, man, what's going on? What's going on?" It's like, "No, man, you know we know them," It's
like, "No, man, you know, we thought they were doing this," or "We thought
something was going to happen, man," you know. So I was like, "No, man."
And one guy had a video camera: "Yeah, we're going to videotape it in case he
did anything to you." I was like, "No, man, you know?" But it's, it's—I know
how they feel, you know. It's just, it has gotten—and to me thinking, you know
there's not that many gangs, as much. And to be thinking that stuff like that
still goes on. It's worse, I guess, than it was when I was around.

BEN: You mean in terms of the police?

JOSÉ: Yeah, in terms of the cops messing with us. So it—like I said, I didn't
know it was that bad now. It trips me out that it's still around. I guess there
are a lot of people that are into drugs and stuff that are driving lowriders, but
it's not—and I have friends at work, too, they just think those are bad people.
And when they found—you know, when I started working there, that's the
first thing they thought. Well, a Mexican with a earring, you know, he's a gang
member.

A lieutenant gave a PowerPoint presentation on Operation Rock-Out, a four-
month undercover operation that had netted fifty-eight arrests of drug dealers.
It targeted various areas in East Austin (for example, 1900 Rosewood, Twelfth
and Chicon, Fourteenth and Chestnut, Seventh and Prospect), and, the lieutenant reported with some evident pride, had resulted higher-than-usual bonds.
The program used "high-profile interdiction," an approach of stopping and
identifying anyone "out there" in the targeted area. The assumption was that
"after a certain time, they're up to no good" in that area. The lieutenant's presentation concluded with a projected image of a perpetrator who could have

been a cholo (marked by his plaid flannel shirt and shaved head) being put in a prowl car.

《 》

"What, there's only four people here with hair?" Somebody made the comment from within a crowd of twenty-five to thirty people gathered early on a Saturday evening in the grocery-store parking lot on Riverside. Sure enough, it was a regular cholo convention, shaved heads and baggy T-shirts in abundance. Most of the Kings were there, along with Lito, several of the Stylistic Syndicate, and some people I had seen before but did not know. When I parked and walked up to the group, I heard one of the Syndicate members talking about fajita meat, the price difference between premarinated and plain. Plans were underway for a "taco plate" benefit picnic.

Taco plates were routine events on the Eastside and a popular means of fund-raising for some cause, such as a neighbor's or friend's hospital bills. People would cook a large amount of food on a given day, then distribute hand-lettered signs advertising an affordable hot lunch, maybe five dollars for a plate. The Kings, who regularly held car washes to raise money for club expenses, had decided with some friends that it would help the lowriders' image to conduct a public charity project, something they had done before by adopting a family at Christmastime. With the idea that public good works might improve traffic encounters with the police, the lowriders were approaching the APD as a possible beneficiary. The department, already connected with numerous charities around town, would be in a position to distribute a sum raised by the taco plate to deserving organizations. Eventually, someone came up with the idea of contributing the taco plate proceeds to a fund benefitting families of officers killed in the line of duty. That option was freighted with particular importance, and some club members speculated that directly contributing to the APD's own charity would benefit everyone in the cruising scene.

After the meeting, Steve was skeptical. "See, it ain't going to make a difference."

Eddie responded, "It won't matter to all of them. It might not matter to the chief, but to one or two, it might matter. And when one of them loses a buddy, so they're getting the benefit of the money, it's like, 'Hey, I appreciate what you're doing.' But it ain't about changing the whole APD. It's about us. About the community, and coming together to do something positive. It might not make a difference to APD. But it makes a difference here." He tapped a finger on Steve's chest, over his heart. "Because you know you're good. You know you're not out shooting people. And so we want to show the community that lowriders ain't about that."

Members of several clubs debated fajita meat or ground beef, crispy tacos or soft. Some members of the Syndicate had relatives who owned a restaurant and could provide steam tables and the food-service license that would allow the clubs to set up on an afternoon in the park. Eddie asked whether their supplier could provide shredded lettuce, recalling the convenience of that product from when he worked at the Motorola cafeteria.

I arrived at the park for the benefit about nine in the morning or so, with two pots of pinto beans as my contribution. The Stylistic Syndicate members' cousin accepted my pots and dumped them into a large pan already simmering on the steam table set up on the grass near the shelter house. There was a canopy set up that Eddie had gotten from his boss for free because it had a small tear in the tarp. It was a good-sized structure with an aluminum-tube frame. Eddie planned to put the feet into cement at his house and park his car under it. For now, it made an excellent temporary shelter. One of the Syndicate members confirmed that the food-service license could be called up if anybody questioned the legality of selling plates. Club members respected this by running the outside operation like a restaurant. A huge cooler full of ice was dedicated to keeping the lettuce cold. They poured off the grease from the meat periodically and hauled it away to the restaurant for disposal. Everyone handling food wore rubber gloves, and nobody with gloves handled money (Figure 5.1).

With serving supposed to begin about eleven, at ten fifteen I took a bunch of tickets and walked over to the pool, where there was a swim meet of tiny kids going on. I approached everyone I saw and told them, "Folks, we're having a taco plate benefit over there to benefit families of APD officers killed in the line of duty. If you need some lunch, come on over. We're serving right over there behind you." Most people told me they were leaving soon, but at least two families eventually came by. I thought I might sell some tickets right there at the meet, but everyone said no or maybe.

A Suburban pulled up, and a man in a cowboy hat and belt buckle got out. He was greeted warmly: someone's cousin. He had called in an order for thirty plates for his workplace. On the assembly line, we worked fast. He loaded piles of Styrofoam containers in through the tailgate.

When things wound down in the afternoon, David of the Stylistic Syndicate counted the money: more than a thousand dollars. The police never showed up, nor did any press, nor any representative of the APD foundation. "Didn't you call them?" Aaron asked Eddie.

"Yeah, but nobody said they'd be here."

"Did you tell them what it was for?"

"Yeah, alls they did was give me an address where to send the check."

Tony was disgusted. "Sure, just send us the money—we want nothin' to do with y'all." Someone mentioned that we could donate the money elsewhere, and people agreed to meet before cruising the next Saturday at Albertson's parking lot to discuss it.

《 》

Weeks later, we gathered at a car wash that sat at the edge of a bluff overlooking Riverside. I hung around the edge of the parking lot with some of the Kings while we waited for the others to polish their rides. "Look at that law down there," said Lito, pointing to an unmarked Chevy Caprice sedan directly below us down a steep grade, parked beside a fast-food taco place. The car's windows were tinted almost completely black, making it impossible to see in.

Figure 5.1. An Eastside taco-plate benefit.

It was Memorial Day weekend, and Eddie had reminded us at the meeting to be careful. There would be a lot of police out, and a lot of drunks. If you are out at 2:00 when the bars start letting out, he had said, it is better just to wait to drive home rather than to share the road with drunk drivers. We cruised onto Riverside heading west and could see a lot of strobe lights ahead, a few blocks east of the highway. Seven police cars stood in the middle of the street, along with a paddy wagon and a van marked "Crime Scene Unit." Rows of orange traffic pylons marked out an area in the center turn lane. At first it looked like an accident, but no wrecks were evident.

We pulled into the parking lot at Club InSane and drove in a small circle around the lot, looking for familiar cars. Four police officers in black fatigues, combat boots, and T-shirts stood near the entrance of the club. We left the In-Sane lot and went to the bingo hall, pulling into a circle to discuss the situation through rolled-down windows. Nobody knew what was up with all the cops, but somebody said they were doing random sobriety checks. Aaron said what I was thinking: "Can they do that?" Nobody knew. Being posted up in the middle of Riverside, they were certainly going to cut down on cruising and import racing. I saw the white van rumored to carry the "jump-out boys," as Smiley called the special police unit, circle Club InSane.

There had been tension lately with the police, or rather, the tension had been escalating. There were rumors that the police had initiated a "zero tolerance" policy on cruising. Smiley said that when the Syndicate was at Pizza Hut the night before, the police came and told them all to get their IDs out and sit on the curb. The police then searched every car. Eddie said, "They can search our cars. They won't find anything." Albert countered this: "If they find my Glock, they won't be too happy." I was not sure whether he was joking about carrying a gun.

Smiley's cell phone rang just as I heard someone say, "Yeah, I saw the jump-out girls." The metaphorical emasculation of the SWAT team reflected the tension of the evening. The cat-and-mouse game was not just an annoyance that night, but felt more like the rumblings before a battle, and no one knew what might raise the stakes.

Smiley hung up his cell phone. "The jump-out boys are headed this way." We all got into our cars to move as the Low Intentions showed up, four club members that I recognized, though they were riding in a stock family sedan. We paused to say hello, but then took off without much delay.

Conclusion

One of the first lowriders I saw in person was a van that I later learned belonged to Chris, and it was covered on all surfaces with wild-style graffiti, rolling on the classic lowrider spoke rims that he would later put on his Skylark. It was the wheels that make me now recall that vehicle as a lowrider, though it was hardly the classic version that a '64 Impala would have been. The graffiti presented me, when I was just beginning to imagine myself as a would-be scholar of popular culture, with an instant allusion to the New York writers and their storied history of contesting public space on the medium of subway and elevated trains (Joe Austin 2001). It was this aesthetic recognition, occurring in a particular context—the heavily student-oriented blocks of Guadalupe Street that run past the University of Texas campus in Austin—that delivered a surge of excitement. The marked vehicle impressed me—registered its affects—not only because of the extent of its aestheticization, but also because of my intuitive sense that it had come from some other, nearby place and was charging into this one as an uninvited guest, one with the urgent message that it was here, like it or not.

My ethnographic engagement with lowriders has been a process of working out this experience and others like it that I engineered by cultivating relationships and doing a great deal of studied hanging out. In retrospect, this first encounter set me on a trajectory toward materialism, since it was not any textual information that produced the excitement I felt. This feeling returned as I learned where to go and how to look for a particularly rare or beautiful car, or one that betrayed that it was riding on hydraulics by the way it bounced over bumps in the road, indicating that it could at any moment bust out with a hop or three-wheel motion.

My efforts to contextualize and theorize these affects began with asking some of the perennial questions that haunt those who see the need for change in the world, and hence for political critique, and who harbor the kind of relationship to aesthetic forms and practices that leads them to hope that such things carried on "after the chores are done" matter. Such questions include the following: How do these things that move us matter? Do the practices that might be called "arts" or "expressive culture" primarily reflect the world, or do they provide instruments for molding it? Are they hand mirrors or small axes? To the last one, the answer one hopes for is that they are both. It was in trying to identify how I could understand a lowrider as being shaped by and at the same time influencing its context that I began to see cultural practice as a production of space.

Lowrider space is a fluid and mobile spatial field, anchored by one or more people in cars marked by their distinctive aesthetics. As aesthetic forms, lowrider cars and lowrider practices do not "express" or "reflect" Mexican American experience so much as they manifest a particular social position. As an event of spatial production, lowrider style generates Mexican American experience. The politics of such an act of aesthetic manifestation is determined less by the intentions of the car's owner and builder than by the forces and precedents that have constructed his or her social position, which is, in Marx's words, "inherited from the past." In other words, the appearance of lowriders in a setting where Mexican Americans have been driven out of town, their stories forgotten, their neighborhood moved, their language punished, and so on down the list of barrioizing events cannot help but be political. It follows that the affective politics of presence need not be clearly articulated or coherent in order to generate and deliver force.

Because lowriders in public space work on the spatial character, and hence the nature and function, of streets, parking lots, parks, and other kinds and scales of spaces, we can see that the politics of lowrider materiality lies in the way that it gives form to and refunctions a specific relation to social structures, or, in Benjamin's Marxian term, "the relation to the means of production"

(Benjamin 1978, 226). "Refunction" refers to *Umfunktionierung*—the Brechtian notion that Benjamin references in "The Author as Producer" to describe the effect that politically engaged artists should seek. The point of political art for Benjamin is not to shovel some ostensibly challenging content through the artistic apparatus of production, allowing the public to be entertained by guilt or gravitas but leaving the apparatus unaffected. The point is precisely to refunction the means of production and, hence, the political position of the artist within the relations of production. In invoking *Umfunktionierung* here, I am influenced both by what I have seen lowriders do with automobility and by the potential for what ethnography can do with scholarship.

But why does everything always have to be political? I can hear the complaint from here. There is at least a small trend in cultural studies to attempt to embrace aesthetics on its own terms, which often coincides with a certain disavowal of the compulsion to unearth political implications in every sphere of creative activity (see, for example, Aldama 2004, 2009; Schloss 2004). Perhaps this is a response to observations that cultural criticism as a broad field has harbored some rather facile claims about the political import of aesthetic objects and texts, an assertion that will not be lost on anyone who has attended his or her share of academic conferences in the humanities. It is also convincing to argue that to map resistance everywhere has the potential to reduce or attenuate the significance that aesthetic forms hold for those who make, use, and consume them. After all, one can expect a devotee of a particular art form to tell you that a piece need not be political to be good. Moreover, we who find fulfillment in excavating critique in surprising places must be held to account for the fact that the exercises of taste cultures do not substitute for voting, organizing a community or a union, or taking part in other forms of political activity or resistance.

But I find such discussions to be based on an overwrought distinction. Surely there are other forms and fields of politics than those we conventionally think of first as real (see Ramírez 2004). More to the point, aesthetics as a discourse or a theory that accounts for events and degrees of affectivity is intimately entwined with any process that creates identity, solidarity, commitment, or understanding. If a piece of aesthetic work is to effect change, the requisite is not that its creator knows that this will happen, and intended it all along, but that the piece of work is effective. Hence Benjamin's argument in "The Author as Producer": even if a work need not be political to be good, it certainly needs to be good to be political. To be "good" aesthetically in this Benjaminian

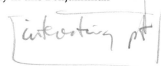

sense means to advance the state of the art, to teach writers something about writing. It is my contention throughout this book that lowriders teach us something about automobility. From that lesson, I would say that "good" in relation to car customization refers to a custom vehicle that is effective in the delivery of certain affects and the satisfaction of particular, conditioned, aesthetic expectations.

This is clearly a conditional and relational, rather than an absolute, notion of the aesthetic. I understand aesthetics to be a field of expectation and action by which people define a zone of cultural activity according to their priorities. To the extent that these priorities are shared with others, and potentially contrast with other priorities shared among other constituencies, we arrive back at politics. Priorities, like Ross Chambers's (1991) notion of "authority," are not in and of themselves the ends of political struggle, but their recognition or dismissal is certainly a political act. It is political, in other words, to recognize when a group of people enact a prioritization of the aesthetic; it is equally political to take that enactment seriously when the message from more canonical quarters is that you need not do so.

As an ethnographer, I endeavor to look and listen elsewhere than in those canonical quarters. With this inclination, I assumed that lowriders mattered to Mexican Americans, at least to some, since there were many Mexican Americans expending considerable time, money, and effort to keep this practice alive. How, then, do they matter, and with what consequence? Space worked its way into an emergent answer to this question as I learned from Henri Lefebvre (1991) that space is socially produced, that this production is the site of political contestation, and that important moments in this process occur in everyday situations. The understanding of space as material, emergent, and contested turned my gaze to urban space, not only in the conventional, infrastructural sense of built environments, roadways, and so on, but also to material practices that give form to imagined cities.

Attending to spatial production gave me the opportunity to see that by constructing particular environments, radiating out from autos and bodies to the extent of their sensorial impact on audiences, lowriders alter the sensoria of their cities. The politics of presence that this effects, refunctioning the spatial dimension of social reproduction, does not, by itself, undo histories of confinement, relegation, surveillance, and displacement. It does, however, momentarily change the relation between the imagined maps of ordered and managed difference and the material formation of sites as they are. Such moments matter precisely because the sensoria of cities are the focus of and the means for many of the processes by which cities are pressed into order—historically an unequal, divided order.

As a cultural practice that intervenes in the production of space, lowriding defines and forms a zone for itself through performative reiteration. The idea of culture as a zone rather than a proposition has driven me to craft representations that emphasize multiplicity, not essence; possibility, not guarantees; and ambivalence, not ideological clarity. I think these characteristics move closer to how lowriding functions in ordinary life than would any depiction that generalizes an interpretation of lowriding as representing a singular, coherent political position. The relationship of people to cultural forms like lowriding is not a matter of "take it or leave it" consumption choices, but instead of an enduring, negotiated, sometimes conflicting relation.

In that way, lowriding is indeed like family, in the sense of people you are stuck being connected with as much as in the positive, mutual-aid sense that lowriders usually mean. It is this kind of relation, I suggest, that drives women to write letters to *Lowrider Magazine* to pour out their relationship woes and grievances against machismo, even as it is propagated in the same pages. It is the same kind of relation that motivates endless debates about aesthetics as well as competing efforts to expand or constrict the boundaries of what qualifies as lowriding. It means that you do not have to love all lowriders or everything about them to love lowriding. The ties that keep these dynamic processes going are not absolutely determined or inevitable, but affective and emergent. They are ties based not on an aesthetic, iconographic, or ideological consensus, but on a shared historical position.

To account for the materiality of these relations, and indeed of the social production of space, in a book requires that the text struggle against its own limitations, for to consider space as historical does not lead to the proposal that material spatial formations are self-evidently legible. Instead, the necessary struggle to effect and yet challenge representations productively stretches the projects of analysis and argument. This is good, since it is precisely in the troubling intersections between lowrider space and intellectual discourse that I would expect theory to have the most to learn from lowriders. One of the key lessons is that if politics is in large part a production of space, expressive culture is in large part a performance of space (see, for example, Feld and Basso 1996; Nash 2000; Sciorra 1996; Stokes 1994; Thrift 2004c). Framed in this way, lowriding concurs with theoretical attempts to avoid reifying space, such as the notion derived from Marx that, like commodities, sites are "*processes* which appear in the *form* of things" (Merrifield 1992, 520), existing both as a field of action and as the basis of action (Munn 1996, 94). Social space is dynamic. It is not a thing, but a form that social relations take in particular locations at particular times.

Perhaps these qualities get at what lowriding does for its participants— what makes it well suited as a practice for engaging in the politics of space. For a car is durable, yet malleable with effort; mobile yet inhabitable; personifiable, though it extends the power and speed of gestures far beyond what a person alone can do. Perhaps lowriding allows for a specific position, a node in social and historical processes, to be manifested in a way that is precise without being delimited, and formidable without being permanent. Perhaps lowriding can do things that books cannot—including this one—such as materialize and give form to an experience, a history, and a perspective enacted from the receiving end of various measures of the social order to reproduce itself.

A famous subject of a very widely read ethnography once complained to "her writer": "I hate that book. . . . I hate it because I change and it doesn't" (K. Brown 2001, 399). Though I have slightly obscured the identities of the lowriders who populate these pages, in order to allow them deniability, I wonder whether they will feel the same. A book's fixing of narratives in type goes against many of the impulses lowriders seem to demonstrate: moving forward, innovating in order to get someone to "trip out," imagining and planning new designs to "come out with."

I trust that they will. Perhaps it will not always be cars. All the members of the club that I call the Custom Kings with whom I keep in touch have moved on to new affiliations or gone solo. Rumor has it that the police on Riverside are prepared to ticket any driver who passes the same point twice in a designated period of time, and that stores conveniently located at the best parts of the cruising strip have run cruisers off. Then again, on a nice spring weekend, I will see news and photos from the park come over the social-networking newsfeeds. Who knows what gas will cost next summer, or how long we as a species can even carry on supporting automobility at the level of the normal. Change will come. But some of those whom I got to know as lowriders will find ways to declare and manifest their presence, to produce the zones in which they can construct and exercise authority, to find pleasure and drama in ordinary times and places, and to affect the shifting contours and textures of social space through which we material beings and our creations flow.

Notes

Introduction

1. A small but steady stream of research produced since the 1970s makes up the lowrider literature. Before her untimely death, the foremost ethnographer of lowriding was Brenda Jo Bright, who published several essays in addition to her MA thesis and dissertation (Bright 1986, 1994, 1995, 1997, 1998). A handful of anthropologists and folklorists published short pieces on lowriders before Bright's more extensive work (e.g., Beck 1980; Gradante 1982, 1985; Griffith 1989; R. Mendoza 2000; Plascencia 1983; Stone 1990; Vigil 1991), and other scholars mention lowriding in work with a broader focus (Cintron 1997; Cross 1993; Rojas 1995; Vigil 1988). Journalists made early contributions to documenting the style (King 1981; Trillin and Koren 1978; West 1976), with Paige Penland in particular writing numerous articles for *Lowrider Magazine* (Penland 2003). Lowrider style has captured the attention of the visual-art world through work like the photography of David Harris and Jack Parsons, and the sculpture and installations of Ruben Ortíz-Torres (Chavoya 2004; Donnelly 2000; Parsons, Padilla, and Arellano 1999). Since Bright's pioneering work, there have been several dissertations focusing on lowriders in the fields of anthropology (Chappell 2003), art history (Chavoya 2002), cultural studies (D. Sandoval 2003b), and education (Cowan 2003), with others in progress. The most recent scholarship on lowriders includes work by Best (2005), Chappell (2006a, 2008, 2010), and Tatum (2011).

2. I use "Mexican American" after the example of José Limón (1994, 6) to denote U.S. residents of Mexican descent, but I keep it unhyphenated to avoid invoking an assimilated "ethnicity," in which one's current legal nationality absorbs and renders merely symbolic a nation of origin or heritage (Gans 1979). The people I call Mexican Americans are indeed largely U.S. citizens but remain "minoritized" within national, cultural, economic, racial,

and other structures of identity (see Sanchez 1995). The lowriders I met for this project would generally fall into the category of "Chicano/a" as that term is typically used by academics, though I almost never heard lowriders use it to describe themselves (they uniformly did refer to the vernacular landmark "Chicano Park"), perhaps because the specific politics that it implies would seem too self-conscious (see Limón [1994, 137] for a similar comment on "*carnalismo*"). But nor would they likely self-identify as "Hispanic," a term that has been undergoing rapid change in the context of current international migration. At the time of my research in Texas, "Hispanic" would have connoted an upwardly mobile class status or aspiration along with probable U.S. citizenship. The everyday lowrider scene that I observed in Austin was overwhelmingly Mexican American, so the need to self-identify was not always pressing. When it did serve the conversation, I often heard people speak of themselves and others as "Mexican," often with a slightly ironic pronunciation that bordered on "Meskin" (Limón 1994, 6), and only once or twice as "*mexicano.*"

3. *Colors*, directed by Dennis Hopper, Orion Pictures, 1988.

4. In an effort to prevent any unintended negative consequences of my study, and to protect the privacy of the people who participated in it, I follow the anthropological convention of using pseudonyms for individuals and clubs. I have chosen these carefully to try to approximate some of the cultural resonances of the names I actually knew people by—English or Spanish forms, nicknames or given names, etc. Hence, I use "Roman" and not "Román," since I met several other people who pronounced their own names in the Anglicized form. Neither version is the real name of the interviewee cited here.

5. A case in point: Joshua Long's ethnographic dissertation on Austin as a "creative city" relies almost entirely on Anglo interlocutors who are generalized as "Austinites" (2008).

6. See, e.g., Joe Austin (2001), Chang (2005), Ferrell (1996), Forman (2002), Rose (1994), Schloss (2004), Susan Stewart (1994, chap. 7).

7. All italics in the quotations in this paragraph are my added emphasis.

8. Scholars who have preceded me in approaching Chicano/a politics through spatiality include Brady (2002), Flores (2002), Rivera (2005), and the authors cited in note 12 below.

9. A similar "culturalist" move to appeal to ethnological legitimacy occurs in the interpretation of hip-hop MCs as "griots" (Bradley 2009, 23), or in lending high-art legitimacy to a graffiti-writing scene by treating it as part of art history (Joe Austin 2001, 193).

10. Mike Taylor in particular stressed this point in a personal conversation.

11. Scholars who have attempted to move beyond textualist understandings of significance include Csordas (1993), Desjarlais (2003), González (1993), Hyams (2003), Inda (2000), Jackson (1993, 1998), Stoller (1997), Young (1995), and others. Particularly influential on this project have been the scholars who, though often working with language, emphasize the productive rather than reflective character of performance (e.g., Abrahams 1977, 1981; J. L. Austin 1962; Bakhtin 1986; Bauman 1984, 1986; Briggs 1986, 1988; Feld 1988; Flores 1995; Harding 2001; Kapchan 1996, 2003; Limón 1994; Paredes 1958, 1993; K. Stewart 1996). Indispensible theoretical arguments regarding the politics of material practice include Bourdieu (1977) and Foucault (1979). For a recent ethnographic project that prioritizes attention to emergence as the inevitable quality of public culture, see K. Stewart (2007).

12. This project originated in the thick of what has been called the "spatial turn" in the human sciences, a proliferation of work animated in large part by Lefebvre's premise that "social space is a social product" (1991). Among the scholars I draw on who engage with Lefebvre are Berland (1992), Crang and Thrift (2000), Gottdiener (1994), Harvey (1989, 1991, 1998b, 2000), Katznelson (1992), Kun (1997), Lawrence and Low (1990), Low (1996, 1999a, 1999b, 2000), Low and Lawrence-Zuñiga (2003), Doreen Massey (1994, 2005), McCann (1999), Merrifield (1992, 1995, 2002a, 2002b), Mitchell (2003), Munn (1996), Rodman (1992), Rogers (2002), Rotenberg (1993, 2001), Savage and Warde (1993), Sciorra (1996), Shields (1996), Soja (1989, 1996), Thrift (1996), Zatz-Díaz (2003, 2005), and Zukin (1995, 1996). Deutsche (1996) provides an indispensable critique of certain Lefebvrian urbanists for their authoritarian tendencies and blindness to gender and sexuality. Translations of Lefebvre continue to appear and have an impact on the Anglophone academy; see Lefebvre (2003, 2004, 2008).

13. Davíd Díaz (2005) notes that work focusing on Mexican American experience is underrepresented in the planning and urbanist literature, especially given the centrality of Los Angeles as the object of discussion (see Soja 2000). Yet the literature on Mexican Americans and urban space is no doubt growing (see, e.g., Arreola 2004; Avila 1998; Davis 2000; S. Rodríguez 1998; Valle and Torres 2000), as is the field of Latino/a spatial studies more generally (see, e.g., Dávila 2004; Dávila and Lao 2001; G. Pérez 2004; Ramos-Zayas 2003).

14. On race and class in Mexican America, see also Alvarez (2007), N. Foley (1997), Menchaca (2001), Montejano (1987), Pérez-Torres (2006), and others.

Chapter 1

1. Bill Rankin has produced an identity map of Chicago by "dot mapping" the concentrations of people self-identifying as one of five ethnic or racial groups (including "other"). See the map at http://www.radicalcartography.net/index.html?chicagodots. Eric Fischer applies a similar method to more than a hundred other cities: http://www.flickr.com/photos/walk ingsf/sets/72157624812674967. The New York Times hosts an interactive site producing similar maps based on the Census Bureau's American Community Survey: http://projects.nytimes.com/census/2010/explorer. These conglomerations of self-reported identities do not necessarily reflect the various identity maps and imagined cities that are salient in social practice, but the clear residential patterns and boundaries they reveal are compelling.

2. What I am calling the "Eastside," after the lowriders' vernacular, includes parts of census tracts 9.02 and 10.00. The census shows these tracts as 87 percent and 84 percent Latino, respectively, with African American populations of 7.3 percent and 1.4 percent. In an earlier analysis of a larger area, the Eastside community activists Susana Almanza and Raúl Alvarez (1997, 110) noted that people of color made up 88 percent of the population of seven census tracts they call "Central East Austin." Five of these tracts had poverty rates exceeding 30 percent, with two exceeding 50 percent.

3. The University of Texas Press is a notable presence in this eastward expansion from the original "Forty Acres" of UT.

4. See the South Austin–oriented website at http://www.austindelsur.com/.

5. This possibility caused a rift between potential allies in community activism during the public debate on a light-rail system for Austin. The development of the East Sixth Street corridor around a light-rail station as a "mixed use" area suggested for some an influx of higher-end condominiums and townhouses. Thus, merchants who owned Mexican restaurants on the street as well as ecology- and transportation-conscious leftists and liberals found themselves pitted against homeowners and tenants of the area concerned about being displaced; see Almanza and Alvarez (1997).

6. Playing "Shave and a Haircut" on a car horn in Mexico can be taken as the profane insult "*Chinga tu madre, cabrón,*" and is even punishable as a traffic violation. It may be that the Cruzers meant to allude to this insult (though their version included an additional note, suggesting "Just Cruzin" in place of "cabrón"), but when I mentioned the Mexican version later to a member of the Kings, he felt that no one in his club took it that way.

7. Originating in Colombia, the cumbia rhythm is common in Mexican popular music.

8. The Austin Police Department concluded from its own study that racial profiling was not a problem, but the lowriders I talked to would clearly have disagreed (see Knee 2003).

9. What lowriders called the "Euro" scene represents a customizing genre whose vehicles are also called "tuners" or "imports." The tuner customizing and street-racing scene has become one of the most widely recognized and popular custom-car genres, supporting a movie franchise in the *Fast and the Furious* films. Many younger Mexican Americans, as well as Anglos and Asian Americans, got into tuners, often to the chagrin of old-school lowriders.

Chapter 2

1. Citing the Economic Policy Institute (EPI), Ehrenreich reports that in the early 1960s, food accounted for 24 percent of the average family budget, and housing 29 percent. In 1999, food absorbed 16 percent and housing 37 percent. The federal poverty level is calculated by tripling the minimum food costs for a family of a given size—in other words, poverty levels assume that food is 33 percent of the budget (Ehrenreich 2001, 200). In 2006, the EPI calculated the pretax income required for a family like José's (one parent, two children) to meet a "safe but modest" standard of living in the Austin–Round Rock area to be $41,577 annually. This was based on the optimistic estimate that housing would require only 25 percent of income (Economic Policy Institute 2008). The EPI's target income is more than twice the federal poverty guideline for a family of three, at $18,310. In 2009, a classified ad for an automotive technician at the garage where one of the lowriders I knew used to work listed a base pay of $10–20/hour, or $20,800 annually at the entry level, assuming forty-hour weeks without overtime or vacation.

2. In her lowrider history, Paige Penland dates this preference back to the 1940s: "Chevrolets, which were slightly less expensive, easier to repair, and perfect for large families, became more popular in the *barrios* than Fords" (2003, 10).

3. Sarah Mahler (1995) describes the *encargado* system in her ethnography of Latin American immigrants on Long Island. Examples of anti-immigrant panic that specifically addresses housing situations are depicted in documentary films such as *Farmingville* (directed

by Carlos Sandoval and Catherine Tambini, Camino Bluff Productions, 2004) and *9500 Liberty* (directed by Eric Byler and Annabel Park, 2009).

4. In later work, Griffith elaborates on the baroque sensibility that he identifies in low-riders and other folk objects in the Southwest. Stepping away from any simplistic notion of survival or revival, he attributes these enduring and widespread principles to "a sense of how things should go together that has been a basic part of Mexican culture since at least the eighteenth century" (1995, 163). This sense is what I am calling an aesthetic, and I do not refute Griffith's take on it here so much as propose that it be considered in dialogue with other aesthetic principles with which lowriders are also engaged.

5. In his essay "Driving while Black," Gilroy, a self-professed "bemused non-driver," worries over the "apparent triumph of anti-political and assertively immoral consumerism in black popular culture," but also notes the necessity of a critical view on how "the automobile appears . . . at the very core of America's complex negotiations with its own absurd racial codings," suggesting that cars have been a part of consumer culture that has "salved the chronic injuries of racialized hierarchy" (2001, 83–84). Thus, he raises questions similar to those animating this project: how can scholars view the critical knowledge that we hope or believe to exist within excorporating, minority-marked practices that are thoroughly enmeshed in a fraught and fetishized consumer culture?

6. *Napoleon Dynamite*, directed by Jared Hess, Fox Searchlight/Paramount, 2004; *Cars*, directed by John Lasseter and Joe Ranft, Walt Disney/Pixar, 2006.

7. Selena was a young Chicana star in the Tejano music scene who was tragically murdered by her fan club president. The Anglo media world was entirely unprepared for the outpouring of grief at her death, even though she and her band had filled the Astrodome in their last performance together (Limón 1999). Tupac Shakur and Biggie Smalls were black rap-music stars who were both gunned down in their prime and who came to be seen as emblematic of a deadly East Coast–West Coast rivalry in the big-time rap game (Dyson 2001; Toop 2000).

8. Such casual references probably overstate the agency of the women involved and certainly elide the brutality of human trafficking, but I suggest that like Benjamin's image, colloquial references to the sex trade are primarily about taking jaded note of the compromising relations underlying the promises of consumer exchange.

9. See http://www.homies.tv.

10. *Friday*, directed by F. Gary Gray, New Line Cinema/Priority Films, 1995.

11. Daytons, or "Ds," wire-spoke wheels manufactured by Dayton Wire Wheels, are known for their high quality and exceptional warranty.

Chapter 3

1. Many lowriders kept active in the scene after becoming parents. Often, in fact, they would build lowrider bikes for their children and enter them in shows. Two mainstays on the Austin scene were a *Blue's Clues*–themed bike and a tricycle named for the girl who owned it, with a custom trailer to haul its stereo system.

2. What I call "lifestyle profiling" here, or racial surveillance based on cultural practices, resembles what other scholars have identified as "new cultural racism." For an influential introduction, see Balibar (1991); for a recent intervention, see Visweswaran (2010).

3. The theme of refusal is also resonant with the work of Hebdige (1979), Limón (1983), and Marcuse (1971), among others.

4. My synopsis of *Lowrider Magazine*'s account of its own history is based on a Paige Penland article in the January 1997 issue (see Penland 1997).

5. Chavez accounts for his own youthful participation in lowriding in an interview reprinted in Penland's (2003) history of *Lowrider Magazine*.

6. Beyond the Chicano movement, the early French situationists likewise won a student election and diverted funds from the University of Strasbourg to publish the landmark pamphlet *On the Poverty of Student Life* (see UNEF Strasbourg 1966).

7. A comparison with *National Geographic*'s affirmative "exploration" discourse is also apt in that Paige Penland, after her work as one of *Lowrider Magazine*'s central staff writers, moved into travel writing, contributing pieces that included passing mentions of car culture in Lonely Planet guides on Los Angeles and New Mexico.

8. An extensive, though not complete, collection of *Lowrider Magazine* issues is held in the Benson Latin American Collection at the University of Texas.

9. Changes in ownership and editorial direction over the history of *Lowrider Magazine* have altered its content in ways that merit detailed study but are well beyond the scope of my engagement with lowrider publishing here.

10. A more reliable and complete account of these events is clearly needed and would require oral-historical accounts from within the movement. Still, the positions I sketch out here will likely be familiar to those conversant with Chicana/o movement history.

11. See Alarcón (1996), Anzaldúa (1987, 27), Gutiérrez (1993), and E. Pérez (1999).

12. The portrayal of women in lowrider iconography is worthy of its own project, which would be attentive to images of not only Malintzin and lowrider models, but also the *Virgen de Guadalupe*, the Tejana music star Selena, pachucas, Aztec princesses, the twentieth-century revolutionaries known as *adelitas*, and other figures.

13. With "media culture industry," I mean to blend views presented by scholars such as Horkheimer and Adorno (1972) and Kellner (1995) to acknowledge that audiences negotiate their engagement with the mediascape, of which lowrider media are a part (Hall 1981), but also to underscore that a large part of the apparatus of production and distribution of such media remain in the control of a class able to deploy considerable resources in the interest of maintaining its privilege. This translates into force behind the aforementioned "norms and requirements," and thus a gravity toward conformity with them. Short of the position that Horkheimer and Adorno have come to signify in debates on popular culture, I do not assume that such conformism is a black hole, inevitably sucking everyone and everything into its exploitative center. Instead, I believe that, as Horkheimer and Adorno recognized about bourgeois art, popular culture can create space for its own resistance (O'Malley 1993).

14. Another example of how "rituals of inversion" fall short of challenging ordinary hierarchies is found in Douglas Foley's classic reading of a high school powder-puff football game in small-town South Texas (Foley 1990, chap. 2).

15. By 2000, Gonzalez had returned to the helm of *Lowrider Magazine* after a series of other editors. Such changes in leadership have affected the look and visual cultural politics of the magazine over time in ways that merit a thorough study, but that I do not think would alter the general characterizations I am making here.

16. BMW no longer offers the films, collectively titled *The Hire*, for download, though they continue to circulate on the web. At this writing, *Star* appears at http://www.youtube.com/watch?v=q1dYv_gKTA8.

17. Cultural mediations that raise critiques of automobility form a rich thread running through modern culture, including work by Andy Warhol, Joan Didion, J. G. Ballard, and many others. A study of this work would be illuminating in its own right, but such a focus on highbrow texts is precisely what I argue cannot stand in for attention to popular uses of automobility. Social, ethnographic, and cultural-historical accounts of automobility constitute a growing interdisciplinary literature (see, e.g., Böhm 2006; Featherstone, Thrift, and Urry 2005; S. Jain 2002, 2004; Miller 2001; Packer 2008; Seiler 2008).

18. While I have not discussed the Ritchie film with lowriders, the reception of the film *The Fast and the Furious* (directed by Rob Cohen, Universal Pictures, 2001), which came out during my fieldwork, is perhaps analogously ambivalent. Several lowriders I knew were in line at the box office on the opening day of this custom-car-themed film, and they discussed it in detail and with interest. Yet the specific genre of customization that was the centerpiece of that film—street racing, or "tuning"—often was a source of contention among lowriders on the street. Lowriders saw tuners, or "Euros," in real life as competitors for space, as irresponsible drivers, and at times as naïve youth making questionable aesthetic choices. Still, they were excited to go see them on the big screen and participate in a larger niche market of automobile-customization enthusiasts.

19. In a few specific moments, I saw lowriders extend to outsiders thought to be gay the general liberal tolerance that they often proclaimed. I consider this situation to be a close analogue of Eminem's position in his fictional film *8 Mile* (directed by Curtis Hanson, Imagine Entertainment/Mikona Productions, 2002), and in subsequent media statements, that he is not antigay, but rather is opposed to the gender transgressions of men who "act like faggots." Such genderphobia (Stephens 2005) suggests an attempt to negotiate between specific modes of performing aggressive masculinity that depend on homophobia and the limited progress made in the larger public culture to discredit homophobia as such.

20. In fact, my practice in this text of referring to members of the Custom Kings as "the Kings" differs from the way club members talked about themselves. Rather than take on the title of a "King," lowriders would most often identify themselves as "with the Kings." In the event that a person should leave the club or switch to another, lowriders would talk about them "getting out" rather than ceasing to be a King.

21. As part of my institutional-review-board-approved plan for the protection of human subjects, I did not interview minors for this project, which is why my consideration of Maria's experience is mediated by a parent.

22. In *The Production of Space*, Lefebvre critiques scholars who, in purporting to address issues of space, seem to "leap" from metaphysical considerations of writing and critique— mental space—to "the social" (1991, 5). For Lefebvre, the realm of the social does not repre-

sent a "macro" scale that can be apprehended only through abstraction, as with statistics, but is coterminous with the material. I do not share entirely in Lefebvre's attack on his contemporaries, several of whom also populate the bibliography here, but his call to the body in 1974 signals a common concern even among professional rivals in the continental intellectual scene (e.g., Bourdieu and Foucault).

Chapter 4

1. Customer self-check lanes have become common in retail, an instance of George Ritzer's "McDonaldization" thesis (1993), according to which customers are increasingly trained to do more of the work involved in consumption themselves. In grocery stores, however, these lines tend to have item limits, suggesting that there is a point at which even unpaid checkers contribute to shrink and it becomes advantageous to have an employee involved.

2. Others included the performance artist Laurie Anderson working as a "cultural spy" in a McDonald's, and a Studs Terkel–style oral history of work that began as a website and was published in book form as *Gig: Americans Talk about their Jobs* (Bowe, Bowe, and Streeter 2000). Low-wage work and the plight of the working poor are also longstanding concerns of the anthropology of work, exemplified in texts such as those by Edin and Lein (1997), Hondagneu-Sotelo (2001), Newman (1999), Romero (1992), and others.

3. Ehrenreich observes that as a white woman with access to cash, medical care, and other aspects of an upper-middle-class position, she will never experience the actual desperation that the working poor face—she has a way out.

4. Cintron's description of the "aura" of art as a construction is ironically compatible with the notion of mechanical reproducibility as the destruction of aura in Benjamin's "The Work of Art in the Age of Mechanical Reproduction" (1968b). Common to both accounts is the idea that the aura is a stake in a struggle. Cintron describes the struggle to establish and defend aura authority through the subjugation of other knowledges.

5. Faith in eternal growth was shattered by the crisis that began in 2007. The bubble bursting was a surprise only to those who had been blissfully ignorant of longstanding critiques of capitalist optimism such as those by Schumacher (1975) or, for that matter, Marx; see also Harvey (2009).

Chapter 5

1. Other material on this story is drawn from articles by Leah Olin that appeared in the paper on May 24, 2000, and May 27, 2000.

2. Gangster aesthetics is part of a much broader array of such intercultural practices (Alvarez 2008; Macías 2008). The attitude and assertion of "dignity" in the face of minoritization in such repertoires of everyday performance provoke panics that then tend to emphasize any potential gang connection.

3. Beyond the aesthetic component, this generalization of gangness depends on a notion of innate, that is, heritable, criminality. This, in turn, has been compounded under coun-

terterrorism regimes of law enforcement and nationalist or nativist strategies of countering gangs by deporting immigrant youth (see Zilberg 2004).

4. See, e.g., the website of the National Alliance of Gang Investigators' Associations, http://www.nagia.org, or the Street Gangs Resource Center, http://www.streetgangs.com.

5. See http://www.ci.austin.tx.us/police/gang.htm. All other references in this paragraph are to the website of Austin Gangbusters, which is archived at http://web.archive.org/web/19990220022741/http://www.austingangbusters.org/members.htm.

6. See http://web.archive.org/web/19990220022741/http://www.austingangbusters.org/members.htm. At the APD townhall meetings in 2000, District Attorney Ronnie Earle announced that crime rates were actually down in the city at large and that Austin had the lowest murder rate in Texas.

7. *American Me*, directed by Edward James Olmos, Olmos Productions/Universal Pictures/YOY, 1992; *Blood In, Blood Out*, directed by Taylor Hackford, Hollywood Pictures/Touchwood Pacific Partners/Vato de Atole Productions, 1993.

8. Ruben Mendoza (2000) relates lowrider clubs to the *mutualistas*, mutual-aid organizations that were crucial in early movements for the civil rights of Mexican Americans. The notion of mutual aid as an ethos honored by clubs was echoed in my conversations with lowriders, albeit not in the same words.

9. *Boyz n the Hood*, directed by John Singleton, Columbia Pictures, 1991; *Boulevard Nights*, directed by Desmond Nakano, Warner Brothers Pictures, 1979.

10. In David Montejano's influential history of Mexicans in Texas since the Treaty of Guadalupe Hidalgo, he frames intercultural and racial conflict between Texas Mexicans and Anglo settlers as a rupture with a prior peace structure, a state of relative stability in the hegemonic processes by which elites established their rule (1987, 34).

11. Police violence was the subject of an alternate town-hall meeting organized by the NAACP and held at Huston-Tillotson College, a historically black institution on the Eastside. Participants in that meeting (almost all black) shared stories of violence at the hands of the police, including at least one death.

12. On LaCresha Murray, see the *Austin American-Statesman*, August 14, 2001. On Cedar Avenue, see the *Austin American-Statesman*, May 26, 2001. On the yogurt shop controversy, see the *Austin American-Statesman*, May 31, 2000. Ramírez was convicted, but the case was later thrown out when it was revealed that the victim had concealed from jurors a civil lawsuit against him; see the *Austin American-Statesman*, May 4, 2001, and August 1, 2002. On the police oversight issue, see the *Austin American-Statesman*, May 30, 2000.

13. This account is by no means a holistic examination of the police policy. I did not approach police officers in order to gain a fuller sense of their perspective, nor am I engaging the criminological and administrative literature on community policing, which is considerable. The reason I did not prioritize these lines of inquiry is that the project here is not to represent community policing in a comprehensive way, or to thoroughly document its implementation, but rather to attempt to render how it became effective "on the ground," from the particular perspective of lowrider space (see Ferguson and Gupta 2002). If readers can take this for what it is—a "partial truth" (Clifford 1986) proffered in the interest of representing a historically

specific context—I hope that it can make a small contribution to a critical understanding and improvement of future interactions between police and barrio communities (see R. Pérez 2006).

14. The meetings occurred before 9/11, and thus foreshadowed such security measures as the TIPS (Terrorism Information and Prevention System) program, through which the government called upon service providers like plumbers and delivery personnel to report anything suspicious they saw in the course of doing their business. Changes in surveillance laws also were effected after 9/11 under the USA PATRIOT Act. Overall, the cult of security in a state permanently at war has allowed for increased public tolerance of surveillance, as long as it is directed at others.

15. The issue of property values marks a class difference between those who view property as an investment and those who see it as a more or less permanent place to live, essentially a real-estate version of exchange and use value. If property is an investment that might be liquidated by selling it, a rise in property values is beneficial as an increase in equity. If property is principally a place to live, however, increased property value can be detrimental if it leads to higher taxes. This issue was palpable at the time of my research, since property values and housing costs were rising around Austin. In the summer of 2001, numerous residents of the Eastside saw their property values increase dramatically overnight, in some cases as much as doubling.

Reference List

Abrahams, Roger. 1977. "Toward an Enactment-Centered Theory of Folklore." In *Frontiers in Folklore*, edited by William Bascom, 79–120. Boulder, Colo.: Westview.

——. 1981. "Shouting Match at the Border: The Folklore of Display Events." In *"And Other Neighborly Names": Social Process and Cultural Image in Texas Folklore*, edited by R. Bauman and R. D. Abrahams, 303–322. Austin: Univ. of Texas Press.

Abu-Lughod. 1991. "Writing against Culture." In *Recapturing Anthropology: Working in the Present*, edited by Richard G. Fox, 137–162. Santa Fe: School of American Research.

Alarcón, Norma. 1991. "The Theoretical Subject(s) of *This Bridge Called My Back* and Anglo-American Feminism." In *Criticism in the Borderlands: Studies in Chicano Literature, Culture, and Ideology*, edited by H. Calderón and J. D. Saldívar, 28–60. Durham, N.C.: Duke Univ. Press.

——. 1996. "Conjugating Subjects in an Age of Multiculturalism." In *Mapping Multiculturalism*, edited by Avery Gordon and Christopher Newfield, 127–148. Minneapolis: Univ. of Minnesota Press.

Alba, Richard, and Victor Nee. 2003. *Remaking the American Mainstream: Assimilation and Contemporary Immigration*. Cambridge, Mass.: Harvard Univ. Press.

Aldama, Frederick Luís. 2004. "Cultural Studies in Today's Chicano/Latino Scholarship: Wishful Thinking, Flatus Voci, or Scientific Endeavor?" *Aztlán* 29, no. 1: 193–218.

——. 2009. *This Is Your Brain on Latino Comics*. Austin: Univ. of Texas Press.

Almanza, Susana, and Raúl Alvarez. 1997. "Empowering Communities of Color: Lessons from Austin." In *Just Transportation: Dismantling Race and Class Barriers to Mobility*, edited by Robert D. Bullard and Glenn S. Johnson, 110–120. Stony Creek, Conn.: New Society.

Alvarez, Luís. 2007. "From Zoot Suits to Hip Hop: Towards a Relational Chicana/o Studies." *Latino Studies* 5, no. 1: 53–75.

——. 2008. *The Power of the Zoot: Youth Culture and Resistance during World War II*. Berkeley and Los Angeles: Univ. of California Press.

Anderson, Benedict. 1991. *Imagined Communities: Reflections on the Origin and Spread of Nationalism*. London: Verso.

Anzaldúa, Gloria. 1987. *Borderlands/La Frontera: The New Mestiza*. San Francisco: Aunt Lute Books.

Aoki, Keith. 1993. "Race, Space, and Place: The Relation between Architectural Modernism, Post-modernism, Urban Planning, and Gentrification." *Fordham Law Journal* 20:699–829.

Appadurai, Arjun. 1996. *Modernity at Large: Cultural Dimensions of Globalization*. Minneapolis: Univ. of Minnesota Press.

Arreola, Daniel, ed. 2004. *Hispanic Spaces, Latino Places: Community and Cultural Diversity in Contemporary America*. Austin: Univ. of Texas Press.

Austin, J. L. 1962. *How to Do Things with Words*. Oxford: Oxford Univ. Press.

Austin, Joe. 2001. *Taking the Train: How Graffiti Art Became an Urban Crisis in New York City*. New York: Columbia Univ. Press.

Avila, Eric R. 1998. "The Folklore of the Freeway: Space, Culture, and Identity in Postwar Los Angeles." *Aztlán* 23, no. 1: 15–31.

Bakhtin, Mikhail M. 1981. *The Dialogic Imagination*. Translated by Vadim Liapunov and Kenneth Brostrom. Austin: Univ. of Texas Press.

——. 1984. *Rabelais and His World*. Translated by Helene Iswolsky. Bloomington: Indiana Univ. Press.

——. 1986. *Speech Genres, and Other Late Essays*. Translated by Vern McGee. Austin: Univ. of Texas Press.

Balibar, Etienne. 1991. "Is There a 'Neo-Racism'?" In *Race, Nation, Class: Ambiguous Identities*, edited by Etienne Balibar and Immanuel Wallerstein, 17–29. London: Verso.

Barthes, Roland. 1972. *Mythologies*. Translated by A. Lavers. New York: Hill and Wang.

——. 1981. *Camera Lucida: Reflections on Photography*. Translated by Richard Howard. New York: Hill and Wang.

Baudrillard, Jean. 1996. *The System of Objects*. Translated by James Benedict. London: Verso.

Bauman, Richard. 1984. *Verbal Art as Performance*. Long Grove, Ill.: Waveland.

——. 1986. *Story, Performance, Event: Contextual Studies in Oral Narrative*. Cambridge: Cambridge Univ. Press.

Beck, Peggy. 1980. "The Low Riders: Folk Art and Emergent Nationalism." *Native Arts/West* 4:25–27.

Benjamin, Walter. 1968a. "Theses on the Philosophy of History." In *Illuminations: Essays and Reflections*, edited by Hannah Arendt and translated by Harry Zohn, 253–264. New York: Schocken.

——. 1968b. "The Work of Art in the Age of Mechanical Reproduction." In *Illuminations: Essays and Reflections*, edited by Hannah Arendt and translated by Harry Zohn, 217–252. New York: Schocken.

——. 1978. "The Author as Producer." In *Reflections: Essays, Aphorisms, Autobiographical*

Writings, edited by Peter Demetz and translated by Edmund Jephcott, 220–238. New York: Schocken.

———. 2002a. *The Arcades Project*. Edited by Rolf Tiedemann. Translated by Howard Eiland and Kevin McLaughlin. Cambridge, Mass.: Belknap Press.

———. 2002b. "A Different Utopian Will." In *Walter Benjamin: Selected Writings*, vol. 3, edited by Howard Eiland and Michael W. Jennings, 134–136. Cambridge, Mass.: Belknap Press.

Bennett, Andy. 1999. "Subcultures or Neo-tribes? Rethinking the Relationship between Youth, Style, and Musical Taste." *Sociology* 33, no. 3: 599–617.

Berger, Michael L. 1991. "The Car's Impact on the American Family." In *The Car and the City: The Automobile, the Built Environment, and Daily Urban Life*, edited by Martin Wachs and Margaret Crawford, 57–74. Ann Arbor: Univ. of Michigan Press.

Berland, Jody. 1992. "Angels Dancing: Cultural Technologies and the Production of Space." In *Cultural Studies*, edited by Lawrence Grossberg, Cary Nelson, and Paula A. Treichler, 38–51. New York: Routledge.

Berlant, Lauren. 2008. "Intuitionists: History and the Affective Event." *New Literary History* 20, no. 4: 845–860.

Best, Amy. 2005. *Fast Cars, Cool Rides: The Accelerating World of Youth and Their Cars*. New York: New York Univ. Press.

Böhm, Steffan, ed. 2006. *Against Automobility*. Malden, Mass.: Blackwell.

Borhek, J. T. 1989. "Rods, Choppers, and Restorations: The Modification and Re-creation of Production Motor Vehicles in America." *Journal of Popular Culture* 22, no. 4: 97–107.

Bourdieu, Pierre. 1977. *Outline of a Theory of Practice*. Translated by Richard Nice. Cambridge: Cambridge Univ. Press.

———. 1984. *Distinction: A Social Critique of the Judgment of Taste*. Translated by Richard Nice. Cambridge. Mass.: Harvard Univ. Press.

———. 1999. *Language and Symbolic Power*. Translated by John B. Thompson. Cambridge, Mass.: Harvard Univ. Press.

Bowe, John, Marisa Bowe, and Sabin C. Streeter. 2000. *Gig: Americans Talk about their Jobs at the Turn of the Millennium*. New York: Crown.

Bradley, Adam. 2009. *Book of Rhymes: The Poetics of Hip Hop*. New York: Nation Books.

Brady, Mary Pat. 2002. *Extinct Lands, Temporal Geographies: Chicana Literature and the Urgency of Space*. Durham, N.C.: Duke Univ. Press.

Brenneis, Donald. 1994. "Discourse and Discipline at the National Research Council: A Bureaucratic Bildungsroman." *Cultural Anthropology* 9, no. 1: 23–36.

Briggs, Charles. 1986. *Learning How to Ask: A Sociolinguistic Appraisal of the Role of the Interview in Social Science Research*. Cambridge: Cambridge Univ. Press.

———. 1988. *Competence in Performance: The Creativity of Tradition in Mexicano Verbal Art*. Philadelphia: Univ. of Pennsylvania Press.

Bright, Brenda Jo. 1986. "Style and Identity: Houston Low Riders." MA thesis, Rice Univ.

———. 1994. "Mexican American Low Riders: An Anthropological Approach to Popular Culture." Phd diss., Rice Univ.

———. 1995. "Remappings: Los Angeles Low Riders." In *Looking High and Low: Art and Cultural Identity*, edited by Brenda Bright and Liza Blakewell, 89–123. Tucson: Univ. of Arizona Press.

———. 1997. "Nightmares in the New Metropolis: The Cinematic Poetics of Low Riders." *Studies in Latin American Popular Culture* 16:13–29.

———. 1998. "'Heart like a Car': Hispano/Chicano Culture in Northern New Mexico." *American Ethnologist* 25, no. 4: 583–609.

Brown, Bill. 2001. "Thing Theory." *Critical Inquiry* 28, no. 1: 1–22.

Brown, Karen McCarthy. 2001. *Mama Lola: A Vodou Priestess in Brooklyn*. Berkeley and Los Angeles: Univ. of California Press.

Buck-Morss, Susan. 1991. *The Dialectics of Seeing: Walter Benjamin and the Arcades Project*. Cambridge, Mass.: MIT Press.

Butler, Judith. 1993a. *Bodies That Matter: On the Discursive Limits of "Sex."* New York: Routledge.

———. 1993b. "Endangered/Endangering: Schematic Racism and White Paranoia." In *Reading Rodney King/Reading Urban Uprising*, edited by Robert Gooding-Williams, 15–22. London: Routledge.

———. 2004. "Imitation and Gender Insubordination." In *The Judith Butler Reader*, edited by Sara Salih, 119–137. Malden, Mass.: Blackwell.

Camarillo, Albert. 1979. *Chicanos in a Changing Society: From Mexican Pueblos to American Barrios in Santa Barbara and Southern California, 1848–1930*. Cambridge, Mass.: Harvard Univ. Press.

Certeau, Michel de. 1984. *The Practice of Everyday Life*. Translated by Steven Rendall. Berkeley and Los Angeles: Univ. of California Press.

Chambers, Ross. 1991. *Room for Maneuver: Reading (the) Oppositional (in) Narrative*. Chicago: Univ. of Chicago Press.

Chang, Jeff. 2005. *Can't Stop Won't Stop: A History of the Hip-Hop Generation*. New York: Macmillan.

Chappell, Ben. 1998. "Making Identity with Cars and Music: Lowriders and Hip-Hop as Urban Chicano Performance." MA report, Univ. of Texas at Austin.

———. 2000. "'Take a Little Trip with Me': Lowriding and the Poetics of Scale." In *Technicolor: Race, Technology, and Daily Life*, edited by Alondra Nelson and Thuy Linh N. Tu, 35–52. New York: New York Univ. Press.

———. 2003. "Lowrider Space: A Critical Encounter of Knowledges." Phd diss., Univ. of Texas at Austin.

———. 2006a. "Lowrider Cruising Spaces." In *Mobile Crossings: Representations of Chicana/o Cultures*, edited by Anja Bandau and Marc Priewe, 51–62. Trier, Germany: Wissenschaftlicher Verlag Trier.

———. 2006b. "Rehearsals of the Sovereign: States of Exception and Threat Governmentality." *Cultural Dynamics* 18, no. 3: 313–334.

———. 2008. "Lowrider Style: Cultural Poetics and the Politics of Scale." In *Cultural Studies: An Anthology*, edited by Michael Ryan, 634–645. Malden, Mass.: Blackwell.

———. 2010. "Custom Contestations: Lowriders and Urban Space." *City and Society* 22, no. 1: 25–47.

Chavoya, C. Ondine. 2000. "Rubén Ortiz Torres: Style Politics and Hydraulic Hijinx." In *Customized: Art Inspired by Hot Rods, Low Riders and American Car Culture*, edited by Nora Donnelly, 43–47. New York: Abrams.

———. 2002. "Orphans of Modernism: Chicano Art, Public Representation, and Spatial Practice in Southern California." Phd diss., Univ. of Rochester.

———. 2004. "The Art of Rubén Ortiz Torres and Lowriding in Southern California." *CR: New Centennial Review* 4, no. 2: 141–184.

Cintron, Ralph. 1997. *Angel's Town: Chero Ways, Gang Life, and Rhetorics of the Everyday*. Boston: Beacon.

Cisneros, Sandra. 1994. *The House on Mango Street*. New York: Knopf.

Clifford, James. 1986. "Introduction: Partial Truths." In *Writing Culture: The Poetics and Politics of Ethnography*, edited by James Clifford and George E. Marcus, 1–26. Berkeley and Los Angeles: Univ. of California Press.

Cohen, Colleen Ballerino, Richard Wilk, and Beverly Stoeltje, eds. 1996. *Beauty Queens on the Global Stage: Gender, Contests, and Power*. London: Routledge.

Conquergood, Dwight. 1991. "Rethinking Ethnography: Toward a Critical Cultural Politics." *Communication Monographs* 58:179–194.

———. 2002. "Performance Studies: Interventions and Radical Research." *Drama Review* 46, no. 2: 145–156.

Copjec, Joan, and Michael Sorkin. 1999. *Giving Ground: The Politics of Propinquity*. New York: Verso.

Cowan, Peter. 2003. "Lowrider Art: Latino Visual Literacy and Border Knowledge." Phd diss., Univ. of California.

Crang, Mike, and Nigel Thrift, eds. 2000. *Thinking Space*. London: Routledge.

Crawford, Michael. 2009. *Shop Class as Soulcraft: An Inquiry into the Value of Work*. New York: Penguin.

Cross, Brian. 1993. *It's Not about a Salary: Rap, Race, and Resistance in Los Angeles*. London: Verso.

Csordas, Thomas. 1993. "Somatic Modes of Attention." *Cultural Anthropology* 8, no. 2: 135–156.

Cummings, Laura. 1991. "Carne con Limón: Reflections on the Construction of Social Harmlessness." *American Ethnologist* 18, no. 2: 370–372.

Dávila, Arlene. 2004. *Barrio Dreams: Puerto Ricans, Latinos, and the Neoliberal City*. Berkeley and Los Angeles: Univ. of California Press.

Dávila, Arlene, and Augustín Lao, eds. 2001. *Mambo Montage: The Latinization of New York*. New York: Columbia Univ. Press.

Davis, Mike. 1990. *City of Quartz: Excavating the Future in Los Angeles*. London: Verso.

———. 2000. *Magical Urbanism: Latinos Reinvent the U.S. City*. London: Verso.

Del Castillo, Adelaida R. 1996. "Gender and Its Discontinuities in Male/Female Domestic Relations: Mexicans in Cross-Cultural Context." In *Chicanas/Chicanos at the Crossroads*, edited by D. Maciel and I. D. Ortíz, 207–230. Tucson: Univ. of Arizona Press.

Desjarlais, Robert. 2003. *Sensory Biographies: Lives and Deaths among Nepal's Yolmo Buddhists*. Berkeley and Los Angeles: Univ. of California Press.

Deutsche, Rosalyn. 1996. *Evictions: Art and Spatial Politics*. Cambridge, Mass.: MIT Press.

Díaz, David. 2005. *Barrio Urbanism: Chicanos, Planning, and American Cities*. New York: Routledge.

Donnelly, Nora, ed. 2000. *Customized: Art Inspired by Hot Rods, Low Riders, and American Car Culture*. New York: Abrams.

Douglas, Mary. 1966. *Purity and Danger: An Analysis of Concepts of Pollution and Taboo*. New York: Penguin.

Dyson, Michael Eric. 2001. *Holler If You Hear Me: Searching for Tupac Shakur*. New York: Basic Civitas Books.

Economic Policy Institute. 2008. "Basic Family Budget Calculator." http://www.epi.org/content/budget_calculator.

Edensor, Tim. 2004. "Automobility and National Identity: Representation, Identity, and Driving Practice." *Theory, Culture, and Society* 21, nos. 4–5: 101–120.

Edin, Kathryn, and Laura Lein. 1997. *Making Ends Meet: How Single Mothers Survive Welfare and Low-Wage Work*. New York: Sage.

Ehrenreich, Barbara. 2001. *Nickel and Dimed: On (Not) Getting By in America*. New York: Metropolitan.

English-Lueck, J. 2002. *Cultures@SiliconValley*. Palo Alto, Calif.: Stanford Univ. Press.

Fears, Mary. 1996. "Chicana behind the Wheel: Women Taking Larger Part in Lowrider Onda." *El Placazo* (Fall).

Featherstone, Michael, Nigel Thrift, and John Urry, eds. 2005. *Automobilities*. London: Sage.

Feld, Steven. 1988. "Aesthetics as Iconicity of Style, or 'Lift-up-over Sounding': Getting into the Kaluli Groove." *Yearbook for Traditional Music* 20:74–114.

———. 1990. *Sound and Sentiment: Birds, Weeping, Poetics, and Song in Kaluli Expression*. Philadelphia: Univ. of Pennsylvania Press.

Feld, Steven, and Keith Basso, eds. 1996. *Senses of Place*. Santa Fe: School of American Research.

Ferguson, James, and Akhil Gupta. 2002. "Spatializing States: Toward an Ethnography of Neoliberal Governmentality." *American Ethnologist* 29, no. 4: 981–1002.

Fernandez, James, and Michael Herzfeld. 1998. "In Search of Meaningful Methods." In *Handbook of Methods in Cultural Anthropology*, edited by H. Russell Bernard, 89–130. Walnut Creek, Calif.: AltaMira.

Ferrell, Jeff. 1996. *Crimes of Style: Urban Graffiti and the Politics of Criminality*. Boston: Northeastern Univ. Press.

Flink, James. 1988. *The Automotive Age*. Cambridge, Mass.: MIT Press.

Flores, Richard. 1995. *Los Pastores: History and Performance in the Mexican American Shepherd's Play of South Texas*. Washington, D.C.: Smithsonian Institution Press.

———. 2002. *Remembering the Alamo: Memory, Modernity, and the Master Symbol*. Austin: Univ. of Texas Press.

Florida, Richard. 2001. *The Rise of the Creative Class and How It's Transforming Work, Leisure, Community, and Everyday Life*. New York: Basic Books.

Foley, Douglas. 1990. *Learning Capitalist Culture: Deep in the Heart of Tejas*. Philadelphia: Univ. of Pennsylvania Press.

Foley, Neil. 1997. "Becoming 'Hispanic': Mexican Americans and the Faustian Bargain with Whiteness." In *Reflexiones: New Directions in Mexican American Studies*, edited by Neil Foley, 53–70. Austin: Center for Mexican American Studies / Univ. of Texas Press.

Forman, Murray. 2002. *The 'Hood Comes First: Race, Space, and Place in Rap and Hip-Hop*. Middletown, Conn.: Wesleyan Univ. Press.

Foucault, Michel. 1979. *Discipline and Punish*. Translated by Alan Sheridan. New York: Vintage.

———. 1980. "Two Lectures." In *Power/Knowledge: Selected Interviews and Other Writings*, edited by Colin Gordon, 78–107. New York: Pantheon.

———. 1982. "The Subject and Power." In *Michel Foucault: Beyond Structuralism and Hermeneutics*, edited by Hubert Dreyfus and Paul Rabinow, 208–226. Chicago: Univ. of Chicago Press.

———. 1986. "Of Other Spaces." *Diacritics* 16 (Spring): 22–27.

———. 1991. "Governmentality." In *The Foucault Effect: Studies in Governmentality*, edited by Graham Burchell, Colin Gordon, and Peter Miller, 87–105. Chicago: Univ. of Chicago Press.

Frow, John. 1995. *Cultural Studies and Cultural Value*. New York: Oxford Univ. Press.

Gans, Herbert. 1979. "Symbolic Ethnicity: The Future of Ethnic Groups and Cultures in America." *Ethnic and Racial Studies* 2, no. 1: 1–20.

Garza-Falcón, Leticia. 1998. *Gente Decente: A Borderlands Response to the Rhetoric of Dominance*. Austin: Univ. of Texas Press.

Gilroy, Paul. 2001. "Driving while Black." In *Car Cultures*, edited by Daniel Miller, 81–104. Oxford: Berg.

Gledhill, Christine. 1999. "Pleasurable Negotiations." In *Feminist Film Theory: A Reader*, edited by Sue Thornham, 166–179. New York: New York Univ. Press.

González, Jennifer. 1993. "Rhetoric of the Object: Material Memory and the Artwork of Amalia Mesa-Bains." *Visual Anthropology Review* 9, no. 1: 62–91.

———. 1995. "Autotopographies." In *Prosthetic Territories: Politics and Hypertechnologies*, edited by G. Brahm and M. Driscoll, 133–150. Boulder, Colo.: Westview.

Gottdiener, Mark. 1994. *The Social Production of Urban Space*. Austin: Univ. of Texas Press.

Gradante, William. 1982. "Low and Slow, Mean and Clean." *Natural History* 91, no. 4: 28–39.

———. 1985. "Art among the Low Riders." In *Folk Art in Texas*, edited by F. E. Abernathy, 70–77. Dallas: Southern Methodist Univ. Press.

Graves-Brown, Paul. 2000. "Always Crashing in the Same Car." In *Matter, Materiality, and Modern Culture*, edited by Paul Graves-Brown, 155–165. London: Routledge.

Gregory, Derek. 1994. *Geographical Imaginations*. Malden, Mass.: Blackwell.

Griffith, James. 1989. "Mexican American Folk Art." In *From the Inside Out*, edited by Karana Hattersley-Drayton, Joyce M. Bishop, and Tomás Ybarra-Frausto, 52–59. San Francisco: Mexican Museum.

———. 1995. *A Shared Space: Folklife in the Arizona-Sonora Borderlands*. Logan: Utah State Univ. Press.

Grossberg, Lawrence. 2006. "Does Cultural Studies Have Futures? Should It? (Or What's the Matter with New York?)." *Cultural Studies* 20, no. 1: 1–32.

Gupta, Akhil, and James Ferguson. 1992. "Beyond 'Culture': Space, Identity, and the Politics of Difference." *Cultural Anthropology* 7, no. 1: 6–23.

———, eds. 1997. *Anthropological Locations: Boundaries and Grounds of a Field Science*. Berkeley and Los Angeles: Univ. of California Press.

Gutiérrez, Ramón. 1993. "Community, Patriarchy, and Individualism: The Politics of Chicano History and the Dream of Equality." *American Quarterly* 45, no. 1: 44–67.

Hall, Stuart. 1981. "Notes on Deconstructing 'The Popular.'" In *People's History and Socialist Theory*, edited by Raphael Samuel, 227–240. London: Routledge and Kegan Paul.

———. 1997. "The Work of Representation." In *Representation: Cultural Representations and Signifying Practices*, edited by Stuart Hall, 13–74. London: Sage.

Harding, Susan. 2001. *The Book of Jerry Falwell: Fundamentalist Language and Politics*. Princeton, N.J.: Princeton Univ. Press.

Harris, Daniel. 1992. "The Conformity of Office Zaniness." In *Media Journal: Reading and Writing about Popular Culture*, edited by J. Harris, J. Rosen, and G. Calpas, 181–183. Boston: Allyn and Bacon.

Harvey, David. 1989. *The Condition of Postmodernity: An Inquiry into the Origins of Cultural Change*. Cambridge: Blackwell.

———. 1991. Afterword to *The Production of Space*, by Henri Lefebvre, 425–434. Oxford: Blackwell.

———. 1998a. "The Body as an Accumulation Strategy." *Environment and Planning D: Society and Space* 16:401–422.

———. 1998b. *Social Justice and the City*. Malden, Mass.: Blackwell.

———. 2000. *Spaces of Hope*. Berkeley and Los Angeles: Univ. of California Press.

———. 2009. "Address to the World Social Forum, Belém, Brazil." *Vice Magazine*. Accessed August 27, 2009. http://vice.typepad.com/vice_magazine/2009/02/belem—-introdu.html.

Hawk, J. D. 2006. "That's Not a Naked Woman; That's My Wife! Car Museum Gives Lowrider Image a Buff and Shine." *La Prensa San Diego*. Accessed April 10, 2010. http://laprensa sandiego.org/archieve/february24-06/lowrider.htm.

Hebdige, Dick. 1979. *Subculture: The Meaning of Style*. London: Routledge.

———. 1988. *Hiding in the Light: On Images and Things*. London: Routledge.

Hondagneu-Sotelo, Pierrette. 2001. *Doméstica: Immigrant Workers Cleaning and Caring in the Shadows of Affluence*. Berkeley and Los Angeles: Univ. of California Press.

hooks, bell. 2003. *We Real Cool: Black Men and Masculinity*. New York: Routledge.

Horkheimer, Max, and Theodor Adorno. 1972. *Dialectic of Enlightenment*. Translated by John Cumming. New York: Seabury.

Hyams, Melissa. 2003. "Adolescent Latina Bodyspaces: Making Homegirls, Homebodies and Homeplaces." *Antipode* 35, no. 3: 536–558.

Inda, Jonathan Xavier. 2000. "Performativity, Materiality, and the Racial Body." *Latino Studies Journal* 11, no. 3: 74–99.

———. 2005. "Analytics of the Modern: An Introduction." In *Anthropologies of Modernity: Foucault, Governmentality, and Life Politics*, edited by Jonathan Xavier Inda, 1–20. Malden, Mass.: Blackwell.

Irwin, Megan. 2006. "Hard Body: Liz Cohen's Infiltrating the Lowrider World—and Calling It Art." *Phoenix New Times*, October 5. Accessed May 12, 2011. http://www.phoenixnewtimes.com/2006-10-05/news/hard-body.

Jackson, Michael. 1993. *Paths toward a Clearing: Radical Empiricism and Ethnographic Inquiry*. Bloomington: Indiana Univ. Press.

———. 1998. *Minima Ethnographica: Intersubjectivity and the Ethnographic Project*. Chicago: Univ. of Chicago Press.

Jain, Anil. 2002. "Capitalism, Inc.—The 'Phagic' Character of Capitalism." In *Postmodern Practices: Beiträge zu einer Vergehenden Epoche*, edited by T. Doerfler and C. Globisch, 59–67. Münster, Germany: LIT.

Jain, Sarah S. Lochlann. 2002. "Urban Errands: The Means of Mobility." *Journal of Consumer Culture* 2, no. 3: 385–404.

———. 2004. "'Dangerous Instrumentality': The Bystander as Subject in Automobility." *Cultural Anthropology* 19, no. 1: 61–94.

———. 2005. "Violent Submission: Gendered Automobility." *Cultural Critique* 61 (Autumn): 186–214.

Jiménez, Tomás. 2010. *Replenishing Ethnicity: Mexican Americans, Immigration, and Identity*. Berkeley and Los Angeles: Univ. of California Press.

Joseph, Miranda. 1999. "The Performance of Production and Consumption." *Social Text* 54 (Spring): 25–61.

Kapchan, Deborah. 1996. *Gender on the Market: Moroccan Women and the Revoicing of Tradition*. Philadelphia: Univ. of Pennsylvania Press.

———. 2003. "Performance." In *Eight Words for the Study of Expressive Culture*, edited by Burt Feintuch, 121–144. Champaign: Univ. of Illinois Press.

Katznelson, Ira. 1992. *Marxism and the City*. Oxford: Clarendon.

Keane, Webb. 2005. "Signs Are Not the Garb of Meaning: On the Social Analysis of Things." In *Materiality*, edited by Daniel Miller, 182–205. Durham, N.C.: Duke Univ. Press.

Kellner, Douglas. 1995. *Media Culture: Cultural Studies, Identity, and Politics between the Modern and the Postmodern*. London: Routledge.

Kelso, John. 2001. "DPS Strikes Out with Ticket Fest at Car Show." *Austin American-Statesman*, July 31.

Kim, Sojin. 1995. *Chicano Graffiti and Murals*. Jackson: Univ. of Mississippi Press.

King, Wayne. 1981. "Low Riders Are Becoming Legion among Chicanos." *New York Times*, May 9. Accessed April 12, 2010. http://www.nytimes.com/1981/05/09/us/low-riders-are-becoming-legion-among-chicanos.html.

Kirshenblatt-Gimlett, Barbara. 1995. "The Aesthetics of Everyday Life: Interview with Suzi

Gablik." In *Conversations before the End of Time*, edited by Suzi Gablik, 410–433. New York: Thames and Hudson.

Knee, Stan. 2003. "Memorandum: Traffic and Pedestrian Stop Data." February 14. Austin Police Department. Accessed February 10, 2010. http://www.ci.austin.tx.us/police/downloads/racialprofilingmemofeb14.pdf.

Koch and Fowler. 1928. *A City Plan for Austin, Texas*. Austin: City Plan Commission.

Kopytoff, Igor. 1986. "The Cultural Biography of Things: Commoditization as Process." In *The Social Life of Things: Commodities in Cultural Perspective*, edited by Arjun Appadurai, 64–94. Cambridge: Cambridge Univ. Press.

Kordas, Ann. 2000. "Losing my Religion: Controlling Gang Violence through Limitations on Freedom of Expression." *Boston University Law Review* 80:1451–1492.

Kracauer, Siegfried. 1995. *The Mass Ornament: Weimar Essays*. Translated by Thomas Y. Levin. Cambridge, Mass.: Harvard Univ. Press.

Kun, Josh. 1997. "Against Easy Listening: Audiotopic Readings and Transnational Soundings." In *Everynight Life: Culture and Dance in Latin/o America*, edited by C. Fraser Delgado and J. E. Muñoz, 288–309. Durham, N.C.: Duke Univ. Press.

Lack, Paul D. 1981. "Slavery and Vigilantism in Austin, Texas, 1840–1860." *Southwestern Historical Quarterly* 85, no. 1: 1–20.

Ladendorf, Kirk. 2009. "Many of Austin's Chip Jobs Gone for Good." *Austin American-Statesman*, September 8. Accessed August 10, 2010. Available at http://www.allbusiness.com/electronics/computer-equipment-computer/12852025-1.html.

Laguerre, Michel. 1999. *Minoritized Space: An Inquiry into the Spatial Order of Things*. Berkeley: Institute for Governmental Studies.

Latino Comedy Project. 2002. *In Memorial: Chuy Mendoza, 1983–2002*. Accessed August 8, 2010. http://www.lcp.org/n_slainHero2.htm.

Lawrence, Denise L., and Setha Low. 1990. "The Built Environment and Spatial Form." *Annual Review of Anthropology* 19:453–505.

Lefebvre, Henri. 1991. *The Production of Space*. Translated by Donald Nicholson-Smith. Oxford: Blackwell.

———. 1992. *Critique of Everyday Life*, vol. 1. Translated by John Moore. London: Verso.

———. 1996. *Writings on Cities*. Translated by Eleonore Kofman and Elizabeth Lebas. Malden, Mass.: Blackwell.

———. 2003. *The Urban Revolution*. Translated by Robert Bononno. Minneapolis: Univ. of Minnesota Press.

———. 2004. *Rhythmanalysis: Space, Time, and Everyday Life*. Translated by Stuart Elden and Gerald Moore. New York: Continuum.

———. 2008. *Critique of Everyday Life*, vols. 1–3. Translated by John Moore. London: Verso.

Limón, José E. 1983. "Western Marxism and Folklore: A Critical Introduction." *Journal of American Folklore* 96, no. 379: 34–52.

———. 1994. *Dancing with the Devil: Society and Cultural Poetics in Mexican-American South Texas*. Madison: Univ. of Wisconsin Press.

———. 1999. *American Encounters: Greater Mexico, the United States, and the Erotics of Culture*. Boston: Beacon.

Lipsitz, George. 1998. *The Possessive Investment in Whiteness: How White People Profit from Identity Politics*. Philadelphia: Temple Univ. Press.

Loewen, James. 2005. *Sundown Towns: A Hidden Dimension of American Racism*. New York: New Press.

Long, Joshua. 2008. "Weird City: Sense of Place and Creative Resistance in Austin, Texas." Phd diss., Univ. of Kansas.

Low, Setha. 1996. "The Anthropology of Cities: Imagining and Theorizing the City." *Annual Review of Anthropology* 25:383–409.

———. 1999a. Introduction to *Theorizing the City: The New Urban Anthropology Reader*, edited by Setha Low, 1–36. New Brunswick, N.J.: Rutgers Univ. Press.

———. 1999b. "Spatializing Culture: The Social Production and Social Construction of Public Space in Costa Rica." In *Theorizing the City: The New Urban Anthropology Reader*, edited by Setha Low, 111–137. New Brunswick, N.J.: Rutgers Univ. Press.

———. 2000. *On the Plaza: The Politics of Public Space and Culture*. Austin: Univ. of Texas Press.

Low, Setha, and Denise Lawrence-Zuñiga, eds. 2003. *The Anthropology of Space and Place: Locating Culture*. Malden, Mass.: Blackwell.

Lubrano, Alfred. 2004. *Limbo: Blue-Collar Roots, White-Collar Dreams*. Malden, Mass.: Wiley.

Lutz, Catherine A., and Jane L. Collins. 1993. *Reading "National Geographic."* Chicago: Univ. of Chicago Press.

Lynch, Kevin. 1960. *The Image of the City*. Cambridge, Mass.: MIT Press.

Macías, Anthony. 2008. *Mexican American Mojo: Popular Music, Dance, and Urban Culture in Los Angeles, 1935–1968*. Durham, N.C.: Duke Univ. Press.

Mahler, Sarah J. 1995. *American Dreaming: Immigrant Life on the Margins*. Princeton, N.J.: Princeton Univ. Press.

Marcuse, Herbert. 1971. *An Essay on Liberation*. Boston: Beacon.

———. 1978. *The Aesthetic Dimension: Toward a Critique of Marxist Aesthetics*. Boston: Beacon.

———. 1991. *One-Dimensional Man: Studies in the Ideology of Advanced Industrial Society*. Boston: Beacon.

Marx, Karl. 1994. *The Eighteenth Brumaire of Louis Bonaparte*. New York: International Publishers.

Massey, Doreen. 1994. *Space, Place, and Gender*. Minneapolis: Univ. of Minnesota Press.

———. 2005. *For Space*. London: Sage.

Massey, Douglas, Jorge Durand, and Nolan J. Malone. 2003. *Beyond Smoke and Mirrors: Mexican Immigration in an Era of Economic Integration*. New York: Sage.

Massumi, Brian. 2002. *Parables for the Virtual: Movement, Affect, Sensation*. Durham, N.C.: Duke Univ. Press.

McCann, Eugene J. 1999. "Race, Protest, and Public Space: Contextualizing Lefebvre in the U.S. City." *Antipode* 31, no. 2: 163–184.

McCarthy, Anna. 2006. "From the Ordinary to the Concrete: Cultural Studies and the Politics of Scale." In *Questions of Method in Cultural Studies*, edited by M. White and J. Schwoch, 21–53. Malden, Mass.: Blackwell.

McDonald, Jason. 2005. "From Bipartite to Tripartite Society: Demographic Change and Realignments in Ethnic Stratification in Austin, Texas." *Patterns of Prejudice* 39, no. 1: 1–25.

McFarland, Pancho. 2008. *Chicano Rap: Gender and Violence in the Postindustrial Barrio*. Austin: Univ. of Texas Press.

Menchaca, Martha. 2001. *Recovering History, Constructing Race: The Indian, Black, and White Roots of Mexican Americans*. Austin: Univ. of Texas Press.

Mendoza, Louis. 2001. "Making Sense of the 'Hood.'" *CR: New Centennial Review* 1, no. 1: 333–343.

Mendoza, Ruben. 2000. "Cruising Art and Culture in Aztlán: Lowriding in the Mexican American Southwest." In *U.S. Latino Literatures and Cultures: Transnational Perspectives*, edited by F. A. Lomelí and K. Ikas, 3–35. Heidelberg, Germany: Universitätsverlag C. Winter.

Mendoza-Denton, Norma. 2008. *Homegirls: Language and Cultural Practice among Latina Youth Gangs*. Malden, Mass.: Blackwell.

Merrifield, Andy. 1992. "Space and Place: A Lefebvrian Reconciliation." *Transactions of the British Institute of Geography* 18:516–531.

———. 1995. "Lefebvre, Anti-logos, and Nietzsche: An Alternative Reading of the Production of Space." *Antipode* 27, no. 3: 294–303.

———. 2002a. *Dialectical Urbanism*. New York: Monthly Review Press.

———. 2002b. *Metromarxism: A Marxist Tale of the City*. London: Routledge.

Merry, Sally Engle. 2001. "Spatial Governmentality and the New Urban Social Order: Controlling Gender Violence through Law." *American Anthropologist* 103, no. 1: 16–29.

Miller, Daniel. 1994. *Modernity: An Ethnographic Approach; Dualism and Mass Culture in Trinidad*. Oxford: Berg.

———. 1995. "Consumption as the Vanguard of History: A Polemic by Way of Introduction." In *Acknowledging Consumption: A Review of New Studies*, edited by Daniel Miller, 1–57. London: Routledge.

———. 2001. *Car Cultures*. Oxford: Berg.

Mitchell, Don. 2003. *The Right to the City: Social Justice and the Fight for Public Space*. New York: Guilford.

Montejano, David. 1987. *Anglos and Mexicans in the Making of Texas, 1836–1936*. Austin: Univ. of Texas Press.

Mulvey, Laura. 1975. "Visual Pleasure and Narrative Cinema." *Screen* 16, no. 3: 6–18.

Munn, Nancy D. 1986. *The Fame of Gawa: A Symbolic Study of Value Transformation in a Massim*. Cambridge: Cambridge Univ. Press.

———. 1996. "Excluded Spaces: The Figure in the Australian Aboriginal Landscape." *Critical Inquiry* 22, no. 3: 446–465.

Nash, Catherine. 2000. "Performativity in Practice: Some Recent Work in Cultural Geography." *Progress in Human Geography* 24, no. 4: 653–664.

Nericcio, William Anthony. 2007. *Tex[t]-Mex: Seductive Hallucinations of "the Mexican" in America*. Austin: Univ. of Texas Press.

Newman, Katherine. 1999. *No Shame in My Game: The Working Poor in the Inner City*. New York: Knopf.

Nichols, Bill. 1994. *Blurred Boundaries: Questions of Meaning in Contemporary Culture*. Bloomington: Indiana Univ. Press.

Noriega, Chon. 2001. "Fashion Crimes." *Aztlán* 26, no. 1: 1–13.

Norst, Joel. 1988. *Colors*. New York: Pocket.

Norton, Anne. 1993. *Republic of Signs: Liberal Theory and American Popular Culture*. Chicago: Univ. of Chicago Press.

O'Dell, John. 2000. "Lowrider Magazine Riding Higher than Ever." *Los Angeles Times*, April 19.

O'Malley, Pat. 1993. "Containing Our Excitement: Commodity Culture and the Crisis of Discipline." *Studies in Law, Politics, and Society* 13:159–186.

Ortíz-Torres, Rubén. 2000. "Cathedrals on Wheels." In *Customized: Art Inspired by Hot Rods, Low Riders, and American Car Culture*, edited by Nora Donnelly, 37–38. New York: Abrams.

Ortner, Sherry. 1984. "Theory in Anthropology since the Sixties." *Comparative Studies in Society and History* 26, no. 1: 126–166.

Our Lady of Guadalupe Catholic Church. n.d. "History of Our Lady of Guadalupe Church" (Austin, Texas). Accessed August 8, 2010. http://www.olgaustin.org/history.shtml.

Packer, Jeremy. 2008. *Mobility without Mayhem: Safety, Cars, and Citizenship*. Durham, N.C.: Duke Univ. Press.

Parchesky, Jennifer. 2006. "Women in the Driver's Seat: The Auto-erotics of Early Women's Films." *Film History* 18, no. 2: 174–184.

Paredes, Américo. 1958. *With His Pistol in His Hand: A Border Ballad and Its Hero*. Austin: Univ. of Texas Press.

———. 1993. "On Ethnographic Work among Minority Groups: A Folklorist's Perspective." In *Folklore and Culture on the Texas-Mexican Border*, edited by Richard Bauman, 73–112. Austin: Univ. of Texas Press.

Parsons, Jack, Carmella Padilla, and Juan Estevan Arellano. 1999. *Low 'n' Slow: Lowriding in New Mexico*. Santa Fe: Museum of New Mexico Press.

Penland, Paige. 1997. "The History of *Lowrider Magazine*: What a Long, Low Trip It's Been." January. *Lowrider*, 74–82.

———. 2003. *Lowrider: History, Pride, Culture*. St. Paul, Minn.: Motorbooks.

Pérez, Emma. 1999. *The Decolonial Imaginary: Writing Chicanas into History*. Bloomington: Indiana Univ. Press.

Pérez, Gina. 2004. *The Near Northwest Side Story: Migration, Displacement, and Puerto Rican Families*. Berkeley and Los Angeles: Univ. of California Press.

Pérez, Ramona. 2006. "The Misunderstanding of Mexican Community Life in Urban Apartment Space: A Case Study in Applied Anthropology and Community Policing." *City and Society* 18, no. 2: 232–259.

Pérez-Torres, Rafael. 2006. *Mestizaje: Critical Uses of Race in Chicano Culture*. Minneapolis: Univ. of Minnesota Press.

Phillips, Susan. 2000. *Wallbangin': Graffiti and Gangs in L.A.* Chicago: Univ. of Chicago Press.

Pile, Steve. 2005. *Real Cities: Modernity, Space, and the Phantasmagorias of City Life.* London: Sage.

Plascencia, Luis F. B. 1983. "Low Riding in the Southwest: Cultural Symbols in the Mexican Community." In *History, Culture, and Society: Chicano Studies in the 1980s*, 141–175. Ypsilanti, Mich.: Bilingual Press.

Rabinow, Paul. 2003. *Anthropos Today: Reflections on Modern Equipment.* Princeton, N.J.: Princeton Univ. Press.

Ramírez, Catherine. 2004. "Representing, Politics, and the Politics of Representation in Gang Studies." *American Quarterly* 56, no. 4: 1135–1146.

———. 2008. *The Woman in the Zoot Suit: Gender, Nationalism, and the Cultural Politics of Memory.* Durham, N.C.: Duke Univ. Press.

Ramos-Zayas, Ana. 2003. *National Performances: The Politics of Class, Race, and Space in Puerto Rican Chicago.* Chicago: Univ. of Chicago Press.

Reynolds, Brian, and Joseph Fitzpatrick. 1999. "The Transversality of Michel de Certeau: Foucault's Panoptic Discourse and the Cartographic Impulse." *Diacritics* 29, no. 3: 63–80.

Rich, Adrienne. 2001. "Notes toward a Politics of Location." In *Arts of the Possible: Essays and Conversations*, 62–82. New York: Norton.

Ritzer, George. 1993. *The McDonaldization of Society.* Newberry Park, Calif.: Pine Forge Press/ Sage.

Rivera, John-Michael. 2005. "'La Memoria de Nuestra Tierra': Landscapes, Mexicans, and the Browning of America." *Aztlán* 30, no. 1: 123–146.

Rodman, Margaret C. 1992. "Empowering Place: Multilocality and Multivocality." In *The Anthropology of Space and Place: Locating Culture*, edited by Setha Low and Denise Lawrence-Zuñiga, 204–223. Malden, Mass.: Blackwell.

Rodríguez, Roberto. 1997. *Justice: A Question of Race.* Tempe: Bilingual Review Press.

Rodríguez, Sylvia. 1998. "Fiesta Time and Plaza Space: Resistance and Accommodation in a Tourist Town." *Journal of American Folklore* 111, no. 439: 39–56.

Rogers, Tim. 2002. "Henri Lefebvre, Space, and Folklore." *Ethnologies* 24, no. 1: 21–44.

Rojas, James. 1995. "The Latino Landscape of East Los Angeles." *NACLA Report on the Americas* 28, no. 4: 32–37.

Romero, Mary. 1992. *Maid in the U.S.A.* New York: Routledge.

Rosaldo, Renato. 1993. *Culture and Truth: The Remaking of Social Analysis.* Boston: Beacon.

Rose, Tricia. 1994. *Black Noise: Rap Music and Black Culture in Contemporary America.* Hanover, N.H.: Univ. Press of New England / Wesleyan Univ. Press.

Ross, Andrew. 2002. *No Collar: The Humane Workplace and its Hidden Costs.* New York: Basic Books.

Rotenberg, Robert. 1993. "On the Salubrity of Sites." In *The Cultural Meaning of Urban Space*, edited by R. Rotenberg and G. McDonogh, 17–30. Wesport, CT: Bergin & Garvey.

———. 2001. "Metropolitanism and the Transformation of Urban Space in Nineteenth-Century Colonial Metropoles." *American Anthropologist* 103, no. 1: 7–15.

Salinas, Raúl R. 1995. *East of the Freeway*. Austin: Red Salmon.

Samuels, David. 2004. *Putting a Song on Top of It: Expression and Identity on the Carlos Apache Reservation*. Tucson: Univ. of Arizona Press.

Sanchez, George. 1995. *Becoming Mexican American: Ethnicity, Culture, and Identity in Chicano Los Angeles, 1900–1945*. New York: Oxford Univ. Press.

Sánchez-Tranquilino, Marcos. 1995. "Space, Power, and Youth Culture: Mexican American Graffiti and Chicano Murals in East Los Angeles, 1972–1978." In *Looking High and Low: Art and Cultural Identity*, edited by Brenda Jo Bright and Liza Bakewell, 55–88. Tucson: Univ. of Arizona Press.

Sánchez-Tranquilino, Marcos, and John Tagg. 1992. "The Pachuco's Flayed Hide: Mobility, Identity, and Buenas Garras." In *Cultural Studies*, edited by Lawrence Grossberg, Cary Nelson, and Paula A. Treichler, 556–570. New York: Routledge.

Sandoval, Chela. 2000. *Methodology of the Oppressed*. Minneapolis: Univ. of Minnesota Press.

Sandoval, Denise. 2003a. "Bajito y Suavecito: The Lowriding Tradition." Smithsonian Institution Virtual Gallery. Accessed 9 April, 2010. http://latino.si.edu/virtualgallery/lowrider/LR_SandovalEssay.htm.

——. 2003b. "Bajito y Suavecito/Low and Slow: Cruising through Lowrider Culture." Phd diss., Claremont Graduate School.

Sandoval, Denise, and Patricia Polk. 2000. *Arte y Estilo: The Lowriding Tradition*. Los Angeles: Peterson Automotive Museum.

Savage, Mike, and Alan Warde. 1993. *Urban Sociology, Capitalism, and Modernity*. London: Macmillan.

Schloss, Joe. 2004. *Making Beats: The Art of Sample-Based Hip-Hop*. Middletown, Conn.: Wesleyan Univ. Press.

——. 2009. *Foundation: B-Boys, B-Girls, and Hip-Hop Culture in New York*. New York: Oxford Univ. Press.

Schulman, Norma. 1994. "The House that Black Built: Television Stand-Up Comedy as Minor Discourse." *Journal of Popular Film and Television* 22, no. 3: 108–115.

Schumacher, E. F. 1975. *Small Is Beautiful: Economics as if People Mattered*. New York: Harper & Row.

Sciorra, Joseph. 1996. "Return to the Future: Puerto Rican Vernacular Architecture in New York City." In *Re-presenting the City: Ethnicity, Capital and Culture in the Twenty-First Century Metropolis*, edited by Anthony King, 60–92. London: Macmillan.

Seiler, Cotton. 2006. "'So That We as a Race Might Have Something Authentic to Travel By': African American Automobility and Cold-War Liberalism." *American Quarterly* 58, no. 4: 1091–1117.

——. 2008. *Republic of Drivers: A Cultural History of Automobility in America*. Chicago: Univ. of Chicago Press.

Sennett, Richard. 2009. *The Craftsman*. New Haven, Conn.: Yale Univ. Press.

Shank, Barry. 1994. *Dissonant Identities: The Rock'n'Roll Scene in Austin, Texas*. Middletown, Conn.: Wesleyan Univ. Press.

Sheller, Mimi, and John Urry. 2000. "The City and the Car." *International Journal of Urban and Regional Research* 24:107–125.

Sheriff, John. 1994. *Charles Peirce's Guess at the Riddle: Grounds for Human Significance.* Bloomington: Indiana Univ. Press.

Shields, Rob. 1996. "A Guide to Urban Representation and What to Do about It: Alternative Traditions of Urban Theory." In *Re-presenting the City: Ethnicity, Capital, and Culture in the Twenty-First Century Metropolis*, edited by Anthony King, 227–252. London: Macmillan.

Smithsonian Institution. n.d. *"Dave's Dream" Lowrider.* Online object entry from collection. Washington, D.C.: National Museum of American History. Accessed August 9, 2010. http://historywired.si.edu/object.cfm?ID=215.

Soja, Edward. 1989. *Postmodern Geographies: The Reassertion of Space in Critical Social Theory.* London: Verso.

———. 1996. *Thirdspace: Journeys to Los Angeles and Other Real-and-Imagined Places.* Oxford: Blackwell.

———. 2000. *Postmetropolis: Critical Studies of Cities and Regions.* Malden, Mass.: Blackwell.

Stallabrass, Julian. 1996. *Gargantua: Manufactured Mass Culture.* London: Verso.

Stallybrass, Peter, and Allon White. 1986. *The Politics and Poetics of Transgression.* Ithaca, N.Y.: Cornell Univ. Press.

Stephens, Vincent. 2005. "Pop Goes the Rapper: A Close Reading of Eminem's Genderphobia." *Popular Music* 24, no. 1: 21–36.

Stewart, Kathleen. 1991. "On the Politics of Cultural Theory: A Case for 'Contaminated' Cultural Critique." *Social Research* 58, no. 2: 395–412.

———. 1996. *A Space on the Side of the Road: Cultural Poetics in an "Other" America.* Princeton, N.J.: Princeton Univ. Press.

———. 2005. "Cultural Poesis: The Generativity of Emergent Things." In *The Sage Handbook of Qualitative Research*, edited by N. Denzin and Y. Lincoln, 1015–1030. London: Sage.

———. 2007. *Ordinary Affects.* Durham, N.C.: Duke Univ. Press.

Stewart, Susan. 1993. *On Longing: Narratives of the Miniature, the Gigantic, the Souvenir, the Collection.* Durham, N.C.: Duke Univ. Press.

———. 1994. *Crimes of Writing: Problems in the Containment of Representation.* Durham, N.C.: Duke Univ. Press.

Stokes, Martin. 1994. "Turkish Arabesk and the City: Urban Popular Culture as Spatial Practice." In *Islam, Globalization, and Postmodernity*, edited by A. Ahmed and H. Donnan, 21–37. London: Routledge.

Stoller, Paul. 1997. *Sensuous Scholarship.* Philadelphia: Univ. of Pennsylvania Press.

Stone, Michael. 1990. "'Bajito y Suavecito': Low Riding and the 'Class' of Class." *Studies in Latin American Popular Culture* 9:85–126.

Striffler, Steve. 2002. "Inside a Poultry Processing Plant: An Ethnographic Portrait." *Labor History* 43, no. 3: 305–313.

Sutton, Jane. 2008. "'Brothel Bus' Makes Last Stop in Miami." Reuters. June 26. Accessed August 9, 2010. http://www.reuters.com/article/idUSN2632464420080626.

Tatum, Charles M. 2011. *Lowriders in Chicano Culture: From Low and Slow to Show*. Santa Barbara, Calif.: Greenwood.

Taylor, Charles. 2004. *Modern Social Imaginaries*. Durham, N.C.: Duke Univ. Press.

Thrift, Nigel. 1996. *Spatial Formations*. London: Sage.

———. 2004a. "Driving in the City." *Theory, Culture, and Society* 21, nos. 4–5: 41–59.

———. 2004b. "Intensities of Feeling: Towards a Spatial Politics of Affect." *Geografiska Annaler* 86 B(1): 57–78.

———. 2004c. "Performance and Performativity: A Geography of Unknown Lands." In *A Companion to Cultural Geography*, edited by J. Duncan, N. Johnson, and R. Schein, 121–136. Malden, Mass.: Blackwell.

Toop, David. 2000. *Rap Attack 3: African Rap to Global Hip-Hop*. London: Serpent's Tail.

Trillin, Calvin, and Edward Koren. 1978. "Low and Slow, Mean and Clean." *New Yorker*. July 10, 70–74.

Turner, Victor. 1986. *The Anthropology of Performance*. New York: PAJ.

UNEF Strasbourg. 1966. *On the Poverty of Student Life: Considered in its Economic, Political, Psychological, Sexual, and Particularly Intellectual Aspects, and a Modest Proposal for its Remedy*. Strasbourg: University of Strasbourg Student Union.

U.S. Census Bureau. 2005. *Texas Becomes Nation's Newest "Majority-minority" State*. Census Bureau Reports. Washington, D.C.: U.S. Census Bureau.

Valle, Victor, and Rodolfo Torres. 2000. *Latino Metropolis*. Minneapolis: Univ. of Minnesota Press.

Vélez-Ibañez, Carlos. 1996. *Border Visions: Mexican Cultures of the Southwest United States*. Tucson: Univ. of Arizona Press.

Vigil, James Diego. 1988. *Barrio Gangs: Street Life and Identity in Southern California*. Austin: Univ. of Texas Press.

———. 1991. "Car Charros: Cruising and Lowriding in the Barrios of East Los Angeles." *Latino Studies Journal* 2, no. 2: 71–79.

Villa, Raúl Homero. 2000. *Barrio Logos: Space and Place in Urban Chicano Literature and Culture*. Austin: Univ. of Texas Press.

Viramontes, Helena Maria. 1995. *The Moths, and Other Stories*. Houston: Arte Publico.

Visweswaran, Kamala. 2010. *Un/common Cultures: Racism and the Rearticulation of Cultural Difference*. Durham, N.C.: Duke Univ. Press.

Volosinov, V. N. 1986. *Marxism and the Philosophy of Language*. Translated by Lasislav Matejka and I. R. Tuitunik. Cambridge, Mass.: Harvard Univ. Press.

Weber, Max. 2003. *The Protestant Ethic and the Spirit of Capitalism*. Translated by Talcott Parsons. Mineola, N.Y.: Dover.

West, Ted. 1976. "Scenes from a Revolution: Low and Slow." *Car and Driver*. August, 47–51.

Willis, Paul. 1978. *Profane Culture*. London: Routledge and Kegan Paul.

Wolfe, Tom. 1971. *The Kandy-Kolored Tangerine-Flake Streamline Baby*. New York: Pocket.

Yarbro-Bejarano, Yvonne. 1994. "Gloria Anzaldúa's *Borderlands/La Frontera*: Cultural Studies, 'Difference,' and the Non-unitary Subject." *Cultural Critique* 28 (Autumn): 5–28.

———. 1999. "Sexuality and Chicana/o Studies: Toward a Theoretical Paradigm for the Twenty-first Century." *Cultural Studies* 13, no. 2: 335–345.

Young, Katherine, ed. 1995. *Bodylore*. Knoxville: Univ. of Tennessee Press.

Zatz-Díaz, Ivan. 2003. "From Movie Palaces to Little Boxes: The Production of Screen Spaces and Everyday Life." Paper presented at the Cultural Studies Association, Pittsburgh.

———. 2005. "The Weight of Nightmares." *Situations* 1, no. 1: 143–159.

Zilberg, Elana. 2004. "Fools Banished from the Kingdom: Remapping Geographies of Gang Violence between the Americas (Los Angeles and San Salvador)." *American Quarterly* 56, no. 3: 759–779.

Zukin, Sharon. 1995. *The Cultures of Cities*. Cambridge: Blackwell.

———. 1996. "Space and Symbols in an Age of Decline." In *Re-presenting the City: Ethnicity, Capital and Culture in the Twenty-First Century Metropolis*, edited by Anthony King, 43–59. London: Macmillan.

———. 2009. *Naked City: The Life and Death of Authentic Urban Places*. Oxford: Oxford Univ. Press.

Index

Page numbers in italics indicate images.

aesthetic experience, 22
aesthetics: bourgeois, 66–67, 78, 80, 92,
    100; defined, 22, 204; funereal, 83,
    85–86; gangster, 169–171, 214n2;
    gendered visual, 79; generative, 202;
    lowrider, 3, 13, 17–18, 21, 68, 79, 87, 92,
    97, 99–100, 169, 201, 205; and politics,
    21–22, 66, 97, 203–204; popular, 2, 8,
    34–35, 75, 81–82, 169, 204; of space, 34,
    75, 169; working-class, 67
affect, 22–24, 33, 87, 107, 174; and politics,
    134–135, 202; and space, 16, 20, 22–25,
    45–46, 51, 97, 202
affectivity, 9, 21–24, 33, 98, 174, 208
Alarcón, Norma, 8
Almanza, Susana, 209n14
Alvarez, Raúl, 209n14
ambivalence, 71, 99–100, 104, 133–134,
    213n18
American Me (1992), 175
Anderson, Benedict, 26, 110

Anzaldúa, Gloria, 134
Appadurai, Arjun, 26
artists, engagement with lowriders, 93, 125,
    213n17
assimilation, 27–28, 100
Austin, *38, 39*; changes in, 37, 142; cruis-
    ing, 32, *34*, 41; diversity of, 6, 11, 33;
    East, 37, 40–42, 45, 52, 72, 194–195,
    209n2; geography, 2, 24, 32–33, 37–38,
    41, 60, 72, 142; Mexican American,
    27–28, 44; North, 192; South, 39–41, 72,
    174, 209n4; West, 25, 39, 90, 162
Austin American-Statesman, 118, 141, 169
Austin Police Department, 172, 191–192,
    201n8, 215n5–6
autotopographies, 7, 75

Bakhtin, Mikhail, 97
baroque, 67–68, 77, 78–79, 80, 85–86, 211n4
barrio, 4, 25–26, 33, 43, 47, 50–51, 100, 110,
    116, 140, 178, 187

barrioization, 25, 36, 44–45, 50, 202

barriology, 25–26, 33, 36, 45, 60, 76, 82, 92, 100, 169, 170–171, 174–175, 186–187

Barthes, Roland, 22, 65

Baudrillard, Jean, 67

Benjamin, Walter, 86, 92, 150, 202–203, 211n8, 214n4

Berland, Jody, 7–8

Berlant, Lauren, 23

Blood In, Blood Out (1993), 175

Boulevard Nights (1979), 106, 188

Bourdieu, Pierre, 67, 81, 208n11

Boyz n the Hood (1991), 94, 188

Bright, Brenda Jo, 88, 121–122, 207n1

Butler, Judith, 172

car culture, U.S., 16, 64, 72, 81, 98, 102, 135

carnivalesque, 63, 92, 123

Cars (2006), 82, 102

Chambers, Ross, 66, 204

Chaplin, Charlie, 89

Chávez, César, 109, 212n5

Chavoya, Ondine, 13

Chicano Park, 9–11, *10–13*, 32, 41, 89–90, 105, 189, 195

Cintron, Ralph, 163–164, 214n4

Cisneros, Sandra, 106

citizenship, 24, 71, 73, 188, 207n2

class, 18; and academia, position of, 111, 118, 138, 139–141, 145; and aesthetics, 67–68, 99; and consumption, 79–82, 87; and lowriders, position of, 28, 53–54, 64, 68, 107, 111, 127–128, 138, 141–142, 165, 180, 208n2; and the "new economy," 165–166; and space, 21–22, 24, 33, 39–41, 48, 71, 74, 96, 192, 216n15; and violence, 21; and work, 139–140, 163, 166. *See also* aesthetics; economy: "new"; work: hierarchical value of

Cohen, Liz, 125

Colors (1988), 4

community policing, 21, 191–195, 215n133

conspicuous production, 88

consumption, 27–28, 64–67, 71, 73, 76, 79–82, 87–89, 92, 98, 100, 205, 211n5, 214n1; gendered, of visual media, 114, 119, 122–123

contestation, 7, 24–25, 34, 60, 166, 169, 181, 201

contests, bikini and hardbody, 117–118, 121–123

counter-cartography, 29, 35, 59–60; and remapping, 50

cruising, 10–13, *13*, 25, 31–35, *34*, 46–51, 60, 63, 73, 105–106, 114, 182, 185, 188–191, 195–196, 199–200, 206

culture: anthropological concept, 6–7; expressive, 15, 18, 172, 202; generative concept, 24, 30, 135, 202, 205, 208n11; media/industry, 14, 29, 65, 82, 89, 103–104, 108–110, 117–118, 121, 123, 126, 128, 212n13; popular, 8, 40, 65, 98, 119, 139, 185–186, 201, 212n13. *See also* consumption

Cuneo, Joan, 129

customization, 2, 6, 8, 14–15, 17, 22, 59, 65–66, 73, 78, 81–82, 87–89, 97, 99, 126

"Dave's Dream" car, 83. *See also* memorial cars

Davis, Mike, 171

Dazza, 116–117

Del Valle, 41, 73

Deutsche, Rosalyn, 209n12

Día de la Raza, 46

dialectics, 36–37, 99–100

discourse, 19–20, 24, 82, 107

Eastside, 11, 25, 43, *38*, 39, 40–45, 72, 41–42, 47–51, 72, 90, 145, 193–195, 197, 209n2, 216n15

Eazy-E, 86

economy: automotive, 66, 76, 81, 82, 87, 140, 151–156, 158; barter and trade,

158–160; housing, 50, 71, 74–75; illegal, 140–141; "new," 9, 29, 141–143, 163–166

Ehrenreich, Barbara, 71–72, 147–150, 210n1, 214n3

8 Mile, 213n19

embodiment, 20, 102–108, 125–127, 130, 133–135, 138, 202, 213n22

emergence, 9, 11, 17, 22, 25, 100, 103, 135, 204–205, 208n11

ethnography. *See* space: and ethnography

Euros, 18, 62, 72–73, 156, 159, 183–184, 210n9, 213n18

experience, 7, 19–20, 22–23, 45, 81, 99, 134, 143, 150–151, 171, 185–186, 202, 206

family, 15–16, 73–75, 80, 83, 85, 144, 187, 205

feelingful signs, 15

fetish, reverse, 89

fetishism, commodity, 81, 88, 100, 164, 211n5

Foucault, Michel, 97–98, 107

Friday (1995), 91, 94–95

gangs: and aesthetics, 18, 75, 96, 169–174, 214n2–3; and barriology, 169, 171, 174–175, 178, 186; lowriders, opposed by, 60, 171, 176–177; police science on, 171–174; and race, 172; and social determinants of, 186; solidarity, 178, 186–187; and space, 170–172, 177–179, 187; stereotyping, 15, 21, 107–108, 142, 174–175, 196; threat, figured as, 5, 50, 168, 172, 188; and violence, 178–180, 186, 189

gender: and automobility, 104, 127–129, 134; determination of research, 102, 111–113, 118–119, 134; homosociality, 130; of lowriding, 102– 123, 125, 129, 134; and normativity, challenges to, 132–133, 185–186; order, 123; race and class, articulated with, 99–100, 128; and space, 102, 209n12; and violence,

21, 127, 187; visual constructions of, 79, 104, 111, 117–118, 121–122, 125–126

genderphobia, 213n19

General Motors (GM), 18, 49, 72, 92, 153, 156

gentrification, 37, 41, 46, 71–72

ghetto, 18, 36, 80, 152

Gilroy, Paul, 81, 211n5

Gonzalez, "El Larry," 109, 125–126, 213n15

governmentality, 24, 188

graffiti, 7, 40, 85, *85*, 94, 132, 173, 178, 201, 208n9

Griffith, James, 77–78, 80, 211n4

Hall, Stuart, 8

Harris, Alex, 93–94

Hebdige, Dick, 174

heterotopia, 97

hip-hop, 1, 7, 13, 14, 41, 65, 69, 80, 94, 105

Homies, 75, 92–93, *94*

hydraulics, 1–2, 32, 58, 61–62, 73, 82, 137, 160, 163, 183, 202

Ice Cube, 94–95

identity maps, 33, 34–35, 37, 60, 209n1

ideology, 81, 102, 127

imagined cities, 26, 29, 34, 36, 204, 209n1

imagined community, 110

Institute of Contemporary Art, Boston, 93

interior: automotive, 2, 29, 68, 71, 76–78, *77*, *78*, 80, 86–87, 93–94, 97, 100, 152; brothel, 86–87; as home, 69, 71, 73, 94–95; upholstery, 2, 77, *77*, *82*, 83, 85, 93

Jain, Sara Lochlann, 111, 127–129

Kelso, John, 118–119

Laguerre, Michel, 35–36

Lefebvre, Henri, 24, 29, 36, 89, 204, 209n12, 213–214n22

Limón, José, 207n2

Lipsitz, George, 33

Low, Setha, 36

lowrider: defined, 2; in media, 82, 102; negative views of, 20; positive image of, 15, 60, 121–122, 131, 134, 142, 170, 176, 178, 187, 189, 195, 198, 205; scholarship on, 207n1; space, 9, 20, 23–27, 32, 34, 37, 126, 129–130, 141, 170, 174, 185, 202, 205; women, 123, 126, 130

Lowrider Magazine, 3, 108–111, *112*, 113–114, 116–117, 119–121, 123, *124*, 125–126, 133, 188, 205, 212n4, 212n8–9, 213n15; readers' critiques of, 114, 119–121

Madrid, Sonny, 109

Mahler, Sarah, 76, 210n3

Marcuse, Herbert, 81

Marx, Karl, 98, 133, 202, 206, 214n5

masculinity, 13, 16, 21, 79–80, 111, 113, 119, 127–128, 130–131, 134, 170, 185–186, 213n19

materiality, 3, 6–9, 15–17, 19–20, 23–30, 36–37, 46, 65–66, 75, 81, 83, 86–87, 97, 102, 104, 106, 108, 127, 129, 131, 133–134, 138–139, 164–165, 202, 204–206, 208n11, 213–214n22

McFarland, Pancho, 185–186

MEChA. See *Movimiento Estudiantíl Chicana/Chicano de Aztlán*

memorial cars, 83–85, *84*. *See also* "Dave's Dream"

Mendoza, Louis, 26

Mendoza-Denton, Norma, 185–186

Mexico, cultural ties to lowriding, 13, 27, 77, 211n4

Miller, Daniel, 99, 102

miniatures, 92

minoritized space, 7, 21, 35–36, 44, 60, 82, 140, 173

model cars, *68*, 69–73, *70*, 92, *93*, 95

model photography, 111, 113–126, *115*, 133

Montopolis, 41, *84*

Movimiento Estudiantíl Chicana/Chicano de Aztlán (MEChA), 109, 120–121

Munn, Nancy, 23

Napoleon Dynamite (2004), 82

1928 Master Plan, 44–45

Norton, Anne, 82

Nuñez, David, 109

oppositionality, 66, 134

Our Lady of Guadalupe Church, Austin, 43

pachucos, 100, 121, 142. *See also* zoot suit

Penland, Paige, 110, 131, 212n7

performance, 8–9, 13, 25, 27, 30, 32, 35, 46, 51, 54, 75, 79, 95, 103, 119, 122, 130, 164, 187, 205, 208n11; of space, 8, 205

Petersen Automotive Museum, 117

pimped-out ride, 86, 106, 160

poetic wisdom, 28, 139, 143

police: controversy, 192, 210n8, 215n11–13; surveillance, 21, 32, 34, 36, 40, 48, 51–52, 56–58, 184, 194, 200; traffic stops, 21, 35, 53–57, 107–108, 175–176, 188, 195–196. *See also* Austin Police Department

politics: cultural, 3, 24–25, 29, 33, 65–66, 104, 118, 120, 122–123, 134–135, 169, 202–204, 213n15; of presence, 25, 34, 73, 134, 202, 204

racial profiling, 54, 81, 107, 187, 210n8

raulrsalinas, 43

resistance, 60, 66, 98–99, 119, 130, 185, 203, 212n13

rims, 10, 17–18, 61, 94–95, 143, 158–159

Ritchie, Guy, 127–128

Riverside Drive, 1–2, 32, *39*, 47–50, 59–60, 69, 72, 90, 114, 182, 184, 200, 206

Robinson Crusoe, 96

Rodriguez, Roberto, 110, 188

Salinas, Raul R. *See* raulrsalinas
Sanchez-Tranquilino, Marcos, 100
Sandoval, Denise, 16, 117, 123, 126, 130, 135
Schloss, Joe, 14
second nature, 27, 65–66, 97, 102
Sedgwick, Eve, 111
segregation, 33, 37, 44–45
significance, 4, 6–9, 14–15, 17, 19–20, 23,
    36, 81, 99, 102, 114, 134, 203; excess, 16,
    22, 67
space: and ethnography, 5–6, 9, 140; and
    memory, 20, 25–26, 45–47, 82, 103, 174;
    policing and regulation of, 187–191,
    200; politics of, 34–35; production
    of, 3–4, 6–9, 11, 23, 25–26, 33, 36–37,
    44–45, 187, 202, 204–205, 213n2; social,
    4, 6–8, 20, 25, 29, 37, 51, 133–134, 139,
    148, 171, 206, 209n12. *See also* perfor-
    mance: of space
spatial fields, 7, 23–24, 34, 75, 202
Star (2001), 127
Stewart, Kathleen, 22, 25
Stewart, Susan, 66–67, 92, 96
subculture, 65

taco plates, 28, 197–199, *199*
Tagg, John, 100
Taylor, Charles, 27
Texas Heat Wave car and truck show, 118
Thrift, Nigel, 23–24
Town Lake, 9, 38, 41, 60, 90

Umfunktionierung, 203
utility, 67, 79, 81, 86

Vélez-Ibañez, Carlos, 8
Villa, Raúl Homero, 25, 26, 36
violence, 21, 106, 127, 170, 172–174, 179, 186,
    188, 192, 215n11

Viramontes, Helena, 106

Willis, Paul, 98
Wolfe, Tom, 98
work: hierarchical value of, 18, 132,
    140–142, 163–164; rationalization of,
    146–147. *See also* class

Xzibit, 105–106

zoot suit, 76, 100, 116, 121–122